Performance Models of Multiprocessor Systems

MIT Press Series in Computer Systems
Herb Schwetman, editor

Metamodeling: A Study of Approximations in Queueing Models, by Subhash Chandra Agrawal, 1985

Logic Testing and Design for Testability, by Hideo Fujiwara, 1985

Performance and Evaluation of Lisp Systems, by Richard P. Gabriel, 1985

The LOCUS Distributed System Architecture, edited by Gerald Popek and Bruce J. Walker, 1985

Analysis of Polling Systems, by Hideaki Takagi, 1986

Performance Analysis of Multiple Access Protocols, by Shuji Tasaka, 1986

Performance Models of Multiprocessor Systems, by M. Ajmone Marsan, G. Balbo, and G. Conte, 1986

Performance Models of Multiprocessor Systems

M. Ajmone Marsan, G. Balbo, and G. Conte

The MIT Press
Cambridge, Massachusetts
London, England

Third Printing, 1990

© 1986 by The Massachusetts Institute of Technology

All rights reserved. No part of this book may be reproduced in any form by any electronic or mechanical means (including photocopying, recording, or information storage and retrieval) without permission in writing from the publisher.

This book was set in Times New Roman by Asco Trade Typesetting Ltd., Hong Kong, and printed and bound by Halliday Lithograph in the United States of America.

Library of Congress Cataloging-in-Publication Data

Ajmone Marsan, M.
  Performance models of multiprocessor systems.

  (MIT Press series in computer systems)
  Includes bibliographies and index.
  1. Multiprocessors—Evaluation. I. Balbo, Gianfranco. II. Conte, Gianni, 1946–.
III. Title. IV. Series.
QA76.5.A346   1986   004'.35   85-23662
ISBN 0-262-01093-3

Contents

	Series Foreword	xi
	Preface	xiii
1	**Introduction**	1

I

2	**Stochastic Processes**	9
2.1	Basic Definitions	9
2.2	Markov Processes	10
2.3	Discrete-Time Markov Chains	12
	2.3.1 Distribution at the nth Step	12
	2.3.2 Steady State Distribution	14
	2.3.3 Matrix Formulation	16
	2.3.4 Example	17
2.4	Continuous-Time Markov Chains	19
	2.4.1 Distribution at Time t	20
	2.4.2 Steady State Distribution	21
	2.4.3 Matrix Formulation	23
	2.4.4 Sojourn and Recurrence Times	24
	2.4.5 The Embedded Markov Chain	25
	2.4.6 The Birth-and-Death Process	27
	2.4.7 The Poisson Process	29
2.5	Aggregation of States in Markov Chains	30
	2.5.1 Aggregation in Discrete-Time Markov Chains	30
	2.5.2 Aggregation in Continuous-Time Markov Chains	33
2.6	Semi-Markov Processes	35
3	**Queuing Models**	39
3.1	The $M/M/1$ Queue	40
3.2	Deterministic Analysis of a Single-Server Queuing System	41
	3.2.1 Little's Formula	42
3.3	Extended Results	44
	3.3.1 The $M/M/m$ Queue	44
	3.3.2 Load-Dependent Server	45
	3.3.3 The $M/M/1/\infty/m$ Queue	46

3.4	The $M/GI/1$ Queue	47
	3.4.1 Coxian Distributions	47
	3.4.2 Embedded Markov Chain	48
3.5	Queuing Networks	50
	3.5.1 Burke's Theorem	50
	3.5.2 Feedforward Queuing Networks	51
	3.5.3 Jackson Queuing Networks	52
	3.5.4 Gordon and Newell Queuing Networks	54
	3.5.5 BCMP Queuing Networks	55
	3.5.5.1 Local Balance Queuing Networks	57
3.6	Computational Aspects of the Solution of BCMP Queuing Networks	59
	3.6.1 The Convolution Method	60
	3.6.2 The Mean Value Analysis Method	62
3.7	The CHW Theorem	65
3.8	Approximation Methods	67
	3.8.1 Nearly Decomposable Systems	67
	3.8.2 Passive Resources	68

4 Stochastic Petri Nets 73

4.1	Standard Petri Nets	73
	4.1.1 Petri Net Marking	74
	4.1.2 Some Extensions to Standard Petri Nets	76
	4.1.3 Some Petri Net Properties	77
4.2	Timed Petri Nets	80
4.3	Stochastic Petri Nets	82
	4.3.1 An Example of a Stochastic Petri Net	85
4.4	Generalized Stochastic Petri Nets	87
	4.4.1 Basic Motivations	87
	4.4.2 An Example of a Generalized Stochastic Petri Net	88
	4.4.3 Evaluation of the Generalized Stochastic Petri Net Steady State Probability Distribution	92
	4.4.4 A Computationally More Efficient Solution Method	95

Contents   vii

II

5	**Multiprocessor Architectures**	101
5.1	Distributed Systems	101
	5.1.1 Computer Networks	101
	5.1.2 Multiprocessor Systems	102
	5.1.3 Special Purpose Machines	102
	5.1.4 Other Classifications of Distributed Systems	103
5.2	Multiprocessor Systems	104
	5.2.1 Multiprocessor Topology	105
	5.2.1.1 Crossbar Switches	107
	5.2.1.2 Shared Bus Systems	107
	5.2.1.3 Multistage Interconnection Networks	109
5.3	The Advantages of a Multiprocessor System	111
5.4	Modeling Assumptions	112
	5.4.1 Level of Abstraction of the Analysis	112
	5.4.2 Formulation of the Workload Model	114

6	**Analysis of Crossbar Multiprocessor Architectures**	119
6.1	Model Classification	121
6.2	Model Discussion	122
	6.2.1 Uniform Memory Reference Pattern	123
	6.2.1.1 Zero-Delay Models—Queued Requests	123
	6.2.1.2 Delay Models—Queued Requests	128
	6.2.1.3 Zero-Delay Models—Lost Requests	129
	6.2.1.4 Delay Models—Lost Requests	130
6.3	Nonuniform Memory Reference Pattern	132

7	**Single-Bus Multiprocessors with External Common Memory**	137
7.1	Performance Indices	141
7.2	Equal Exponentially Distributed Active and Access Times ($M_e/M_e/*$)	143
7.3	Equal Exponentially Distributed Active Times and Equal Generally Distributed Access Times—FCFS ($M_e/G_e/$FCFS)	144
7.4	Different Generally Distributed Active Times and Equal Exponentially Distributed Access Times—FCFS and PS ($G_d/M_e/$FCFS and PS)	145

7.5	Different Generally Distributed Active and Access Times—PS (G_d/G_d/PS)	146
7.6	Different Exponentially Distributed Active Times and Generally Distributed Access Times—FCFS and FP (M_d/G_d/FCFS and FP)	147
7.7	Different Generally Distributed Active and Access Times—FCFS (G_d/G_d/FCFS)	151
7.8	Numerical Results	153

8 Multiple-Bus Multiprocessors with External Common Memory — 158

8.1	Continuous-Time Markov Chain Models	160
8.2	Generalized Stochastic Petri Net Models	161
	8.2.1 Detailed Model	163
	8.2.2 Alternative Representation of Memory Subnets	165
	8.2.3 Folding of the Detailed Model	167
	8.2.4 Compact Model	169
	8.2.5 Remarks	172
8.3	Product Form Solution	173
8.4	Simple Queuing Bounds	179
	8.4.1 Upper Bound	179
	8.4.2 Lower Bound	181
8.5	Numerical Results	185

9 Single-Bus Multiprocessors with Distributed Common Memory — 191

9.1	Modeling Assumptions	191
9.2	Architecture 1	194
9.3	Architecture 2	195
9.4	Architecture 3	200
9.5	Architecture 4	202
	9.5.1 Continuous-Time Markov Chain Models	205
	9.5.2 Generalized Stochastic Petri Net Models	207
9.6	Architecture Comparison	215

10	**Multiple-Bus Multiprocessors with Distributed Common Memory**	224
10.1	Architecture 1	224
10.2	Architecture 2a	224
10.3	Architecture 2b	233
10.4	Architecture 3	244
10.5	Architecture 4	245
10.6	Numerical Results	251
11	**Other Aspects of Multiprocessor Performance Evaluation**	258
11.1	Synchronization of Tasks	259
11.2	Failure of System Components	266
11.3	Prototype Measurements and Model Validation	272
	Index	279

Series Foreword

This series is devoted to all aspects of computer systems. This means that subjects ranging from circuit components and microprocessors to architecture to supercomputers and systems programming will be appropriate. Analysis of systems will be important as well. System theories are developing, theories that permit deeper understandings of complex interrelationships and their effects on performance, reliability, and usefulness.

We expect to offer books that not only develop new material but also describe projects and systems. In addition to understanding concepts, we need to benefit from the decision making that goes into actual development projects; selection from various alternatives can be crucial to success. We are soliciting contributions in which several aspects of systems are classified and compared. A better understanding of both the similarities and the differences found in systems is needed.

It is an exciting time in the area of computer systems. New technologies mean that architectures that were at one time interesting but not feasible are now feasible. Better software engineering means that we can consider several software alternatives, instead of "more of the same old thing," in terms of operating systems and system software. Faster and cheaper communications mean that intercomponent distances are less important. We hope that this series contributes to this excitement in the area of computer systems by chronicling past achievements and publicizing new concepts. The format allows publication of lengthy presentations that are of interest to a select readership.

Herb Schwetman

Preface

Computer science is a young scientific discipline facing the challenge of a revolutionary technological progress that results in enormous improvements in processing capabilities and induces unprecedented requirements for even higher processing power.

Distributed computing systems allow the requests of demanding applications to be met by exploiting very large scale integration technologies and advanced communication facilities.

The lack of a unified theory characterizing the properties of distributed computation and guiding design has not prevented many real distributed systems from being built. This fact has a twofold implication since it provides strong motivations for progress in understanding these systems, and in some cases leads to the construction of systems that do not reach their initial performance goals.

Powerful tools are urgently needed to help the designer in evaluating the ways in which these systems behave, and judging the advantages that certain architectural choices may yield with respect to others. While the development of a mathematics capable of answering all the questions that arise during the design of a system seems far from reaching a satisfactory stage, ad hoc techniques exist for the analysis of specific aspects of the problem. Performance evaluation techniques offer effective tools useful in predicting the efficiency of distributed systems since the early stages of their development.

Several books devoted to computer systems modeling and performance evaluation have recently been published. Although in some of them it is possible to find models of multiprocessor systems, they are always regarded as examples of applications of general modeling techniques rather than as the main object of the study.

This book is instead entirely devoted to the problem of modeling and performance evaluation of multiprocessor systems using analytical methods. Among the multiprocessor features studied, special attention is given to contention for physical system resources, such as shared devices and interconnection networks. The modeling of other important system characteristics, such as failures of components and synchronizations at the software level, is briefly overviewed. In fact, only a few results have been published on these subjects, although it is clear that they have a very significant impact on multiprocessor performance.

To make the book self-contained, a first methodological part has been devoted to the discussion of the modeling techniques used throughout the rest of the book. The second part addresses the specific topic of the evaluation of the efficiency of multiprocessor systems, basing most of the analysis on the research work that the authors have done in this field during recent years.

Many persons have contributed to the derivation of the results presented in this book. Special thanks go to G. Chiola for his contribution to the derivation of the closed form results of chapter 8 (together with S. Donatelli), and of some of the GSPN models of chapters 8, 9, and 11. Chapter 10 is mainly based on the doctoral thesis of G. Carra. The measurements on the prototype multiprocessor system were performed by F. Gregoretti. G. Chiola and G. Ciardo developed a software package for the analysis of GSPN models. The figures were carefully drawn by L. Brino.

Most of the authors' research in the field of multiprocessor system performance evaluation was supported by the Italian National Research Council in the framework of the Computer Science Program, MUMICRO Project. NATO provided some financial support through Research Grants 012.81 and 280.81. The Electronics Department of Politecnico di Torino and the Computer Science Department of Università di Torino are also credited for their support.

Performance Models of Multiprocessor Systems

1 Introduction

Recent progress in VLSI technology has allowed the production of single-chip computing units with processing power comparable to that of mainframes of ten to twenty years ago. A consequence of this innovation has been the possibility of designing and implementing distributed computing systems inspired by the physical distribution and by the intrinsic parallelism of many applications.

Different goals often suggest the development of distributed computing systems with quite different structural characteristics. Multiprocessor systems are a special class of distributed computing systems that appear to represent the most promising way of obtaining the high-performance computers needed in many application fields, such as artificial intelligence, CAD, expert systems, and large-scale system simulation. Characteristics such as fault tolerance, flexibility, functional upgrading, and cost effectiveness are other motivations that have spurred the realization of multiprocessor systems. To pursue these goals, a variety of multiprocessor architectures with different design alternatives have been proposed, implemented, and made commercially available, but their relative merits are not yet fully understood. It is thus very important to develop methodologies and tools for the prediction of the performance of multiprocessor architectures, so that system designers can verify how well different alternatives suit certain given performance specifications.

The area of performance evaluation of computing systems has been the object of extensive research studies since the early days of computer science, and many good books exist on this subject (see, for example, [FERR78, KOBA78, GELE80, CHAN81, TRIV82, LAVE83]). All of these references are characterized by the common goal of discussing theory and application of very general performance evaluation techniques, thus leaving little space for the development of special models such as those needed for the analysis of multiprocessor systems. On the other hand, the few books on multiprocessor architectures that are currently available (see, for example, [ENSL74, SATY80, WAIT80, PAKE83, HWAN84]) give very little emphasis to the performance subject. To fill this gap, if only partially, this book explicitly addresses the topic of performance evaluation of multiprocessor systems, presenting evaluation and modeling techniques that are well suited for the analysis of these systems, and providing several examples of their application to some specific architectures.

Performance evaluation techniques can be classified into two main areas, which we shall call measuring and modeling, respectively. There are three techniques in the first performance evaluation area: measurements, benchmarking, and prototyping. Measurements are performed on a real system under real operating conditions, and thus provide very accurate performance figures with respect to the specific system under investigation, and to its workload. When the need to compare the performances of different computing systems arises, it is necessary to perform measurements using the same workload on the different machines. The artificial workloads (selected application programs or specially built ones) that are used in this case are called benchmarks, and the technique itself is named benchmarking. Note that in both cases the performance is directly measured on the computing systems under study. When the performance evaluation study refers to a computing system that is not physically available yet, it is necessary either to build a prototype or to use models. Prototypes are approximations of the real system (built either in hardware or in software—in the latter case they are often referred to as emulators) that can be used to perform measurements, possibly with benchmark programs.

The design of computing systems whose specifications include performance objectives requires the preliminary evaluation of alternatives that may be only in a first stage of definition. In this case the techniques of measurement and benchmarking must obviously be discarded, since the object of measurement is not available yet. However, even prototyping is of little use, since the development of a prototype or of an emulator requires the definition of many details that may be far from being decided at this stage of the design. It is thus necessary to resort to modeling techniques that pertain to the second performance evaluation area, and that allow the designer to choose the level of abstraction of its representation of the real system.

A model of a multiprocessor, and in general of any computing system, usually consists of two parts: the description of the architecture, and the definition of the workload under which performance predictions should be obtained. The key elements in the model development are the choice of the level of abstraction used to describe the system, the selection of the system features to be included in the model, the assignment of numerical values to the model parameters, and the definition of appropriate performance indices. The choice of the system features to be included in the model is a very important step in the modeling process, since it must ensure the adequacy of the description without introducing unneeded complexity. A good deal of experience, ingenuity, and natural skill is required to accomplish this task, which is intrinsically nonscientific.

Models can be divided into two classes: simulation models and analytical models. Simulation models are computer programs in which system behavior and workload are described using proper algorithms. Special high-level programming languages are usually employed for the construction of these models, whose performance indices are obtained by monitoring program execution. Analytical models, instead, describe system operations and workloads in mathematical terms. Performance estimates are obtained by either analytical or numerical solution of the resulting mathematical model.

Models can be either deterministic or probabilistic. In the latter case, a very large number of complex phenomena that take place inside the system are described by means of macroscopic probabilistic assumptions, neglecting the actual behavior details. This approach can be advantageous for several reasons: the details may not be completely known at the moment of the model development; the inclusion in the model of all the details of system behavior may lead to unmanageable complexity; the use of simple and inexpensive models may provide sufficient accuracy in the performance evaluation of systems during the early design stages.

The development of a simulation model can proceed with hardly any constraint on the model structure. A simulation model can thus be more detailed than an analytical one, but it is often less general and versatile. Moreover, simulation is a costly technique that usually requires large amounts of computer time for the reliable estimation of performance indices. Indeed, the sampling nature of simulation requires that confidence intervals be computed for each performance estimate using methods that may be difficult to apply. Because of this, simulation often seems very appealing to the naive user, who believes it is trivial to employ as a modeling technique, while its correct use may entail several difficulties.

In the development of an analytical model it is often necessary to use a higher level of abstraction than required by simulation, since in order to be able to solve the model some constraints on its structure must be accepted. In the simpler cases it is possible to obtain closed form solutions useful for studying the impact that different model parameters have on performance indices, i.e., to perform a sensitivity analysis. In the more complex cases the model solution can be obtained only numerically, and the sensitivity analysis is possible only at the expense of a large number of numerical solutions, computed for different values of the model parameters. In extreme cases, the computational complexity, the storage requirements, and the numerical problems may make the solution of an analytical model more cumbersome and expensive than simulation.

A class of models that is widely used due to their limited mathematical complexity is based on the theory of a subclass of stochastic processes named Markov chains. Markovian models are used throughout this book, and a quick review of the main results on which these models are based is presented in chapter 2, where the terminology and the notation that we have consistently used throughout the whole book is introduced.

A limit on the use of Markovian models of complex computer systems comes from the fact that their direct construction often requires some familiarity with the basic results of the underlying theory. Indeed, in these cases it is necessary to identify all the system states and the speeds or the probabilities with which the system moves from one state to another. This task may be particularly difficult, and ad hoc techniques may be required for its accomplishment.

A more convenient approach is that of using one of the high-level model description tools that have been proposed in the literature. The two best known such techniques are queuing networks and stochastic Petri nets, which are reviewed in chapters 3 and 4, respectively. Their advantage is that they allow the model to be constructed in a natural way from the description of the system components and operation rules: the model is specified in a graphical form rather than in a mathematical one. Both queuing networks and stochastic Petri nets are then analyzed by studying their underlying Markovian model, but the system designer need not be aware of the theory and of the methods that are necessary for obtaining the model solution. Indeed, software packages are available that hide these details, that help the designer in the model definition through a user friendly graphical interface, and that numerically solve the underlying Markovian model after automatically generating it from the model description. Queuing networks provide the further advantage that in several cases it is possible to obtain directly the closed form model solution without solving the underlying Markovian model. This is not yet possible with stochastic Petri nets, which are a much more recent modeling tool. However, we hope that some breakthrough results will eventually provide this capability also for certain types of stochastic Petri nets. The availability of such results would be extremely useful in the performance evaluation of multiprocessor systems, since stochastic Petri nets allow a natural representation of parallelism and synchronization.

The most common architectures of distributed computing systems are described in chapter 5, with a special emphasis on multiprocessors. In multiprocessor systems, the data exchange among computing units and shared resources is made possible by an interconnection network that characterizes the architecture and plays a crucial role in the overall performance of the system. Chapters 6–10 present many performance results for multiprocessor systems with either crossbar or bus-oriented interconnection networks. Crossbar systems are considered in chapter 6, and their presentation is included mainly for historical reasons. Indeed, crossbar multiprocessor architectures were studied first, starting in the late '60s, when the first multiprocessor system prototypes were being implemented around a crossbar switch. In those days multiprocessor machines were made of very tightly coupled processors, so that the models that were developed for their analysis assume a synchronization at the level of the instruction execution, and hence use a rather low level of abstraction. The goal of these analyses was the study of the performance degradation due to interference in the execution of atomic transactions such as main memory accesses for fetching instructions and data.

Similar models were also developed for the analysis of bus-oriented multiprocessor architectures. However, most of the recent standards of backplane buses for multiprocessor systems [INTE83] assume that processors and memories communicate through a protocol that allows the exchange of variable size messages. This implies that the interaction among modules results from complex operations rather than from atomic transactions such as single memory accesses. Chapters 7–10 thus describe models of bus-oriented multiprocessor systems in which the level of abstraction used for the description of the system behavior is coherent with these indications. Several different multiprocessor architectures are considered in the different chapters, presenting results that were originally published by the authors in several papers which are listed among the references at the end of this chapter.

Many very interesting issues had to be left out of this book due to space constraints. The most noticeable omission from the architectural point of view concerns the whole field of multiprocessor system architectures in which the interconnection is provided by a multistage network. Moreover, we only considered the analysis of performance models of multiprocessor systems accounting for the physical interactions among modules, but neglecting the impact that software has on the efficiency of the system due, for example, to overhead, mutual exclusion, and synchronization of tasks. Furthermore, we did not consider the aspects related to reliability and fault tolerance, as well as the combined aspects of performance and reliability that are often referred to by the name "performability." As a partial correction to these omissions we have included in chapter 11 some results concerning the performance degradation due to the synchronization of tasks and to the failure of system components, together with a section that presents the validation of some of the models discussed in a previous chapter by means of measurements performed on a prototype multiprocessor system implemented at the Electronics Department of Politecnico di Torino. The performance parameters that were measured on this prototype are in very good agreement with the theoretical estimates. We hope that this last section succeeds in imparting to the reader some confidence in the validity of analytical modeling in the performance prediction of multiprocessor computer systems.

References

[AJMO82a] Ajmone Marsan, M., and Gerla, M., "Markov Models for Multiple Bus Multiprocessor Systems", *IEEE Transactions on Computers* C-31(3) (March 1982) 239–248.

[AJMO82b] Ajmone Marsan, M., "Bounds on Bus and Memory Interference in a Class of Multiple Bus

Multiprocessor Systems", *Third International Conference on Distributed Computing Systems*, Ft. Lauderdale, USA, October 1982.

[AJMO82c] Ajmone Marsan, M., Balbo, G., and Conte, G., "Comparative Performance Analysis of Single Bus Multiprocessor Architectures", *IEEE Transactions on Computers* C-31(12) (December 1982) 1179–1191.

[AJMO83] Ajmone Marsan, M., Balbo, G., Conte, G., and Gregoretti, F., "Modeling Bus Contention and Memory Interference in a Multiprocessor System", *IEEE Transactions on Computers* C-32(1) (January 1983) 60–72.

[AJMO84a] Ajmone Marsan, M., Bobbio, A., Conte, G., and Cumani, A. "Performance Analysis of Degradable Multiprocessor Systems Using Generalized Stochastic Petri Nets", *IEEE Distributed Processing Technical Committee Newsletter* 6(SI-1) (January 1984) 47–54.

[AJMO84b] Ajmone Marsan, M., and Carra, G., "Bus and Memory Interference in Double Bus Multiprocessor Systems", *Microprocessing and Microprogramming* 13(2) (February 1984) 73–96.

[AJMO84c] Ajmone Marsan, M., Balbo, G., and Conte, G., "A Class of Generalized Stochastic Petri Nets for the Performance Evaluation of Multiprocessor Systems", *ACM Transactions on Computer Systems* 2(2) (May 1984) 93–122.

[AJMO84d] Ajmone Marsan, M., Chiola, G., and Conte, G., "Performance Models of Task Synchronization in Computer Systems", *First International Conference on Computers and Applications*, Peking, China, June 1984.

[AJMO84e] Ajmone Marsan, M., Balbo, G., Chiola, G., and Donatelli, S., "On the Product Form Solution of a Class of Multiple Bus Multiprocessor System Models", *International Workshop on Modeling and Performance Evaluation of Parallel Systems*, Grenoble, France, December 1984.

[AJMO85] Ajmone Marsan, M., and Chiola, G., "Construction of Generalized Stochastic Petri Net Models of Bus Oriented Multiprocessor Systems by Stepwise Refinements: a Case Study", *International Conference on Modeling Techniques and Tools for Performance Analysis*, Sophia Antipolis, France, June 1985.

[CHAN81] Chandy, K. M., and Sauer, C. H., *Computer Systems Performance Modeling*, Prentice-Hall, Englewood Cliffs, NJ, 1981.

[ENSL74] Enslow, P. H. *Multiprocessors and Parallel Processing*, Wiley-Interscience, New York, 1974.

[FERR78] Ferrari, D., *Computer System Performance Evaluation*, Prentice-Hall, Englewood Cliffs, NJ, 1978.

[GELE80] Gelenbe E., and Mitrani, I., *Analysis and Synthesis of Computer Systems*, Academic Press, London, 1980.

[HWAN84] Hwang, K., and Briggs, F. A., *Computer Architectures and Parallel Processing*, McGraw-Hill, New York, 1984.

[INTE83] INTEL, "MULTIBUS II Bus Architecture Specification," Intel Corporation, 1983.

[KOBA78] Kobayashi, H., *Modeling and Analysis: An Introduction to System Performance Evaluation Methodology*, Addison-Wesley, Reading, MA, 1978.

[LAVE83] Lavenberg, S., *Computer Performance Modeling Handbook*, Academic Press, London, 1983.

[PAKE83] Paker, Y., *Multi-microprocessor Systems*, Academic Press, London, 1983.

[SATY80] Satyanarayanan, M., *Multiprocessors: A Comparative Study*, Prentice-Hall, Englewood Cliffs, NJ, 1980.

[TRIV82] Trivedi, K. S., *Probability and Statistics with Reliability, Queueing, and Computer Science Applications*, Prentice-Hall, Englewood Cliffs, NJ, 1982.

[WAIT80] Waitzman, C., *Distributed Micro/Minicomputer Systems*, Prentice-Hall, Englewood Cliffs, NJ, 1980.

I

2 Stochastic Processes

Stochastic processes are mathematical models useful for the description of random phenomena as functions of a parameter that usually has the meaning of time.

In this chapter we informally introduce some results of the theory of stochastic processes that are necessary for the construction and the solution of the stochastic models of multiprocessor system behavior presented in the second part of this book. Readers who desire a more formal and complete treatment of the theory of stochastic processes are referred to the vast literature that exists on this subject (see, for example, [KEME60, PARZ62, COXM65, FELL66, HOWA71, CINL75, KARL75]).

2.1 Basic Definitions

From a mathematical point of view, a *stochastic process* is a family of random variables $\{X(t), t \in T\}$ defined over the same probability space, indexed by the parameter t, and taking values in the set S. The values assumed by the stochastic process are called *states*, so that the set S is called the *state space* of the process.

Alternatively, we can view the stochastic process as a set of time functions, one for each element of the probability space. These time functions are called either *sample functions*, sample paths, or realizations of the stochastic process.

The probabilistic description of a stochastic process is given by means of either the joint *probability distribution function*[1] (PDF—also known as cumulative distribution function) of the random variables $\{X(t_i), i = 1, 2, \ldots, n\}$,

$$F_{\mathbf{x}}(\mathbf{x}; \mathbf{t}) = P\{X(t_1) \leq x_1, X(t_2) \leq x_2, \ldots, X(t_n) \leq x_n\}, \tag{2.1}$$

or, alternatively, of the joint *probability density function* (pdf),

$$f_{\mathbf{x}}(\mathbf{x}; \mathbf{t}) = \frac{\delta F_{\mathbf{x}}(\mathbf{x}; \mathbf{t})}{\delta \mathbf{x}}. \tag{2.2}$$

The complete probabilistic description of the process $X(t)$ requires the specification of either one of these two functions for all values of n, and for all possible n-tuples $(t_1, t_2, \ldots, t_n)$.

The state space of the process can be either discrete or continuous. In the former case we have a *discrete-space* stochastic process, often referred to as a *chain*. In the latter case we have a *continuous-space* process. The state space of a chain is usually the set of natural integers $\mathbb{N} = \{0, 1, 2, \ldots\}$, or a subset of it.

If the index (time) parameter t is continuous, we have a *continuous-time* process.

---

[1] Note that throughout the book we use the notation $P\{A\}$ to indicate the probability of event A.

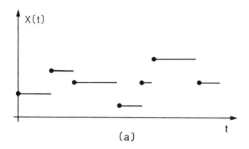

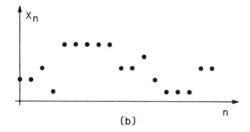

Figure 2.1
Possible sample functions of discrete-space stochastic processes: (a) continuous-time; (b) discrete-time.

Otherwise the stochastic process is said to be a *discrete-time* process, and is often referred to as a stochastic *sequence*, denoted $\{X_n, n = 0, 1, 2, \ldots\}$.

In this book we are interested in stochastic processes with a discrete (most of the times finite) state space, both in continuous and in discrete time. In this case the probabilities $P\{X(t) = s_i\}, \forall s_i \in S$, form the *probability mass function* (pmf) from which the corresponding PDF and pdf are immediately derived. Like many authors, we informally refer to the pmf using the term distribution.

Possible sample functions of discrete-space stochastic processes are shown in figures 2.1a and 2.1b in the continuous- and discrete-time cases, respectively. The process is observed to spend a random time in each state before a transition to a new one. Note that in the continuous-time case the sample functions are assumed to be right continuous.

2.2 Markov Processes

Markov processes owe their name to the Russian mathematician A. A. Markov, who studied the class of stochastic processes whose conditional PDF is such that

$$P\{X(t) \leq x | X(t_n) = x_n, X(t_{n-1}) = x_{n-1}, \ldots, X(t_0) = x_0\}$$
$$= P\{X(t) \leq x | X(t_n) = x_n\}, \qquad t > t_n > t_{n-1} > \cdots > t_0. \tag{2.3}$$

The above condition is known as the *Markov property*. A stochastic process $\{X(t), t \in T\}$ for which the above condition holds is said to be a *Markov process*. For the sake of simplicity we assume that T is the set of real non-negative numbers, i.e., $T = \mathbb{R}^+ = [0, \infty)$.

In this book we consider only discrete-space Markov processes, which are known under the name of *Markov chains* (MC). MC can be either continuous-time or discrete-time, depending on the values that the index parameter t can assume. We thus consider both *discrete-time Markov chains* (DTMC), and *continuous-time Markov chains* (CTMC).

The application areas that we consider in this book allow a further assumption on the conditional PDF to be made. Indeed, we can assume that the behavior of the systems that we study does not depend on the time of observation. We can thus arbitrarily choose the origin of the time axis. Hence it is possible to state that

$$P\{X(t) \leq x | X(t_n) = x_n\} = P\{X(t - t_n) \leq x | X(0) = x_n\}. \tag{2.4}$$

An MC for which the above condition holds is said to be (time) *homogeneous*. In this book we restrict our presentation to homogeneous MC.

The Markov property can be intuitively explained by saying that the future evolution of the process, from the instant t_n on, is independent of the past history of the process; i.e., the state $X(t_n)$ contains all relevant information about the past process history. For a homogeneous MC it is not necessary to know t_n, and we can thus say that the future of the process is completely determined (in a probabilistic sense) by the knowledge of the present state.

An important implication of the Markov property is that the distribution of the *sojourn time* in any state must be memoryless. Indeed, if the future evolution depends on the present state only, it cannot depend on the amount of time already spent by the process in the state. This, coupled with the observation that for a continuous random variable W the only pdf that satisfies the memoryless property

$$P\{W \geq t + \tau | W \geq t\} = P\{W \geq \tau\} \tag{2.5}$$

is the negative exponential

$$f_W(\omega) = ae^{-a\omega}, \qquad \omega \geq 0, \tag{2.6}$$

leads to the conclusion that sojourn times in CTMC states must be exponentially distributed random variables.

Similarly, in the case of DTMC, sojourn times in states must be geometrically distributed random variables:

$$P\{W = i\} = p^{i-1}(1 - p), \qquad i = 1, 2, 3, \ldots. \tag{2.7}$$

The importance of the memoryless distribution of the times spent in states can be better understood by noting that in order to check whether a stochastic process satisfies the Markov property, it suffices to check whether the distributions of sojourn times are memoryless, and whether the probabilities of going from one state to another only depend on the state the process is leaving and on the destination state.

2.3 Discrete-Time Markov Chains

By specializing the Markov property to the discrete-time, discrete-space case we obtain the definition of a DTMC:

DEFINITION The stochastic sequence $\{X_n, n = 0, 1, 2, \ldots\}$ is a DTMC provided that

$$P\{X_{n+1} = x_{n+1} | X_n = x_n, X_{n-1} = x_{n-1}, \ldots, X_0 = x_0\} = P\{X_{n+1} = x_{n+1} | X_n = x_n\} \tag{2.8}$$

for all $n \in \mathbb{N}$, and all $x_k \in S$.

The expression on the right-hand side of the above equation is the (one-step) *transition probability* of the chain, and it denotes the probability that the process goes from state x_n to state x_{n+1} when the index parameter is increased from n to $n + 1$. We use the following notation:

$$p_{ij}(n) = P\{X_{n+1} = j | X_n = i\}. \tag{2.9}$$

If the DTMC is time homogeneous, the above probabilities do not depend on n, so that we may simplify the notation by dropping the variable n, and thus denote transition probabilities as

$$p_{ij} = P\{X_{n+1} = j | X_n = i\}. \tag{2.10}$$

This quantity provides the probability of being in state j at the next step, given that the present state is i. Note that, on summing the probabilities p_{ij} over all possible states j in the state space S, the result is 1.

2.3.1 Distribution at the nth Step

One of the goals of the study of DTMC is to evaluate the probability that the process is in state i at a given step n. This *state probability* is denoted

$$\pi_i(n) = P\{X_n = i\}, \tag{2.11}$$

and it can be evaluated from the knowledge of the transition probabilities and of the initial distribution at time 0. Indeed, using the theorem of total probability,

$$\pi_i(n) = \sum_{j \in S} P\{X_n = i | X_0 = j\} \pi_j(0). \tag{2.12}$$

The quantities that multiply $\pi_j(0)$ in the summation are the probabilities of being in state i at step n, given that the process started out in state j at time 0. They are called *n-step transition probabilities*, and, due to the homogeneity of the DTMC, they are defined as

$$p_{ji}^{(n)} = P\{X_{n+m} = i | X_m = j\}. \tag{2.13}$$

Hence we can rewrite (2.12) as

$$\pi_i(n) = \sum_{j \in S} p_{ji}^{(n)} \pi_j(0). \tag{2.14}$$

Using the Markov property (2.8), it is possible to show that the n-step transition probabilities satisfy the following relation,

$$p_{ji}^{(n)} = \sum_{k \in S} p_{jk}^{(n-l)} p_{ki}^{(l)}, \tag{2.15}$$

which is known as the Chapman-Kolmogorov equation for homogeneous DTMC. It states that it is possible to write any n-step transition probability as the sum of products of $(n-l)$-step and l-step transition probabilities. Indeed, to go from j to i in n steps, it is necessary to go from j to an intermediate state k in $n-l$ steps, and then from k to i in the remaining l steps. By summing over all possible intermediate states k, we consider all possible distinct paths leading from j to i in n steps.

In particular, if we choose either $l = 1$ or $l = n - 1$, we have

$$p_{ji}^{(n)} = \sum_{k \in S} p_{jk}^{(n-1)} p_{ki} = \sum_{k \in S} p_{jk} p_{ki}^{(n-1)}. \tag{2.16}$$

These relations provide recursive expressions for the calculation of n-step transition probabilities from one-step transition probabilities.

The probability that the process is in state i at a given step n, $\pi_i(n)$, can thus be evaluated once the initial distribution is known and transition probabilities are given.

Note that the knowledge of the n-step transition probabilities allows also the evaluation of the joint PDF of the random variables extracted from the process at any set of instants, given the initial PDF. Since the n-step transition probabilities can be found in terms of the one-step transition probabilities, we can conclude that the probabilistic behavior of the process is completely described by the initial distribution and by the one-step transition probabilities.

2.3.2 Steady State Distribution

A second important problem that arises in the study of DTMC concerns the existence and the evaluation of the steady state distribution. This problem is of particular interest to us, since most of the results on multiprocessor system performance presented in the second part of this book are based on steady state analysis.

In order to present the main results concerning the steady state analysis of DTMC we must introduce several definitions concerning the chain and its states.

Let

$$f_j^{(n)} = P\{\text{first return in state } j \text{ occurs } n \text{ steps after leaving it}\} \tag{2.17}$$

and

$$f_j = \sum_{n=1}^{\infty} f_j^{(n)} = P\{\text{ever returning in state } j\}. \tag{2.18}$$

A state j is said to be *transient* if $f_j < 1$, i.e., if there is a nonzero probability of never returning to state j after leaving it. A state j is said to be *recurrent* if $f_j = 1$, i.e., if the process returns to state j with probability one after leaving it.

For a recurrent state j the n-step transition probability $p_{jj}^{(n)}$ must be larger than zero for some $n > 0$.

Define the *period* of a state j, d_j, as the greatest common divisor of all positive integers n such that $p_{jj}^{(n)} > 0$. A recurrent state j is said to be *periodic* with period d_j if $d_j > 1$.

A state j is said to be *absorbing* if $p_{jj} = 1$. An absorbing state is recurrent.

For a recurrent state j define the *mean recurrence time* M_j as

$$M_j = \sum_{n=1}^{\infty} n f_j^{(n)}. \tag{2.19}$$

The mean recurrence time is the average number of steps needed to return to state j for the first time after leaving it.

Recurrent states for which $M_j < \infty$ are said to be *recurrent nonnull*. Recurrent states for which the mean recurrence time is infinite are said to be *recurrent null*.

A subset A of the state space S is said to be *closed* if no transition is possible from states in A to states in $\bar{A}$ (the complement of set A), i.e., if

$$\sum_{i \in A} \sum_{j \in \bar{A}} p_{ij} = 0. \tag{2.20}$$

A DTMC is said to be *irreducible* if S is closed and if no proper subset of S is closed. This implies that every state of the chain can be reached from every other state. Thus, for each pair of states i and j there must be at least one n for which $p_{ij}^{(n)} > 0$.

It can be shown that all states of an irreducible DTMC are of the same type; thus they can be either all transient, all recurrent null, or all recurrent nonnull. Note that an irreducible chain cannot comprise absorbing states. Moreover, either all states are aperiodic or they all have the same period d. In the former case the chain itself is said to be aperiodic, and it is said to be periodic with period d in the latter case.

A distribution $\{z_i, i \in S\}$ defined on the DTMC states is said to be *stationary* if

$$z_i = \sum_{j \in S} z_j p_{ji}, \qquad \forall i \in S, \tag{2.21}$$

that is, if, once this distribution is reached, for all successive steps this is the distribution of the process.

Define the *limiting probabilities* $\{\pi_j, j \in S\}$ as

$$\pi_j = \lim_{n \to \infty} \pi_j(n). \tag{2.22}$$

It can be shown that for all aperiodic, homogeneous DTMC these limits exist. Moreover, if the DTMC is irreducible, the limits are independent of the initial distribution $\{\pi_j(0), j \in S\}$. Furthermore, if all states of the chain are either transient or recurrent null, then

$$\pi_j = 0, \qquad \forall j \in S. \tag{2.23}$$

Instead, if all states are recurrent nonnull, then

$$\pi_j > 0, \qquad \forall j \in S, \tag{2.24}$$

and the limiting probabilities $\{\pi_j, j \in S\}$ form a stationary distribution.

In the latter case all states are said to be *ergodic* and the DTMC itself is said to be ergodic; moreover, the limiting probabilities $\{\pi_j, j \in S\}$ are unique. They can be obtained by solving the system of linear equations

$$\pi_j = \sum_{i \in S} \pi_i p_{ij}, \tag{2.25a}$$

$$\sum_{j \in S} \pi_j = 1. \tag{2.25b}$$

Furthermore, in this case a very simple relation exists between the state limiting probabilities and the state mean recurrence times:

$$\pi_j = \frac{1}{M_j}. \qquad (2.26)$$

The limiting probabilities of an ergodic DTMC are often called also equilibrium or steady state probabilities.

It is easy to show that the steady state probabilities of an ergodic DTMC also satisfy the relationship

$$\pi_j = \lim_{n \to \infty} p_{ij}^{(n)}, \qquad \forall i \in S; \qquad (2.27)$$

i.e., they represent the limit for n going to infinity of the n-step transition probabilities from a state i toward any state j.

The average time spent by the process in state j in a period of fixed duration τ at steady state, $v_j(\tau)$, can be obtained as the product of the steady state probability of state j by the duration of the observation period:

$$v_j(\tau) = \pi_j \tau. \qquad (2.28)$$

The average time spent by the process in state i at steady state, between two successive visits to state j, v_{ij}, can be shown to equal the ratio of the steady state probabilities of states i and j:

$$v_{ij} = \frac{\pi_i}{\pi_j}. \qquad (2.29)$$

The term *visit* can be explained as follows. We say that the process visits state i at time n if $X_n = i$. The quantity v_{ij} is called *visit ratio* since it indicates the average number of visits to state i between two successive visits to state j.

In this book we are particularly interested in stochastic processes having a finite number of states, since the models we develop in part II always comprise a finite number of states. An MC comprising a finite number of states is called a *finite Markov chain*. It is easy to show that all states of a finite aperiodic irreducible DTMC are ergodic.

2.3.3 Matrix Formulation

The use of a matrix notation can be particularly convenient since it simplifies many of the above results. Define the transition probability matrix **P**,

$$\mathbf{P} = [p_{ij}], \qquad (2.30)$$

as well as the vector $\pi(n)$ whose entries are the state probabilities at the nth step:

$$\pi(n) = \{\pi_1(n), \pi_2(n), \ldots\}. \tag{2.31}$$

From (2.16) we obtain that the matrix of the n-step transition probabilities can be expressed as the nth power of the matrix $\mathbf{P}$, and hence (2.14) can be written in matrix form as

$$\pi(n) = \pi(0)\mathbf{P}^n. \tag{2.32}$$

This equation can be used to evaluate the distribution of the DTMC at the nth step, given the transition probability matrix $\mathbf{P}$, and the initial distribution vector $\pi(0)$. Note that the matrices $\mathbf{P}^n$ are stochastic for all values of n.

If the DTMC is ergodic, the steady state probability distribution,

$$\pi = \lim_{n \to \infty} \pi(n), \tag{2.33}$$

can be evaluated from the matrix equation,

$$\pi = \pi \mathbf{P}, \tag{2.34}$$

that is, the matrix form of (2.25a). As before, the normalizing condition (2.25b) must be used in conjunction with (2.34) to identify the unique steady state probability distribution.

As a final comment on the properties of DTMC we remark that, as said before, the sojourn time in state i is a geometrically distributed random variable W_i with

$$P\{W_i = k\} = p_{ii}^{k-1}(1 - p_{ii}), \qquad k = 1, 2, \ldots. \tag{2.35}$$

Indeed, given that the process is in state i, at each step the probability of leaving state i is $(1 - p_{ii})$, and the choice is repeated independently at each step. The average number of steps spent in state i before going to another state each time the process enters state i is then

$$E[W_i] = \frac{1}{1 - p_{ii}}. \tag{2.36}$$

2.3.4 Example

Assume that in some country the weather can be described every day as either sunny, cloudy, or rainy. Moreover, assume that the weather on a given day depends in a probabilistic manner only upon the weather on the previous day. If we indicate the

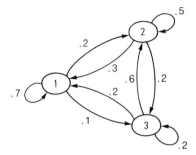

Figure 2.2
State transition diagram of the DTMC weather model.

three weather conditions as 1, 2, and 3, respectively, for sunny, cloudy, and rainy, the probabilities associated with the next day's weather (given today's weather) can be described by a matrix such as

$$\mathbf{P} = \begin{bmatrix} .7 & .2 & .1 \\ .3 & .5 & .2 \\ .2 & .6 & .2 \end{bmatrix}.$$

It is straightforward to check that this weather model satisfies the Markov property. Moreover, since the process is discrete-time and discrete-space, we can interpret the above matrix as the transition probability matrix of a finite, ergodic, DTMC (from the matrix we can see that the process is homogeneous, irreducible, and aperiodic).

The two-step transition probability matrix can be found as the square of the matrix $\mathbf{P}$:

$$\mathbf{P}^2 = [p_{ij}^{(2)}] = \begin{bmatrix} .57 & .30 & .13 \\ .40 & .43 & .17 \\ .36 & .46 & .18 \end{bmatrix}.$$

Higher powers of matrix $\mathbf{P}$ give the n-step transition probability matrix for $n > 2$. The matrix $\mathbf{P}^2$ tells us, for example, that, given that today the weather is rainy, there is a 36% chance of sun on the day after tomorrow.

The DTMC can also be described by means of the graph in figure 2.2, which conveys the same information as the transition probability matrix. Indeed, each of the two representations can be derived from the other. The graphical representation is often called the state (transition) diagram of the DTMC.

Chapter 2

The steady state distribution of the DTMC can be found by solving the system of linear equations

$$\pi_1 = .7\pi_1 + .3\pi_2 + .2\pi_3,$$
$$\pi_2 = .2\pi_1 + .5\pi_2 + .6\pi_3,$$
$$\pi_3 = .1\pi_1 + .2\pi_2 + .2\pi_3,$$
$$\pi_1 + \pi_2 + \pi_3 = 1.$$

Note that the first three equations are linearly dependent, so that one can be discarded.

The steady state distribution can be found to be

$$\pi = \left| \frac{28}{59}, \frac{22}{59}, \frac{9}{59} \right|;$$

this means that at steady state the probability of a sunny day is .47, that the mean recurrence time of sunny days is 2.1 days, and that the average number of sunny days between two consecutive rainy days is 3.11. Moreover, if today the sun is shining, we can expect 2.33 more sunny days before the weather changes.

2.4 Continuous-Time Markov Chains

By specializing the Markov property to the continuous-time, discrete-space case we obtain the definition of a CTMC:

DEFINITION   The stochastic process $\{X(t), t \geq 0\}$ is a CTMC provided that

$$P\{X(t_{n+1}) = x_{n+1} | X(t_n) = x_n, X(t_{n-1}) = x_{n-1}, \ldots, X(t_0) = x_0\}$$
$$= P\{X(t_{n+1}) = x_{n+1} | X(t_n) = x_n\}, \qquad t_{n+1} > t_n > \cdots > t_0, \qquad (2.37)$$

for all $n \in \mathbb{N}$, all $x_k \in S$, and all sequences $\{t_0, t_1, \ldots, t_{n+1}\}$ such that $t_0 < t_1 < \cdots < t_{n+1}$.

This definition is the continuous-time version of (2.8), and also in this case the right-hand side of the equation is the transition probability of the chain.

We use the following notation,

$$p_{ij}(t, \theta) = P\{X(\theta) = j | X(t) = i\}, \qquad (2.38)$$

to identify the probability that the process be in state j at time θ, given that it is in state i at time t, assuming $\theta > t$. When $\theta = t$ we define

$$p_{ij}(t,t) = \begin{cases} 1, & i = j \\ 0, & \text{otherwise.} \end{cases} \tag{2.39}$$

If the CTMC is time-homogeneous, the transition probabilities only depend on the time difference $\tau = \theta - t$, so that we can simplify the notation by writing

$$p_{ij}(\tau) = P\{X(t+\tau) = j | X(t) = i\} \tag{2.40}$$

to denote the probability that the process be in state j after an interval of length τ, given that at present it is in state i.

Also in this case, summing $p_{ij}(\tau)$ over all possible states j in the state space S, we must obtain as a result 1 for all values of τ.

2.4.1 Distribution at Time t

As in the discrete-time case, one of the goals of CTMC analysis is to evaluate the probability that the process be in state i at a given time t. Such probability is denoted.

$$\pi_i(t) = P\{X(t) = i\}. \tag{2.41}$$

Also in this case we can evaluate $\pi_i(t)$ from the transition probabilities and from the initial distribution of the process. Using the theorem of total probability, we have

$$\pi_i(t) = \sum_{j \in S} p_{ji}(t) \pi_j(0). \tag{2.42}$$

Furthermore, it can be shown that the initial distribution, together with the transition probabilities, allows the computation of the joint PDF of any set of random variables extracted from the process. This implies that the complete probabilistic description of the process only depends on the initial distribution and on the transition probabilities.

Using the Markov property (2.37), it is possible to obtain the Chapman-Kolmogorov equation for homogeneous CTMC:

$$p_{ij}(t) = \sum_{k \in S} p_{ik}(t - \theta) p_{kj}(\theta). \tag{2.43}$$

In the continuous-time case, in order to obtain the transition probabilities it is necessary to solve a system of differential equations that is derived from the Chapman-Kolmogorov equation. Define

$$q_{ij} = \lim_{\Delta t \to 0} \frac{p_{ij}(\Delta t)}{\Delta t}, \quad i \neq j, \tag{2.44a}$$

$$q_{ii} = \lim_{\Delta t \to 0} \frac{p_{ii}(\Delta t) - 1}{\Delta t}. \tag{2.44b}$$

Such limits can be shown to exist under certain regularly conditions. The intuitive interpretation of these two quantities is as follows. Given that the system is in state i at some time t, the probability that a transition occur to state j in a period of duration Δt is $q_{ij}\Delta t + o(\Delta t)$. The rate at which the process moves from state i to state j thus equals q_{ij}. Similarly, $-q_{ii}\Delta t + o(\Delta t)$ is the probability that the process move out of state i toward any other state in a period of duration Δt. Thus, $-q_{ii}$ is the rate at which the process leaves state i. We shall assume that q_{ij} is finite for all $i, j \in S$. Note that

$$\sum_{j \in S} q_{ij} = 0. \qquad \forall i \in S. \tag{2.45}$$

From (2.43) we can write

$$p_{ij}(t + \Delta t) - p_{ij}(t) = \sum_{k \in S} [p_{ik}(t + \Delta t - \theta) - p_{ik}(t - \theta)] p_{kj}(\theta). \tag{2.46}$$

Dividing both sides by Δt and taking the limit for $\Delta t \to 0$ and $\theta \to t$, we find

$$\frac{dp_{ij}(t)}{dt} = \sum_{k \in S} q_{ik} p_{kj}(t). \tag{2.47}$$

This equation is known as the Kolmogorov backward equation. Similarly, it is possible to derive the Kolmogorov forward equation:

$$\frac{dp_{ij}(t)}{dt} = \sum_{k \in S} q_{kj} p_{ik}(t). \tag{2.48}$$

These results, together with (2.42), can be used to obtain a system of differential equations whose solution yields the distribution of the process over the state space S at an arbitrary time t:

$$\frac{d\pi_i(t)}{dt} = \sum_{j \in S} q_{ji} \pi_j(t). \tag{2.49}$$

The explicit solution of this system of differential equations is difficult in many cases, so that the time-dependent solution of many interesting CTMC models can only be obtained through numerical integration.

Often, however, it is not necessary to solve for the time-dependent distribution: when a steady state solution exists, it may be of interest for many practical applications.

2.4.2 Steady State Distribution

The conditions for the existence of the steady state distribution depend, as in the discrete-time case, on the structure of the chain and on the classification of states.

Define h_j to be the *first hitting time* of state j, i.e., the instant in which the process enters state j for the first time after leaving the present state. Moreover, let

$$f_{ij} = P\{h_j < \infty | X(0) = i\}. \tag{2.50}$$

A state j is said to be transient if $f_{jj} < 1$, i.e., if there is a positive probability that the process never return to state j after leaving it. A state j is said to be recurrent if $f_{jj} = 1$, i.e., if the process returns to state j in a finite time with probability 1. A state i is said to be absorbing if $q_{ij} = 0$ for all $j \neq i$, hence if $q_{ii} = 0$. A subset A of the state space S is said to be closed if

$$\sum_{i \in A} \sum_{j \in \bar{A}} q_{ij} = 0. \tag{2.51}$$

In this case $p_{ij}(t) = 0$ for all $i \in A$, all $j \in \bar{A}$, and all $t > 0$. The states in $\bar{A}$ are thus not reachable from states in A.

A CTMC is said to be irreducible if S is closed and no proper subset of S is closed, hence if every state of S is reachable from any other state.

Define the limiting probabilities $\{\pi_j, j \in S\}$ as

$$\pi_j = \lim_{t \to \infty} \pi_j(t). \tag{2.52}$$

It can be shown that for all irreducible, homogeneous CTMC the above limits exist and are independent of the initial distribution $\{\pi_j(0), j \in S\}$; moreover, when the limits exist,

$$\lim_{t \to \infty} \frac{d\pi_j(t)}{dt} = 0, \tag{2.53}$$

so that from (2.49) we obtain the system of linear equations

$$\sum_{j \in S} q_{ji} \pi_j = 0. \tag{2.54}$$

Since this is a homogeneous system, one possible solution is that $\pi_i = 0$ for all $i \in S$. If this is the only solution of the system, then no stationary distribution exists for the CTMC. If, instead, other solutions exist, then the unique limiting distribution of the CTMC is found by imposing the normalization condition:

$$\sum_{i \in S} \pi_i = 1. \tag{2.55}$$

In this case the states of the CTMC are recurrent nonnull and ergodic, so that the chain itself is said to be ergodic.

Also in the continuous-time case the limiting probabilities of an ergodic MC satisfy the relationship

$$\pi_j = \lim_{t \to \infty} p_{ij}(t). \tag{2.56}$$

The limiting distribution of an ergodic CTMC is also called either equilibrium or steady state distribution.

The mean recurrence time for a state j, M_j, is defined as the average time elapsing between two successive instants at which the process enters state j. It can be shown that

$$M_j = \frac{1}{\pi_j q_{jj}}. \tag{2.57}$$

2.4.3 Matrix Formulation

Define the transition probability matrix $\mathbf{P}(t)$ as

$$\mathbf{P}(t) = [p_{ij}(t)], \qquad \mathbf{P}(0) = \mathbf{I}, \tag{2.58}$$

and define the vector $\boldsymbol{\pi}(t)$, whose entries are the state probabilities at time t, as

$$\boldsymbol{\pi}(t) = \{\pi_1(t), \pi_2(t), \ldots\}. \tag{2.59}$$

Equation (2.42) can be written in matrix form as

$$\boldsymbol{\pi}(t) = \boldsymbol{\pi}(0) \mathbf{P}(t), \tag{2.60}$$

and the Chapman-Kolmogorov equation (2.43) becomes

$$\mathbf{P}(t) = \mathbf{P}(t - \theta) \mathbf{P}(\theta). \tag{2.61}$$

We can also define the matrix

$$\mathbf{Q} = [q_{ij}], \tag{2.62}$$

which is called either the *infinitesimal generator* of the transition probability matrix $\mathbf{P}(t)$ or the *transition rate matrix*. The backward and forward Kolmogorov equations can then be put in matrix form, obtaining, respectively,

$$\frac{d\mathbf{P}(t)}{dt} = \mathbf{Q}\mathbf{P}(t), \tag{2.63}$$

$$\frac{d\mathbf{P}(t)}{dt} = \mathbf{P}(t)\mathbf{Q}. \tag{2.64}$$

These equations admit the general solution

$$\mathbf{P}(t) = e^{\mathbf{Q}t}, \tag{2.65}$$

which is rather elegant from a formal point of view, but relatively difficult to evaluate.

The differential equations (2.49) defining the state probabilities at time t can be rewritten as

$$\frac{d\pi(t)}{dt} = \pi(t)\mathbf{Q}. \tag{2.66}$$

Finally, the matrix equation defining the steady state distribution of an ergodic CTMC together with (2.55) is

$$\pi\mathbf{Q} = 0, \tag{2.67}$$

where π is the vector

$$\pi = \{\pi_1, \pi_2, \ldots\}. \tag{2.68}$$

2.4.4 Sojourn and Recurrence Times

Sojourn times in CTMC states are exponentially distributed random variables, as was previously noted, because the Markov property requires the distribution of sojourn times to be memoryless, and the only continuous memoryless distribution is the negative exponential. In particular, denoting by W_i the sojourn time in state $i \in S$, it can be shown that

$$f_{W_i}(\omega_i) = -q_{ii} e^{q_{ii}\omega_i}, \qquad \omega_i \geq 0. \tag{2.69}$$

The average sojourn time in state i is thus

$$E[W_i] = -\frac{1}{q_{ii}}. \tag{2.70}$$

Moreover, if we define the *forward recurrence time* at time t, $\phi(t)$, as the amount of time that the process will still spend in the state occupied at t, or, equivalently, as the length of the time period from t to the next change of state, i.e.,

$$\phi(t) = \min\{\theta > 0 : X(t + \theta) \neq X(t)\}, \tag{2.71}$$

due to the memoryless PDF of sojourn times in states, it is possible to show that

$$P\{\phi(t) > x | X(t) = i\} = e^{q_{ii}x}, \qquad x \geq 0. \tag{2.72}$$

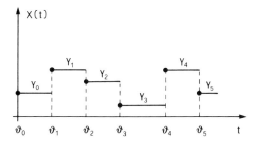

Figure 2.3
Possible sample function of a CTMC (or SMP) from which an EMC can be derived.

Hence the forward recurrence time is exponentially distributed with the same PDF as the sojourn time. The same can be shown to be true for the *backward recurrence time*, defined as the time the process has already spent in the present state at time t, provided that the set T in which the parameter t takes values is $T = (-\infty, \infty)$. The distribution of the backward recurrence time is instead a truncated exponential in the usual case $T = [0, \infty)$. In any case, both the forward and the backward recurrence times are exponentially distributed in the limit for $t \to \infty$.

2.4.5 The Embedded Markov Chain

Consider the sample function of the CTMC $\{X(t), t \geq 0\}$ shown in figure 2.3. The stochastic sequence $\{Y_n, n \geq 0\}$ is a DTMC, and it is called the *embedded Markov chain* (EMC) of the process $X(t)$.

The transition probabilities of the EMC, r_{ij}, are defined as

$$r_{ij} = P\{Y_{n+1} = j | Y_n = i\}. \tag{2.73}$$

Note that, for all times t,

$$r_{ij} = P\{X(t + \phi(t)) = j | X(t) = i\}. \tag{2.74}$$

Using the properties of CTMC it is easy to show that

$$P\{Y_{n+1} = j, \theta_{n+1} - \theta_n > \tau | Y_n = i\} = r_{ij} e^{q_{ii}\tau}, \quad \tau \geq 0, \tag{2.75}$$

and that the transition probabilities r_{ij} can be obtained as a function of the transition rates q_{ij}. Indeed, in the case of an ergodic CTMC,

$$r_{ij} = \begin{cases} -q_{ij}/q_{ii}, & i \neq j \\ 0 & i = j. \end{cases} \tag{2.76}$$

If the CTMC $\{X(t), t \geq 0\}$ is ergodic, then the DTMC $\{Y_n, n \geq 0\}$ is irreducible recurrent (possibly periodic), and the steady state distribution of the process $X(t)$ can be determined from the stationary distribution of the sequence Y_n. Let

$$\pi_j^{(X)} = \lim_{t \to \infty} P\{X(t) = j\} \tag{2.77}$$

and let the quantities $\pi_j^{(Y)}$ be obtained by solving the system of linear equations that gives the stationary distribution for the DTMC $\{Y_n, n \geq 0\}$:

$$\pi_j^{(Y)} = \sum_{i \in S} \pi_i^{(Y)} r_{ij}, \tag{2.78}$$

$$\sum_{i \in S} \pi_i^{(Y)} = 1. \tag{2.79}$$

The steady state probabilities for the CTMC $X(t)$ can then be shown to be

$$\pi_j^{(X)} = \frac{(\pi_j^{(Y)}/-q_{jj})}{\sum_{i \in S}(\pi_i^{(Y)}/-q_{ii})}. \tag{2.80}$$

Or, equivalently,

$$\pi_j^{(X)} = \frac{(1/-q_{jj})}{\sum_{i \in S}(\pi_i^{(Y)}/-q_{ii}\pi_j^{(Y)})} = \frac{E[W_j^{(X)}]}{\sum_{i \in S} v_{ij} E[W_i^{(X)}]}, \tag{2.81}$$

where $W_j^{(X)}$ is the average sojourn time in state j measured on the process $X(t)$, and the v_{ij} are the visit ratios relative to the EMC. Thus the steady state probability of any state j in a CTMC can be evaluated as the ratio of the average sojourn time in state j to the sum of the products of the average sojourn times in all states i in the state space S multiplied by the visit ratios v_{ij}, i.e., by the average number of times that the process visits state i between two successive visits to state j. Note that we are considering a portion of the process that begins with the entrance into state j and ends just before the next entrance into state j. Call this portion of process a *cycle*. The steady state probability of state j is obtained by dividing the average amount of time spent in state j during a cycle by the average cycle duration. Note, moreover, that, if we define a linear function of the steady state probabilities of the CTMC, such as

$$g = \sum_{j \in S} g_j \pi_j^{(X)}, \tag{2.82}$$

as we normally do when calculating steady state averages, this function can be evaluated as

$$g = \sum_{j \in S} \frac{g_j E[W_j]}{\sum_{i \in S} v_{ij} E[W_i]} = \frac{\sum_{j \in S} g_j \pi_j^{(Y)} E[W_j]}{\sum_{i \in S} \pi_i^{(Y)} E[W_i]}. \tag{2.83}$$

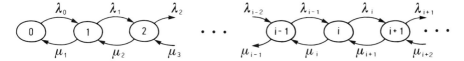

Figure 2.4
State transition rate diagram of a B-D process.

2.4.6 The Birth-and-Death Process

As an example of a CTMC we analyze the *birth-and-death* (B-D) process. A B-D process is a CTMC defined over the state space $S = \{0, 1, 2, \ldots\}$ that can experience only jumps of magnitude ± 1. It is thus possible to write the elements of the transition rate matrix as

$$q_{ij} = \begin{cases} \lambda_i, & j = i + 1 \\ \mu_i, & j = i - 1 \\ -(\lambda_i + \mu_i), & j = i \\ 0, & \text{otherwise,} \end{cases} \quad (2.84)$$

for all $i, j \in S$. The parameters λ_i and μ_i are the birth and death rates from state i, and they represent the rates at which the process leaves state i toward states $i + 1$ and $i - 1$, respectively. We assume that $\lambda_i > 0$ for all $i \in S$, that $\mu_0 = 0$, and that $\mu_i > 0$ for all $i > 0$.

The name of this process originates from the fact that it is a very convenient model for describing the evolution of the size of a population of items.

The B-D process can also be represented by means of its state transition rate diagram, shown in figure 2.4. Each oval represents the state whose number is written inside the oval. Arrows indicate that a transition from one state to another is possible. Transition rates are used to label arrows. Note that, due to the structure of the B-D process, only nearest neighbor transitions are possible. If a state transition rate diagram is used to describe a general CTMC, arrows connect also non-nearest neighbor states. Note also that it is possible to obtain the state transition diagram of the EMC simply by dividing the label of each arrow starting from any state i by $-q_{ii}$.

The state probabilities at time t can be found by solving the set of differential equations

$$\frac{d\pi_i(t)}{dt} = -(\lambda_i + \mu_i)\pi_i(t) + \lambda_{i-1}\pi_{i-1}(t) + \mu_{i+1}\pi_{i+1}(t), \quad i \geq 1,$$

$$\frac{d\pi_0(t)}{dt} = -\lambda_0 \pi_0(t) + \mu_1 \pi_1(t), \quad (2.85)$$

which is obtained by specializing (2.49) to this case. Solving this system explicitly in the general case is difficult. We shall provide a solution in a simple special case later on.

The limiting state probabilities of the B-D process, defined in (2.52), surely exist, since the B-D process is a homogeneous irreducible CTMC. It is thus possible to specialize (2.54) to this case and find

$$-(\lambda_i + \mu_i)\pi_i + \lambda_{i-1}\pi_{i-1} + \mu_{i+1}\pi_{i+1} = 0, \quad i \geq 1,$$
$$-\lambda_0\pi_0 + \mu_1\pi_1 = 0. \tag{2.86}$$

Note that these equations can be obtained directly from the state transition rate diagram by equating the rates of flow into and out from each state. Indeed, the flow into state i comes from state $i-1$ at rate λ_{i-1}, and from state $i+1$ at rate μ_{i+1}. The total flow into state i is the sum of the rates weighted by the probabilities of the origin states. We thus obtain

$$\text{flow into state } i = \lambda_{i-1}\pi_{i-1} + \mu_{i+1}\pi_{i+1}. \tag{2.87}$$

The flow out of state i is the product of the probability of state i and of the sum of the rates out of state i:

$$\text{flow out of state } i = (\lambda_i + \mu_i)\pi_i. \tag{2.88}$$

Equating the flows, using the observation that $\mu_0 = \lambda_{-1} = 0$, and rearranging the terms, we find the pair of equations (2.86).

The recursive solution of (2.86) leads to the result

$$\pi_{i+1} = \frac{\lambda_i}{\mu_{i+1}}\pi_i \tag{2.89}$$

for all $i \in S$.

Note that also these equations can be directly derived from the state transition rate diagram of figure 2.4 by equating the rates traversing each vertical section of the diagram between two neighboring states. We can further substitute recursively to obtain

$$\pi_i = \pi_0 \prod_{k=0}^{i-1} \frac{\lambda_k}{\mu_{k+1}} \tag{2.90}$$

for all $i \in S$.

By imposing the normalizing condition (2.55) we finally obtain

$$\pi_0 = \left[1 + \sum_{\substack{k \in S \\ k \neq 0}} \prod_{j=0}^{k-1} \frac{\lambda_j}{\mu_{j+1}}\right]^{-1}. \tag{2.91}$$

Thus a limiting distribution exists, provided that

$$\sum_{\substack{k \in S \\ k \neq 0}} \prod_{j=0}^{k-1} \frac{\lambda_j}{\mu_{j+1}} < \infty. \tag{2.92}$$

In this case the B-D process is ergodic, and the steady state probabilities are given by

$$\pi_i = \left[\prod_{k=0}^{i-1} \frac{\lambda_k}{\mu_{k+1}}\right] \bigg/ \left[1 + \sum_{\substack{k \in S \\ k \neq 0}} \prod_{j=0}^{k-1} \frac{\lambda_j}{\mu_{j+1}}\right] \tag{2.93}$$

for all $i \in S$.

2.4.7 The Poisson Process

As a further simplification consider a pure birth process with constant birth rate λ. We can view this process as a very special case of a B-D process, since it is obtained by letting $\mu_i = 0$ for all i, and $\lambda_i = \lambda$ for all $i \geq 0$. This process is known as the *Poisson process*. Obviously, since no death is possible, the process experiences only jumps of magnitude $+1$; thus, after leaving a state, it is impossible to return to it. All states are transient and no steady state distribution exists.

In this simple case it is possible, however, to solve explicitly the set of differential equations (2.85), which reduces to

$$\begin{aligned} \frac{d\pi_i(t)}{dt} &= -\lambda \pi_i(t) + \lambda \pi_{i-1}(t), \quad i \geq 1, \\ \frac{d\pi_0(t)}{dt} &= -\lambda \pi_0(t). \end{aligned} \tag{2.94}$$

Assuming that the process starts out from state 0 at time $t = 0$, i.e., that

$$\pi_i(0) = \begin{cases} 1, & i = 0 \\ 0, & i \neq 0, \end{cases} \tag{2.95}$$

it is possible to solve the second differential equation, obtaining

$$\pi_0(t) = e^{-\lambda t}, \quad t \geq 0. \tag{2.96}$$

Using this result, it is possible to solve all other equations recursively, obtaining in the general case

$$\pi_i(t) = \frac{(\lambda t)^i}{i!} e^{-\lambda t}, \qquad t \geq 0, \tag{2.97}$$

for all $i \in S$. The above probabilities originate a Poisson distribution with parameter λt.

An alternative definition of a Poisson process is the following. A Poisson process is a continuous-time stochastic process with state space $S = \{0, 1, 2, \ldots\}$ that can experience only jumps of magnitude $+1$, in which the intervals between jumps are independent, identically distributed random variables whose PDF is exponential with parameter λ.

2.5 Aggregation of States in Markov Chains

Very often Markovian models of real systems comprise a quite large number of states, so that the numerical evaluation of the steady state distribution is computationally very expensive, and in some cases is even infeasible. On the other hand, the equilibrium solution is often used to derive specific quantities by performing a weighted summation of steady state probabilities. In most of these cases, the weights are not different for each state, so that the same result could be achieved by solving a reduced problem in which the model comprises fewer macrostates, each macrostate containing all (or some) of the states for which the associated performance measure is the same.

In this section we address this problem by giving conditions for the existence of a compact aggregate Markovian model.

2.5.1 Aggregation in Discrete-Time Markov Chains

Consider first a finite, ergodic DTMC $\{X_n, n = 0, 1, \ldots\}$ with state space $S = \{1, 2, \ldots, N\}$, transition probability matrix $\mathbf{P}$, state distribution $\pi(n)$, and steady state distribution π.

Define a partition of S by aggregating states into macrostates A_I such that

$$S = \bigcup_{I=1}^{M} A_I \quad \text{and} \quad A_I \cap A_J = \emptyset, \quad \forall I \neq J. \tag{2.98}$$

A new stochastic sequence $\{Y_n, n = 0, 1, \ldots\}$ can be defined on the set of macrostates, with state space $S' = \{A_1, A_2, \ldots, A_M\}$. In order to determine whether this new stochastic sequence is an ergodic DTMC, it is necessary to examine the conditional probabilities

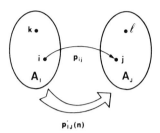

Figure 2.5
Transition probabilities between states and macrostates.

$$P\{Y_{n+1} = A_J | Y_n = A_I, Y_{n-1} = A_K, \ldots, Y_0 = A_L\}. \tag{2.99}$$

If such conditional probabilities only depend on the most recent macrostate A_I, we recognize that $\{Y_n, n \geq 0\}$ is a DTMC, with transition probabilities (see figure 2.5)

$$p'_{IJ}(n) = P\{Y_{n+1} = A_J | Y_n = A_I\}.$$

Summing over all states i in A_I and all states j in A_J, we obtain

$$p'_{IJ}(n) = \sum_{i \in A_I} \sum_{j \in A_J} p_{ij} v_{i|I}(n), \tag{2.100a}$$

where

$$v_{i|I}(n) = \frac{\pi_i(n)}{\sum_{k \in A_I} \pi_k(n)} \tag{2.100b}$$

represents the conditional probability of being in state $i \in A_I$ given that the process is in macrostate A_I. Note that a necessary and sufficient condition for the process $\{Y_n, n \geq 0\}$ to be an ergodic DTMC is that

$$\sum_{j \in A_J} p_{ij} = p'_{IJ}(n) \tag{2.101}$$

for all $i \in A_I$ and for all n. Indeed, in this case the conditional probabilities (2.99) depend only on the present (macro)state, and the dependence on n in (2.100) disappears. Condition (2.101) is the *lumpability condition* of the DTMC $\{X_n, n \geq 0\}$ with respect to the partition S'. The DTMC $\{Y_n, n \geq 0\}$ is then called the *lumped* Markov chain.

If only the steady state behavior is of interest, it is possible to write for the DTMC $\{X_n, n \geq 0\}$

$$\pi_j = \sum_{i \in S} \pi_i p_{ij}, \tag{2.102a}$$

$$\sum_{j \in S} \pi_j = 1. \tag{2.102b}$$

Summing (2.102a) over all states j in macrostate A_J, we obtain

$$\pi'_J = \sum_{A_I \in S'} \pi'_I p'_{IJ} \tag{2.103a}$$

for all $A_J \in S'$, and also

$$\sum_{A_J \in S'} \pi'_J = 1, \tag{2.103b}$$

where

$$\pi'_J = \lim_{n \to \infty} P\{X_n \in A_J\} = \sum_{j \in A_J} \pi_j, \tag{2.104}$$

$$p'_{IJ} = \sum_{i \in A_I} \sum_{j \in A_J} p_{ij} v_{i|I}, \tag{2.105a}$$

$$v_{i|I} = \frac{\pi_i}{\sum_{k \in A_I} \pi_k}. \tag{2.105b}$$

Note that equations (2.102)–(2.105) hold for all DTMC, regardless of the fulfillment of the lumpability condition, so that it is possible to evaluate the steady state distribution over macrostates from (2.103) provided that we can evaluate the quantities p'_{IJ} from (2.105). Obviously, we do not want to evaluate the steady state distribution of the process $\{X_n, n \geq 0\}$ and then plug the result into (2.105), since the reason to aggregate states into macrostates is exactly to avoid the solution of this problem due to the large number of states. In some cases, however, it is possible to evaluate the p'_{IJ} without solving for the π_i.

The first case that we consider is when the lumpability condition (2.101) is satisfied. In this case (2.103a) becomes

$$\pi'_J = \sum_{A_I \in S'} \pi'_I \sum_{j \in A_J} p_{ij}, \quad i \in A_I. \tag{2.106}$$

The second case of interest is when it is known a priori that all states in A_I have equal steady state probability. In this case

$$v_{i|I} = \frac{1}{|A_I|}, \tag{2.107}$$

where $|A_I|$ denotes the number of states comprised in macrostate A_I. Hence (2.103a) becomes

$$\pi'_J = \sum_{A_I \in S'} \frac{\pi'_I}{|A_I|} \sum_{i \in A_I} \sum_{j \in A_J} p_{ij}. \tag{2.108}$$

The third case of interest (a generalization of the previous one) is when it is known a priori that the probabilities of all states in A_I are integer multiples of a fixed (possibly not known) quantity γ. In this case we set

$$\pi_i = n_i \gamma \tag{2.109}$$

for all $i \in A_I$, and from (2.105) we find

$$v_{i|I} = \frac{n_i}{\sum_{k \in A_I} n_k}. \tag{2.110}$$

Hence (2.103a) becomes

$$\pi'_J = \sum_{A_I \in S'} \pi'_I \sum_{i \in A_I} \frac{n_i}{\sum_{k \in A_I} n_k} \sum_{j \in A_J} p_{ij}. \tag{2.111}$$

The solution of (2.106), (2.108), and (2.111), respectively, in the three cases considered, together with (2.103b), provides the steady state distribution on macrostates $\pi' = \{\pi'_1, \pi'_2, \ldots, \pi'_M\}$, although the stochastic sequence over macrostates in the latter two cases is not a DTMC.

2.5.2 Aggregation in Continuous-Time Markov Chains

Consider now a finite, ergodic CTMC $\{X(t), t \geq 0\}$ with state space $S = \{1, 2, \ldots, N\}$, infinitesimal generator $\mathbf{Q}$, transition probability matrix $\mathbf{P}(t)$, state distribution $\pi(t)$, and equilibrium distribution π.

Define also in this case a partition of S by aggregating states into macrostates A_I such that (2.98) holds.

A new stochastic process $\{Y(t), t \geq 0\}$ can be defined on the set of macrostates, with state space $S' = \{A_1, A_2, \ldots, A_M\}$. It can be shown that the condition for this new process to be an ergodic CTMC is

$$\sum_{j \in A_J} q_{ij} = q'_{IJ}, \quad \forall i \in A_I. \tag{2.112}$$

The q'_{IJ} are the entries of the infinitesimal generator $\mathbf{Q}'$ of the process $\{Y(t), t \geq 0\}$. This equation represents the condition for the lumpability of the CTMC $\{X(t), t \geq 0\}$

with respect to the partition S'. This condition also implies that

$$\sum_{j \in A_J} p_{ij}(t) = p'_{IJ}(t), \qquad \forall i \in A_I, \tag{2.113}$$

where the $p'_{IJ}(t)$ are the elements of the transition probability matrix $\mathbf{P}'(t)$ of the process $\{Y(t), t \geq 0\}$.

If we are only interested in the analysis of the steady state probabilities of macrostates defined as

$$\pi'_I = \lim_{t \to \infty} P\{X(t) \in A_I\} = \sum_{i \in A_I} \pi_i, \tag{2.114}$$

we can, as in the discrete-time case, write the following equation for the process $\{X(t), t \geq 0\}$,

$$\sum_{i \in S} \pi_i q_{ij} = 0 \tag{2.115a}$$

for all $j \in S$, and

$$\sum_{i \in S} \pi_i = 1. \tag{2.115b}$$

Summing (2.115a) over all states $j \in A_J$ we obtain

$$\sum_{A_I \in S'} \pi'_I q'_{IJ} = 0 \tag{2.116a}$$

for all $A_J \in S'$, and

$$\sum_{A_I \in S'} \pi'_I = 1, \tag{2.116b}$$

where

$$q'_{IJ} = \sum_{i \in A_I} \sum_{j \in A_J} q_{ij} v_{i|I}. \tag{2.117}$$

Also in this case equations (2.114)–(2.117) hold, regardless of the fulfillment of the lumpability condition, so that we can directly evaluate the steady state distribution of macrostates from (2.116) provided that we can evaluate the q'_{IJ} from (2.117) without solving for the steady state distribution of the CTMC $\{X(t), t \geq 0\}$.

As before, three cases can be considered.

First, if the CTMC $\{X(t), t \geq 0\}$ is lumpable with respect to the partition S', then (2.112) holds, and (2.116a) reduces to

$$\sum_{A_I \in S'} \pi'_I \sum_{j \in A_J} q_{ij} = 0, \qquad i \in A_I. \tag{2.118}$$

Second, if all states in A_I are known to have equal steady state probabilities, (2.116a) becomes

$$\sum_{A_I \in S'} \frac{\pi'_I}{|A_I|} \sum_{i \in A_I} \sum_{j \in A_J} q_{ij} = 0. \tag{2.119}$$

Third, if all states in A_I have steady state probabilities that are integer multiples of a fixed (possibly not known) quantity γ, as in (2.109), then (2.116a) reduces to

$$\sum_{A_I \in S'} \pi'_I \sum_{i \in A_I} \frac{n_i}{\sum_{k \in A_I} n_k} \sum_{j \in A_J} q_{ij} = 0. \tag{2.120}$$

The solution of (2.118), (2.119), and (2.120), respectively, in the three cases, together with (2.116b), provides the steady state distribution over macrostates.

2.6 Semi-Markov Processes

Consider the stochastic process sample function shown in figure 2.3. Assume that the process $\{X(t), t \geq 0\}$ is a finite state continuous-time homogeneous process that changes state at instants θ_n, $n = 0, 1, \ldots$, assuming the value Y_n in the interval $[\theta_n, \theta_{n+1})$ and such that

$$\begin{aligned} P\{Y_{n+1} = j, \theta_{n+1} - \theta_n \leq \tau | Y_0 = k, \ldots, Y_n = i, \theta_0 = t_0, \ldots, \theta_n = t_n\} \\ = P\{Y_{n+1} = j, \theta_{n+1} - \theta_n \leq \tau | Y_n = i\} = H_{ij}(\tau), \end{aligned} \tag{2.121}$$

and let

$$p_{ij} = \lim_{\tau \to \infty} H_{ij}(\tau). \tag{2.122}$$

In this stochastic process, sojourn times in states can be arbitrarily distributed; moreover, their PDF may depend on the next state as well as on the present one. This class of stochastic processes is called semi-Markov processes (SMP).

The PDF of the time spent in state i given that the next state is going to be j is given by

$$G_{ij}(\tau) = \begin{cases} H_{ij}(\tau)/p_{ij} & \text{if } p_{ij} > 0 \\ 0 & \text{if } p_{ij} = 0. \end{cases} \tag{2.123}$$

The stochastic sequence $\{Y_n, n \geq 0\}$ is a DTMC and is called the EMC of the SMP $\{X(t), t \geq 0\}$.

The transition probabilities of the EMC are defined as in (2.73). It can be shown that

$$r_{ij} = p_{ij}, \qquad (2.124)$$

with p_{ij} given by (2.122).

Note that in this case it is not necessary to exclude the possibility of a transition from state i to itself, hence not necessarily $r_{ii} = 0$.

The classification of the states of the process $\{X(t), t \geq 0\}$ can be done by observing whether the DTMC $\{Y_n, n \geq 0\}$ comprises either transient or recurrent states. Also the irreducibility question can be answered by observing the EMC. The periodicity of the process $\{X(t), t \geq 0\}$ is, instead, to be examined independently of the periodicity of the EMC. A state i of the SMP is said to be periodic if the process can return to it only at integer multiples of a given time δ. The maximum such δ is the period of the state. Note that a state may be aperiodic in the SMP and periodic in the EMC, and vice versa.

Assume, for simplicity, that all states of the SMP $\{X(t), t \geq 0\}$ are recurrent aperiodic. The average sojourn time in state i can be found as

$$E[W_i] = \int_0^\infty \left[1 - \sum_{k \in S} H_{jk}(t)\right] dt. \qquad (2.125)$$

Let the quantities $\pi_j^{(Y)}$ represent the stationary probabilities of the EMC $\{Y_n, n \geq 0\}$, defined as in (2.78) and (2.79). The limiting probabilities of the SMP $\{X(t), t \geq 0\}$, defined as in (2.77), can be found as

$$\pi_j^{(X)} = \frac{\pi_j^{(Y)} E[W_j]}{\sum_{k \in S} \pi_k^{(Y)} E[W_k]}, \qquad (2.126)$$

which is analogous to (2.80). The EMC technique thus allows the steady state analysis of a broader class of stochastic processes than was previously considered, namely, of SMP.

The mean recurrence time of state j, defined as the average time elapsing between two successive visits to state j, is

$$M_j = \frac{E[W_j]}{\pi_j^{(X)}}. \qquad (2.127)$$

Note that also this equation is an extension of (2.57).

The class of SMP comprises the class of CTMC, but SMP themselves are a subset of a more general class of stochastic processes, named semiregenerative processes. We shall not venture into the analysis of semiregenerative processes, but it is useful to derive one result that, obviously, is valid for all SMP and CTMC.

Consider the SMP sample function shown in figure 2.3. From (2.121) it follows that the time instants at which a jump occurs are such that the future evolution of the process is independent of the past, given the present state, even if the sojourn time in the present state is not an exponentially distributed random variable. This is sufficient to recognize that the process is a semiregenerative stochastic process.

In this case the characteristics of the process can be determined from the behavior in the period comprised between two instants at which jumps occur. This time period is called a cycle. The cycle duration is a random variable C whose average is

$$E[C] = \sum_{j \in S} \pi_j^{(Y)} E[W_j]. \tag{2.128}$$

Indeed, the cycle duration equals the sojourn time in state j provided that the state at the beginning of the cycle is j. Using the total probability theorem, we obtain (2.128).

The limiting state probabilities of a semiregenerative process can be found as the ratio of the average time spent in a state in a cycle divided by the average cycle duration. This provides another method for the derivation of (2.126).

The cycle analysis can also be performed in a slightly different manner. Consider as initial cycle times the instants at which the process enters state j. In this case the average cycle duration is obtained as

$$E[C] = \sum_{k \in S} v_{kj} E[W_k] = \sum_{k \in S} \frac{\pi_k^{(Y)}}{\pi_j^{(Y)}} E[W_k], \tag{2.129}$$

where v_{kj} gives the average number of visits to state k between two successive visits to state j, and is given by (2.29). The average time spent in state j in a cycle is obviously equal to $E[W_j]$, so that we again find the result (2.126).

Note that in this latter case the future evolution of the process, given that we are at the beginning of a cycle, is independent of the past history, and of the present state. The process is thus said to be regenerative with respect to these new cycle starting instants.

This cycle analysis will be used in later chapters to evaluate the steady state distribution of regenerative discrete-time stochastic processes; equation (2.129) will be applied for the computation of the average cycle time, and the steady state probabilities of the continuous-time process will be computed using (2.126).

References

[CINL75] Cinlar, E., *Introduction to Stochastic Processes*, Prentice-Hall, Englewood Cliffs, NJ, 1975.

[COXM65] Cox, D. R., and Miller, H. D., *The theory of Stochastic Processes*, Chapman and Hall, London, 1965.

[FELL66] Feller, W., *An Introduction to Probability Theory and Its Applications*, Vol. 2, Wiley, New York, 1966.

[HOWA71] Howard, R. A., *Dynamic Probabilistic Systems*, Vols. 1 and 2, Wiley, New York, 1971.

[KARL75] Karlin, S., and Taylor, H. M., *A First Course in Stochastic Processes*, Academic Press, New York, 1975.

[KEME60] Kemeni, G., and Snell, J. L., *Finite Markov Chains*, Van Nostrand, Princeton, NJ, 1960.

[PARZ62] Parzen, E., *Stochastic Processes*, Holden Day, San Francisco, 1962.

3 Queuing Models

Queuing models are useful tools for the analysis of systems in which conflicts develop when several entities try simultaneously to access the same resource thus causing a loss of time to take place.

Several books exist in the literature in which the analysis and the application of queuing models are discussed in depth (see, for example, [COHE69, COOP72, KLEI75, KOBA78, GELE80, SAUE81, LAVE83, LAZO84]). In this chapter we briefly review those results that will be useful later on in this book. We start the discussion of queuing models by first studying the behavior of a single queue in isolation. Subsequently the results are extended to models in which several interconnected queues exist.

A *queue* is a system to which *customers* arrive to receive *service*. When the system is busy serving other customers, incoming customers *wait* for their turn. Upon completion of a service, the customer that must be served next is selected according to some *queuing policy*. No customers are allowed to leave the queue before having received service.

Figure 3.1 provides a pictorial representation of such a system. A probabilistic representation of this system is a model in wich the time between successive arrivals of customers and the time needed to serve each customer are assumed to be random variables. Parameters of the model are thus the parameters of the arrival and service processes. In the rest of this chapter, we use the symbols ε and σ to denote these two random variables, respectively. $F_\varepsilon(t) = P\{\varepsilon \leq t\}$ and $F_\sigma(s) = P\{\sigma \leq s\}$ represent the cumulative distributions of interarrival and service times.

The number of customers in the system at any instant of time is the stochastic process that we want to study. The behavior of this stochastic process depends on the type of distributions characterizing the arrival and service processes. The shorthand notation $A/B/c/d/e$ was introduced by Kendall [KEND51] to classify the different types of models that derive from the combination of various types of interarrival and service time distributions, and of different service characteristics. A and B refer to the types

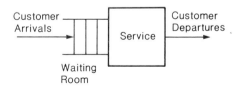

Figure 3.1
A single queue.

of the arrival and service processes, and can either assume the values M or GI to indicate a Markovian (negative exponential distribution) or a general independent (nonexponential distribution) process respectively. The number of parallel identical servers forming the service station is denoted by the symbol c. The sizes of the finite waiting room (when it exists) and of the customer population are the fourth and fifth symbols sometimes appearing in the notation.

3.1 The $M/M/1$ Queue

Let $N(t)$ represent the number of customers in the system (customers in queue and/or receiving service) at time t. The simplest way of making this stochastic process Markovian is that of assuming that interarrival times are independent, exponentially distributed random variables with mean $1/\lambda$, and that service times are independent exponentially distributed random variables with mean $1/\mu$. Moreover, let us assume that interarrival times and service times are mutually independent random variables and that they are independent of the number of customers in the system. The memoryless property of the exponential distributions of the random variables appearing in this model implies that

$$P\{N(t+\tau) = j | N(t) = i\} = p_{ij}(\tau), \qquad i, j = 0, 1, \ldots, \tag{3.1}$$

independently of t and of the past history of the process.

The stochastic process $N(t)$ is a special case of the birth-and-death (B-D) process discussed in the previous chapter. The birth rate is constant, and equals the rate of arrival of customers to the system: $\lambda_i = \lambda$ ($i = 0, 1, \ldots$). The death rate is again constant, and equals the rate of service of customers by the system: $\mu_i = \mu$ ($i = 1, 2, \ldots$).

The necessary and sufficient condition for a steady state solution to exist is that $\rho (= \lambda/\mu) < 1$. When this condition is satisfied, the result obtained in chapter 2 applies [see equation (2.93)] and the steady state distribution of the number of customers in the system is given by

$$\pi_i = \lim_{t \to \infty} P\{N(t) = i\} = \rho^i(1 - \rho) \qquad i = 0, 1, \ldots, \tag{3.2}$$

from which the mean number of customers in the system at steady state is easily obtained:

$$E[N] = \sum_{i=1}^{\infty} i\pi_i = \frac{\rho}{1 - \rho}. \tag{3.3}$$

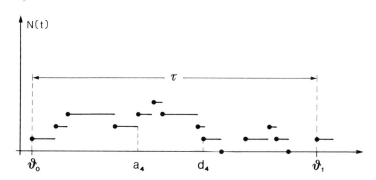

Figure 3.2
Typical sample path of the stochastic process $N(t)$.

From (3.2) we see that $\pi_0 = 1 - \rho$, and it is then straighforward to conclude that ρ represents the system utilization. Observing that λ is the average number of customers arriving to the system per unit of time, that $1/\mu$ can be interpreted as the average number of work units carried to the system by each customer, and assuming that the service capacity (or service speed) of the system is of one work unit per unit of time, ρ can be easily interpreted also as traffic intensity.

3.2 Deterministic Analysis of a Single-Server Queuing System

Results similar to those just discussed can be obtained using a different approach based on the analysis of a sample path of the stochastic process [DENN78].

Suppose we observe the system for an interval of time of length τ (from time θ_0 to time θ_1) such that

$$N(\theta_0^-) = N(\theta_1^-) = 0. \tag{3.4}$$

Figure 3.2 depicts a sample path of the process (a possible behavior of the system) during this observation period. Let A denote the total number of arrivals and D the total number of departures registered during this observation period. A_i can be used to denote the number of customers who found the system in state i (with i customers in it) upon their arrivals and made system state move from i to $i + 1$. Similarly let D_{i+1} represent the number of departures that left behind a system with i customers inside. Because of our equilibrium assumption (3.4),

$$A_i = D_{i+1}. \tag{3.5}$$

Denote by τ_i the time spent by the system in state i during the observation period. Obviously $p_i = \tau_i/\tau$ represents the fraction of time spent in state i, and (3.5) can be rewritten as

$$p_i \frac{A_i}{\tau_i} = p_{i+1} \frac{D_{i+1}}{\tau_{i+1}}. \tag{3.6}$$

In the above expression A_i/τ_i represents the rate of transition from state i to state $i + 1$, (i.e., the arrival rate conditioned on the state of the system being i). Similarly, D_{i+1}/τ_{i+1} denotes the rate of transition of the system from state $i + 1$ to state i (i.e., the departure rate, conditional on $i + 1$ being the state of the system). Denoting by λ_i and μ_{i+1} these two rates, (3.6) can be rewritten as

$$p_i \lambda_i = p_{i+1} \mu_{i+1}, \quad i = 0, 1, \ldots, \tag{3.7}$$

whose solution is

$$p_i = p_0 \prod_{k=0}^{i-1} \frac{\lambda_k}{\mu_{k+1}}, \quad i = 1, 2, \ldots. \tag{3.8}$$

Assuming once again that $\lambda_i = \lambda$ ($i = 0, 1, \ldots$), and $\mu_i = \mu$ ($i = 1, 2, \ldots$), and that $\rho = \lambda/\mu$, it is possible to rewrite this expression to obtain the following form:

$$p_i = \rho^i(1 - \rho) \quad i = 0, 1, \ldots. \tag{3.9}$$

Even though (3.9) and (3.2) are formally identical, they are substantially different. Equation (3.2) describes a property of the stochastic process obtained by introducing a set of probabilistic assumptions on the nature of interarrival and service time distributions. Equation (3.9) describes a relationship that holds between quantities defined over the sample path of figure 3.2 independently of the probabilistic properties of the stochastic process that produced such a sample path. The results derived from the analysis of such a sample path are valid for any sample path of this type, but are meaningless when referred to the underlying stochastic process.

3.2.1 Little's Formula

Using the notation introduced in the previous section, we now derive an important result, whose validity extends far beyond the framework we use for its derivation. Extending slightly the notation, let $A(t)$ and $D(t)$ denote the number of arrivals and of departures (respectively) registered in the system from time 0 up to time t.

Introducing the hypothesis that the time origin coincides with the beginning of the observation interval ($\theta_0 = 0$) and that $A(0) = D(0) = 0$, we can denote the number of customers in the system at time t by $N(t)$, and write the following relation:

$$N(t) = A(t) - D(t). \tag{3.10}$$

If a_i and d_i represent the arrival and departure times of the ith customer, we can define $w_i = d_i - a_i$, the waiting time of the same customer (notice that we call waiting time the time spent by the customer in service as well as in queue).

To simplify matters, assume that the time instants are chosen such that $N(\theta_0^-) = N(\theta_1^-) = 0$ and that $N(\theta_0) = N(\theta_1) = 1$, then we have $\theta_0 \leq a_i, d_i \leq \theta_1$ for all i. The mean number of customers observed in the system during the observation period of length τ is

$$\bar{n} = \frac{1}{\tau} \int_0^\tau N(t)\, dt. \tag{3.11}$$

The mean waiting time experienced by the customers that used the system during the same period is

$$\bar{w} = \frac{1}{A(\tau)} \sum_{i=1}^{A(\tau)} w_i. \tag{3.12}$$

Defining $\lambda = A(\tau)/\tau$, we can also write

$$\bar{w} = \frac{1}{\lambda} \frac{1}{\tau} \sum_{i=1}^{A(\tau)} w_i. \tag{3.13}$$

Let $I_i(t)$ be the presence function of the ith customer

$$I_i(t) = \begin{cases} 1, & a_i \leq t \leq d_i \\ 0, & \text{elsewhere.} \end{cases} \tag{3.14}$$

Then we can write

$$w_i = \int_0^\tau I_i(t)\, dt \tag{3.15}$$

and

$$N(t) = \sum_{i=1}^{A(\tau)} I_i(t). \tag{3.16}$$

Then

$$\int_0^\tau N(t)\,dt = \int_0^\tau \left(\sum_{i=1}^{A(\tau)} I_i(t)\right) dt$$
$$= \sum_{i=1}^{A(\tau)} \int_0^\tau I_i(t)\,dt = \sum_{i=1}^{A(\tau)} w_i, \tag{3.17}$$

from which follows

$$\bar{n} = \lambda \bar{w}. \tag{3.18}$$

Equation (3.18) is known as Little's formula [LITT61] for this deterministic case. Equation (3.18) says that the mean number of customers in the system and the corresponding mean waiting time are always related via the arrival rate of customers λ.

Since in the above derivation no explicit reference to the concept of queue has been made, Little's result holds for any stable system in which the number of customers, the waiting times, and the interarrival times all have finite means. A formally identical result, in which these means are replaced by statistical averages,

$$E[N] = \lambda E[W],$$

holds also for stochastic systems satisfying similarly weak conditions. The formal extension of the previous proof to a more general stochastic process $N(t)$ can be done using renewal arguments. Indeed Little's formula holds for any regenerative stochastic process, i.e., for any stochastic process in which interarrival and service times are both independent, identically distributed random variables and for which an infinite sequence of points such as θ_0 or θ_1, defined before, exists.

3.3 Extended Results

Simple extensions of the results concerning the single-server queue analyzed in section 3.1 can be obtained by generalizing the service station to be either a multiple server, or a device with service speed dependent on the number of customers in the queue (load dependent), as well as by limiting the population of customers using the system.

3.3.1 The $M/M/m$ Queue

Assume that the service center comprises m parallel servers so that the system is now capable of processing up to m units of work per unit of time. Denoting by i the number of customers in the system, the capacity of this service center is represented by the following function:

$$C_i = \begin{cases} i \text{ units of work per unit of time,} & i < m \\ m \text{ units of work per unit of time,} & i \geq m. \end{cases} \quad (3.19)$$

Assuming, as before, that λ represents the rate of customer arrivals, and that $1/\mu$ represents the average amount of work units carried to the system by each customer, the departure rate (conditional on having at least one customer in the system) becomes

$$\mu_i = C_i \mu = \begin{cases} i\mu, & i < m \\ m\mu, & i \geq m. \end{cases} \quad (3.20)$$

The stochastic process underlying this new service system can be seen as a special kind of B-D process in which $\lambda_i = \lambda$, and in which the death rate is defined by (3.20). Having defined ρ in the usual way as λ/μ, and assuming that the stability condition $\lambda/m\mu < 1$ is satisfied, the steady state probability distribution of the number of customers in the system becomes

$$\pi_i = \begin{cases} \pi_0 \dfrac{\rho^i}{i!}, & i < m \\[1em] \pi_0 \dfrac{\rho^i}{m!\, m^{i-m}}, & i \geq m, \end{cases} \quad (3.21)$$

where

$$\pi_0 = \left(\sum_{j=0}^{m-1} \frac{\rho^j}{j!} + \frac{m\rho^m}{(m-\rho)m!} \right)^{-1}. \quad (3.22)$$

Equations (3.21) and (3.22) are particular cases of the more general results derived in chapter 2 [see equations (2.90) and (2.91)] in which also the birth rate, respresenting in our case the parameter of the arrival process, was allowed to depend on the state of the system.

3.3.2 Load-Dependent Server

Using the same arguments, we can further generalize the previous result by assuming that the server has a load-dependent speed, that is, by saying that its capacity (the number of work units processed per unit of time) changes with the number of customers present at the server. As in the previous case, we then obtain a B-D process characterized by a constant birth rate and by the following death rate:

$$\mu_i = \mu C_i. \quad (3.23)$$

The expression of the load-dependent service rates of this type is often referred to as *service function*. The steady state distribution of the number of customers in the system (when it exists) is given by the following expression:

$$\pi_i = \pi_0 \frac{\rho^i}{\prod_{j=1}^{i} C_j}, \qquad i = 1, 2, \ldots, \tag{3.24}$$

where

$$\pi_0 = \left(\sum_{i=0}^{\infty} \frac{\rho^i}{\prod_{j=1}^{i} C_j} \right)^{-1}. \tag{3.25}$$

The stability condition for this system (i.e., the condition for the existence of the steady state distribution) is represented by having a value of $\pi_0 > 0$. This corresponds to the existence of value J such that for any $i > J$ the relationship $\lambda/(\mu C_i) < 1$ is satisfied.

3.3.3 The $M/M/1/\infty/m$ Queue

A third extension of the results derived for the $M/M/1$ queue can be obtained by limiting the number of customers in the system. In this case each customer is characterized by two states: either in the system or "arriving" for a new service. As customers leave the system upon completion of service, they enter into the arriving condition that makes them join the queue again, after a period that is a random variable with negative exponential distribution with parameter λ. It then happens that at any point in time, if i customers are in the system (either receiving or waiting for service), the other $m - i$ customers are arriving, so that the total average arrival rate becomes $(m - i)\lambda$.

This system is modeled quite properly by a special type of B-D process in which the birth rate is expressed by the following function,

$$\lambda_i = \begin{cases} (m - i)\lambda, & 0 \leq i \leq m \\ 0, & \text{otherwise}, \end{cases} \tag{3.26}$$

and the death rate is constant, $\mu_i = \mu$, $i = 1, 2, \ldots$.

No stability conditions need to be checked for this sytem, which is always ergodic. Denoting once again by ρ the ratio λ/μ, the steady state probability distribution of the number of customers can be derived from (2.90) and (2.91), which after a little manipulation become

$$\pi_i = \begin{cases} \pi_0 \rho^i \dfrac{m!}{(m - i)!}, & 0 < i \leq m \\ 0, & i > m, \end{cases} \tag{3.27}$$

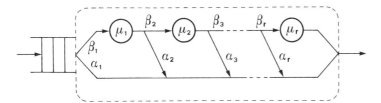

Figure 3.3
Representation of a single queue with Coxian distribution of the service time.

and

$$\pi_0 = \left(\sum_{i=0}^{m} \rho^i \frac{m!}{(m-i)!} \right)^{-1}. \tag{3.28}$$

3.4 The $M/GI/1$ Queue

The service systems analyzed in the previous sections shared the common property that the stochastic process representing the number of customers in the system was a Markov chain. An obvious generalization of the model is that of relaxing the hypothesis of exponentially distributed service times, allowing the number of work units carried to the system by each customer to be generally distributed, but independent of the interarrival times. By so doing, the process $N(t)$, which counts the number of customers in the system, does not enjoy the Markov property, and the (relatively) simple method of analysis of the previous sections cannot be applied.

3.4.1 Coxian Distributions

A Markov chain analysis of this more general problem is, however, still possible when the general distribution of the service time is of Coxian type. A *Coxian distribution* can be expressed as a composition of exponential stages. A single server queuing system with service times distributed according to a Coxian distribution is depicted in figure 3.3, where only one customer is allowed to stay in the service area (enclosed by a dashed line) at any given time.

The service of a customer consists of a sequence of service stages (each one requiring an exponentially distributed time). The solution of the problem can still be obtained using standard Markov chain methods, provided that we analyze a stochastic process whose generic state is a pair representing the number of customers in the system and the stage of service of the customer being served at any given time:

$$(N(t), S(t)). \tag{3.29}$$

Indeed, in this case, given that at time t we observe the system with $N(t)$ customers and with the customer in service at stage $S(t)$, the future behavior of the system is completely determined by this information, and is instead independent of the time already spent in this state.

Because of the memoryless property of the interarrival time distribution and of the distribution of each stage of service, this new stochastic process is Markovian. Closed form, explicit expressions for the distribution of the number of customers in the system are difficult to obtain, but for very simple cases [KLEI75]. However, this representation is very well suited for a numerical solution of the problem.

3.4.2 Embedded Markov Chain

A more general approach to the solution of this same problem is that of recognizing in the process $N(t)$ an embedded Markov chain. For this purpose, we can observe the system only at specific points in time represented by the instants of departure of customers. Assuming that Y_n represents the number of customers in the system left behind by the departure of the nth customer, the future evolution of the system [i.e., the number of customers left behind by the departure of the $(n + 1)$th customer] is completely determined by the present state, and by the distributions of the interarrival and service times. Let Z_{n+1} represent the number of customers arriving at the system during the service of the $(n + 1)$th customer; then

$$Y_{n+1} = Y_n + Z_{n+1} - u(Y_n), \tag{3.30}$$

where

$$u(k) = \begin{cases} 0, & k \leq 0 \\ 1, & k > 0. \end{cases}$$

The stochastic sequence $\{Y_n, n \geq 1\}$, counting the number of customers observed in the system just after the departure of customers, is thus a discrete-time Markov chain, usually referred as the *embedded Markov chain*, whose transition probability matrix is easily computed in terms of the probabilistic characteristics of the arrival and service processes.

In order to derive the transition probabilities, we must compute first the probability that during the service of a customer, j other customers arrive at the station. Let $P\{Z_n = j, \sigma_n = s\}$ denote the probability that j customers arrive during the service of the nth customer that lasts s units of time. The independence between the arrival and service processes allows one to express the above probability as

$$P\{Z_n = j, \sigma_n = s\} = P\{Z_n = j|s\}P\{\sigma_n = s\}, \qquad (3.31)$$

in which the right-hand side is made up of the Poisson distribution [see (2.97)] of the number of arrivals during a given interval multiplied by the density function of the service times. By integration, the probability of j arrivals during the nth service is

$$P\{Z_n = j\} = \hat{p}_j = \int_0^\infty P\{Z_n = j, \sigma_n = s\}\,ds$$
$$= \int_0^\infty \frac{(\lambda s)^j}{j!} e^{-\lambda s} f_\sigma(s)\,ds. \qquad (3.32)$$

The explicit expression of $\hat{p}_j$ depends on the form of the density function $f_\sigma(s)$ of the service time. We thus obtain

$$P\{Y_{n+1} = j | Y_n = i\} = p_{ij}(n) = \hat{p}_{j-i+u(i)}. \qquad (3.33)$$

Because of the homogeneity and mutual independence of service times, the sequence index n of the transition probability $p_{ij}(n)$ can be dropped without loss of generality. The transition probability matrix of the embedded Markov chain assumes then the following form:

$$\mathbf{P} = \begin{bmatrix} \hat{p}_0 & \hat{p}_1 & \hat{p}_2 & \hat{p}_3 & \cdot & \cdot & \cdot \\ \hat{p}_0 & \hat{p}_1 & \hat{p}_2 & \hat{p}_3 & \cdot & \cdot & \cdot \\ 0 & \hat{p}_0 & \hat{p}_1 & \hat{p}_2 & \cdot & \cdot & \cdot \\ 0 & 0 & \hat{p}_0 & \hat{p}_1 & \cdot & \cdot & \cdot \\ \cdot & \cdot & \cdot & \cdot & \cdot & \cdot & \cdot \\ \cdot & \cdot & \cdot & \cdot & \cdot & \cdot & \cdot \\ \cdot & \cdot & \cdot & \cdot & \cdot & \cdot & \cdot \end{bmatrix}. \qquad (3.34)$$

The equilibrium distribution of the number of customers in the system at departure instants, obtained as solution of the embedded Markov chain, is also the steady state distribution of customers in the system, because of the memoryless property of the Poisson arrival process. Indeed, it is possible to show that the distribution at departure instants equals the distribution at arrival instants, provided that the system is stable. It can also be shown that the distribution at arrival instants equals the distribution at random points in time because a Poisson arrival behaves like a random observer.

Starting from (3.30), which represents the fundamental equation of the embedded Markov chain characterizing the $M/GI/1$ queue, expressions for the distribution and the mean of the number of customers in the system can be obtained by simple arguments. In particular, using the symbols CV_σ to denote the coefficient of variation of the distribution of the service times of the queue and ρ to represent the product $\lambda E[\sigma]$, the explicit expression of the mean number of customers in the system turns out to be the following,

$$E[N] = \rho + \rho^2 \frac{(1 + CV_\sigma^2)}{2(1 - \rho)}, \tag{3.35}$$

which is the well known Pollaczek-Khintchin mean value formula.

The analysis of more general single-server queuing systems becomes much more complex and goes beyond the scope of this book; moreover, few explicit results for these more general systems exist.

3.5 Queuing Networks

The behavior of many real systems is characterized by the presence of several congestion points, which refer to the sharing of different types of resources. In these cases it is difficult (and often too restrictive) to represent the complex behavior of the system with a single queue model of the types discussed so far. It is, instead, appealing explicitly to reflect in the model the different congestion points of the system. The model hence becomes a *queuing network* (QN), i.e., a network of interconnected queues that, in general, behave in a dependent manner.

It is easy to realize that the study of such a complex probabilistic model is usually much more difficult than that of a single queue in isolation. Several special cases characterized by the structure of the queue interconnection and by the distributions of the many arrival and service processes have been analyzed in the literature, and found to be solvable with relatively simple mathematical tools. In the following sections we discuss some of these cases, starting with the easiest ones and arriving at more complex ones, which can be treated only with the help of approximation techniques.

3.5.1 Burke's Theorem

Before starting the discussion of the behavior of networks of interconnected queues, we mention an interesting result due to Burke [BURK56] concerning the first queuing model we analyzed at the beginning of this chapter.

Chapter 3   51

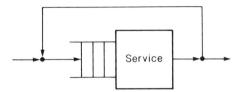

Figure 3.4
A single queue with feedback.

THEOREM   The departure process from a stable single-server queue with exponentially distributed service times and exponentially distributed interarrival times is Poisson with the same parameter of the input process.

This theorem says that, under certain conditions, and despite the appearance of an interference induced by the server on the arrival process (interference that is made explicit by the queue formed in front of the server), the output process maintains the characteristics of the input process, so that an outside observer sees it as if it was unaffected by the service center.

The key property that is used to prove this result is the independence between the arrival and the service processes. This result extends easily to the case of a multiple server queue ($M/M/m$); however, it already ceases to hold for the simple case of an $M/M/1$ queue with feedback (see figure 3.4), in which the previous independence condition is not satisfied.

3.5.2 Feedforward Queuing Networks

Consider now a QN model comprising M ($M/M/m$) stations connected so that they can be numbered in such a way that if j is the index of a server receiving input from server i, then $i < j$. Arrivals from the outside world occur according to Poisson processes and may directly join any server in the network. The service time distributions at all the stations in the network are negative exponential, with the possibility of different parameters for each station.

Customers travel through the network so that upon departure from station i, p_{ij} represents the probability of joining station j ($j > i$). The index 0 is used to represent the outside world, so that p_{i0} is the probability that a customer leaving station i completes its service from the network and "disappears." New customers join the network according to a Poisson arrival process of parameter λ_0. The arrivals from the outside world to the individual stations of the network occur then with parameters $\lambda_0 p_{0i}$.

Since superpositions of independent Poisson processes yield Poisson processes and splittings of Poisson processes yield individual Poission processes, it is easy to see that in feedforward networks each server is fed by a Poission input process, thus behaving like an $M/M/m$ queue in isolation. The characteristics of the network are captured by the parameters of the Poisson input processes of each server that must satisfy the following relation:

$$\lambda_i = \lambda_0 p_{0i} + \sum_{j<i} \lambda_j p_{ji}. \tag{3.36}$$

This system of equations is triangular and admits a unique solution. The whole network is said to be stable if each individual server is stable. Indicating by μ_i and m_i the service rate and the number of servers of the ith station of the network, respectively, the stability condition is the following:

$$\frac{\lambda_i}{m_i \mu_i} < 1, \quad i = 1, 2, \ldots, M. \tag{3.37}$$

The solution of the queuing network is assumed to be the steady state probability distribution of customers over the stations. Let $\mathbf{N}$ be an M component vector whose elements represent the number of customers at each station, and let $\pi(\mathbf{N})$ be the joint steady state probability of finding N_i customers at the ith station ($i = 1, 2, \ldots, M$). Since each server behaves like an $M/M/m$ queue in isolation, the individual queue lengths appear to be independent of each other and we obtain

$$\pi(\mathbf{N}) = \prod_{i=1}^{M} \pi_i(N_i), \tag{3.38}$$

where $\pi_i(N_i)$ represents the probability of finding N_i customers in an $M/M/m_i$ queue characterized by a mean service time of $1/\mu_i$ and by an input Poisson process with parameter λ_i. Equation (3.38) is called a *product form solution*, since the global solution is made up of M components, each one depending on the characteristics of an individual station.

3.5.3 Jackson Queuing Networks

Vital to the derivation of the product form solution (3.38) for feedforward networks was the application of Burke's theorem, made possible by the fact that no cycles were present in such networks. As we observed before, Burke's theorem stops holding as soon as a feedback exists between the output and the input of a server, or, more generally, a feedback exists in a chain of "exponential" service stations. In spite of this negative result, the pioneering work of Jackson [JACK63] showed that the product form solution (3.38) holds for a more general class of networks in which cycles between stations are allowed, i.e., in which a customer is allowed to visit several times the same station before leaving the network. These networks are known as Jackson networks. Jackson theorem states that if the system of equations

$$\lambda_i = \lambda_0 p_{0i} + \sum_{i=1}^{M} \lambda_j p_{ji}, \qquad i = 1, 2, \ldots, M, \tag{3.39}$$

balancing the flows of customers entering and exiting from each individual station has a solution, and if this solution is such that the stability conditions are satisfied, then the product form solution holds.

Proving that the product form solution exists for these networks is no simple matter. The model is analyzed by recognizing that the time behavior of the state of the network (distribution of customers over the stations) is a Markov chain and that the equations for the steady state solution of the model can be written balancing the probability of entering a state with the probability of exiting from the same state. As described in chapter 2, these equations, which are called global balance equations, can be written directly to balance the flow in and out of any network state. Because of the exponential distribution of the service times and of the Poisson arrival process, the set of states adjacent to a given state is relatively small.

Using the following notation to represent particular states,

$$\begin{aligned}
\mathbf{N} &= (N_1, \ldots, N_i, \ldots, N_j, \ldots, N_M), \\
\mathbf{N}_{i0} &= (N_1, \ldots, N_i + 1, \ldots, N_j, \ldots, N_M), \\
\mathbf{N}_{0j} &= (N_1, \ldots, N_i, \ldots, N_j - 1, \ldots, N_M), \\
\mathbf{N}_{ij} &= (N_1, \ldots, N_i + 1, \ldots, N_j - 1, \ldots, N_M),
\end{aligned} \tag{3.40}$$

the following are the only transitions allowed in the network:

$\mathbf{N}_{0j} \to \mathbf{N}$: a customer arrives from the outside world to station j;
$\mathbf{N}_{i0} \to \mathbf{N}$: a customer departs from station i and leaves the system;
$\mathbf{N}_{ij} \to \mathbf{N}$: a customer departs from station i and joins station j.

Assuming that the service speed of all stations is queue length independent and that all the Poisson arrival processes are homogeneous, we can write the following set of balance equations:

$$\sum_{i,j} \pi(\mathbf{N}_{ij})\mu_i p_{ij} u(N_j) + \sum_j \pi(\mathbf{N}_{0j})\lambda_0 p_{0j} u(N_j) + \sum_i \pi(\mathbf{N}_{i0})\mu_i p_{i0}$$

$$= \pi(\mathbf{N}) \left[\sum_i \mu_i u(N_i) + \lambda_0 \right] \quad \text{for all } \mathbf{N},$$
(3.41)

where $u(k)$ is the unity step function defined in (3.30). By inspection it is possible to verify that the product from solution (3.38) indeed satisfies this set of balance equations.

3.5.4 Gordon and Newell Queuing Networks

A particular case of the Jackson networks presented in the previous section is represented by networks in which no arrivals from the outside world are allowed, so that the number of customers in the network $\hat{N}$ is kept constant.

Networks of this type can be used to model systems in which new customers are allowed to enter only upon the departure of another customer. All customers are statistically identical, so that this exchange is transparent to the outside observer, who sees the number of customers in the system as remaining constant. Even though the distribution of every service is assumed to be exponential, none of the arrival processes observed in input to the stations of the network is now Poisson. Gordon and Newell [GORD67] analyzed this class of networks, showing once again that the solution for the steady state distribution of customers in the network is of the product form type. The balance equations are in this case (formally) simpler than those of (3.41), since the terms concerning arrivals from the outside world and departures toward the outside world are now dropped. Moreover, the number of feasible states of the network is now finite (a state is feasible when it satisfies the conditions $\sum_{i=1}^{M} N_i = \hat{N}$; $N_i \geq 0$, $i = 1, 2, \ldots, M$). The product form solution in this case assumes a slightly different form,

$$\pi(\mathbf{N}) = \frac{1}{G} \prod_{i=1}^{M} h_i(N_i),$$
(3.42)

where the term G is a normalization constant introduced to account for the dependence that now exists among the stations of the network. The function $h_i(N_i)$ is an unnormalized queue length distribution at the ith station obtained by solving the same station in isolation, subject to an arrival process with rate satisfying the following equation:

$$\lambda_i = \sum_{j=1}^{M} \lambda_j p_{ji}, \quad i = 1, 2, \ldots, M.$$
(3.43)

It is interesting to observe that this system of equations is homogeneous and hence admits an infinite number of solutions. These solutions differ for a multiplicative constant, and any one of them is equally well suited for computing the product form solution of the network in which the influence of the multiplicative constant is canceled. As long as the transition probability matrix between the stations of the network defines an ergodic discrete time Markov chain, the network admits a product form solution and no stability conditions need to be checked. The network is in some sense *self-adaptive*. One possible solution of the flow balance equations (3.43) is that of computing the arrival rates to all the stations of the network in terms of the arrival rate to the first station:

$$V_i = \frac{\lambda_i}{\lambda_1}, \qquad i = 1, 2, \ldots, M. \tag{3.44}$$

In this case the solution of the flow balance equations are called visit ratios and the ith component of the solution can be interpreted as the mean number of visits that each customer makes to the ith station between two subsequent visits to the first station.[1] The first station becomes a reference station. Once again this product form solution is difficult to prove and can only be verified to satisfy the global balance equations of the network.

3.5.5 BCMP Queuing Networks

Several extensions of the work of Jackson and of Gordon and Newell have been proposed, all leading to QN with product form solution. These extensions concern the possibility of grouping the customers of the network in classes with different use characteristics, the possibility of having different service disciplines for managing the various queues, and the possibility of specifying service time distributions different from the negative exponential.

This wider class of QN models is defined by the following theorem, which resulted from the combined effort of several authors (Baskett, Chandy, Muntz, and Palacios—see [BASK75]), whose initials appear in the name of the theorem.

BCMP THEOREM   The class of networks under consideration contains an arbitrary but finite number M of service stations. There is an arbitrary but finite number R of different classes of customers. Customers travel through the network and change class according to transition probabilities. Thus a customer of class r who completes service

---

[1] Notice that the term *visit ratio* was already introduced in chapter 2 during the discussion of the solution of Markov chains, but with a different meaning, since there was referred to visits to states of the stochastic process instead of visits to stations of the QN.

at station i will next require service at station j in class s with a certain probability denoted $p_{ir,js}$. The transition matrix $\mathbf{P} = [p_{ir,js}]$ can be considered as defining a discrete-time Markov chain whose states are labeled by pairs (i, r). The Markov chain is assumed to be decomposable into U ergodic subchains, so that the symbols EC_1, $EC_2, \ldots, EC_U$ can be used to denote the sets of classes pertaining to each of these subchains. Every time jobs of a given class are allowed to change class membership, the number U of subchains is smaller than R. When instead no change of class membership exists, $U = R$. The possible states of a network of this type are defined by the double vector $\underline{\mathbf{N}} = (\mathbf{N}_1, \mathbf{N}_2, \ldots, \mathbf{N}_M)$ which lists, for each station of the network, the number of customers of the different classes present at the station. Let N_{ir} be the number of customers of class r at station i in the state $\underline{\mathbf{N}}$ of the model, then a closed system is characterized by

$$\sum_{i=1}^{M} \sum_{r \in EC_q} N_{ir} = \hat{N}_q, \qquad q = 1, 2, \ldots, U.$$

In an open system customers may arrive to the network from the outside world. Two general types of state dependent arrival processes are considered. In the first case the total arrival to the network is Poisson with mean rate dependent on the total number of customers in the network. In the second type of arrival process there are up to U Poisson arrival streams, corresponding to the U subchains defined earlier with mean rate dependent on the total number of customers in the network of that specific subchain.

A service station is referred to as of type 1, 2, 3, or 4 according to which condition it satisfies:

Type 1. The service discipline is FCFS; all customers have the same service time distribution at this station, and the service time distribution is a negative exponential. The service rate can depend on the total number of customers at the station.

Type 2. There is a single server at the station, the service discipline is processor sharing (i.e., when there are n customers in the station each is receiving service at rate of $1/n$ units of work per unit of time), and each class of customers may have a distinct service time distribution. The service time distributions have rational Laplace transforms.

Type 3. The number of servers in the station is larger than or equal to the maximum number of customers that can be queued at this station in a feasible state, and each class of customers may have a distinct service time distribution. The service time distributions have rational Laplace transforms.

Type 4. There is a single server at the station, the queuing discipline is preemptive-resume LCFS, and each class of customers may have a distinct service time distribution. The service time distributions have rational Laplace transforms.

The steady state solution of any queuing network satisfying these conditions can be written in a product form

$$\pi(\underline{N}) = \frac{1}{G} \prod_{i=1}^{M} h_i(\mathbf{N}_i), \qquad (3.45)$$

in which each function $h_i(\mathbf{N}_i)$ represents the unnormalized queue length distribution of the ith station obtained by solving the same station in isolation, subject to arrival processes with rates satisfying the following set of flow equations:

$$\lambda_{ir} = \lambda_{0r} p_{0r,ir} + \sum_{j=1}^{M} \sum_{s=1}^{R} \lambda_{js} p_{js,ir}, \qquad i = 1, \ldots, M, \quad r = 1, \ldots, R. \qquad (3.46)$$

The explicit expressions for the functions $h_i(\mathbf{N}_i)$ can be found in the paper where this theorem was first published [BASK75]. In the particular case of a queuing network satisfying the conditions stated before, and in which every station has a load independent service rate and customers are not allowed to change class membership, the functions $h_i(\mathbf{N}_i)$ assume the following form:

$$h_i(\mathbf{N}_i) = \begin{cases} N_i! \prod_{r=1}^{R} \frac{1}{N_{ir}!} (\lambda_{ir})^{N_{ir}} \left(\frac{1}{\mu_i}\right)^{N_i} & \text{(stations of type 1),} \\ N_i! \prod_{r=1}^{R} \frac{1}{N_{ir}!} \left(\frac{\lambda_{ir}}{\mu_{ir}}\right)^{N_{ir}} & \text{(stations of type 2 or 4),} \\ \prod_{r=1}^{R} \frac{1}{N_{ir}!} \left(\frac{\lambda_{ir}}{\mu_{ir}}\right)^{N_{ir}} & \text{(stations of type 3).} \end{cases} \qquad (3.47)$$

where $N_i = \sum_{i=1}^{R} N_{ir}$.

An observation on the results of this theorem is that general service distributions of the Coxian type are allowed only in conjunction with service disciplines that reduce their influence by making the solution to be affected only by the their means (the detailed description of these distributions; i.e., their higher moments disappear from the solution). When the queue of a server is managed with an FCFS policy, all the characteristics of the corresponding service time distribution need to be taken into account, and a product form solution is in this case preserved if and only if the service time distributions of all customers (independently of their class) is the same negative exponential distribution. At first look this seems to make the BCMP theorem a trivial extension of the work of Jackson and of Gordon and Newell when the FCFS discipline is used at all the stations of the network; however, this is not the case if we observe that, by allowing customers to change class membership, it is possible, upon completion of service from a station, to allow the customer to choose the station to join next based on the stations visited before. In this way the matrix containing the probabilities of transition among stations corresponding to customers pertaining to a subchain (set of communicating classes) may characterize a high-order discrete time Markov chain. Of course Jackson networks and Gordon and Newell networks can be considered as particular cases of BCMP networks. As in the case of the results of Jackson and of Gordon and Newell, a proof of the theorem can only be made by inspection, observing that indeed the proposed product form solution satisfies the global balance equations characterizing this more complex model.

3.5.5.1 Local Balance Queuing Networks

A sufficient condition for the proof of the BCMP theorem is the following: To have a product form solution, a queuing network must be made up of service stations, each one satisfying the *local balance* property. A single queue (in isolation) is said to satisfy the local balance property when its underlying Markov process has a solution that, besides obviously satisfying the balance equations for the flows in and out of each of its states, satisfies also a larger set of equations, called *local balance equations*. Local balance equations are obtained by balancing the rate of transition out of a state due to the arrival of a customer of class r to the rate of transition into the same state due to the departure of a customer of the same class r.

In order to relate better this concept to the QN that we are considering in this section, let us apply the idea of local balance to a single class QN. Consider, for instance, the QN depicted in figure 3.5, comprising 3 $M/M/1$ queues visited by 3

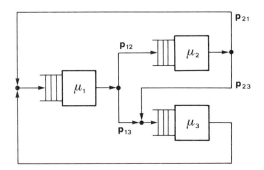

Figure 3.5
A 3-station queuing network.

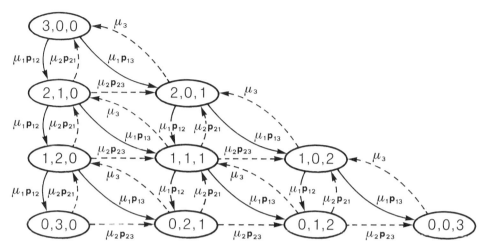

Figure 3.6
State transition rate diagram for the queuing network of figure 3.5.

customers. The state of this network is represented by the vector $\mathbf{N} = (N_1, N_2, N_3)$. The queuing network state transition rate diagram is depicted in figure 3.6. As usual, μ_i represents the service rate of station i, and p_{ij} the probability that a customer join station j upon completion of its service from station i. If we consider state $(1, 1, 1)$, we can write the following global balance equation:

$$P\{(2,1,0)\}\mu_1 p_{13} + P\{(1,2,0)\}\mu_2 p_{23}$$
$$+ P\{(2,0,1)\}\mu_1 p_{12} + P\{(0,2,1)\}\mu_2 p_{21} + P\{(0,1,2)\}\mu_3 \qquad (3.48)$$
$$= P\{(1,1,1)\}(\mu_1 + \mu_2 + \mu_3).$$

A sufficient condition for the steady state probability distribution to satisfy this global balance equation is that the following flows be individually balanced:

$$P\{(2,1,0)\}\mu_1 p_{13} + P\{(1,2,0)\}\mu_2 p_{23} = P\{(1,1,1)\}\mu_3,$$
$$P\{(2,0,1)\}\mu_1 p_{12} = P\{(1,1,1)\}\mu_2, \qquad (3.49)$$
$$P\{(0,2,1)\}\mu_2 p_{21} + P\{(0,1,2)\}\mu_3 = P\{(1,1,1)\}\mu_1.$$

The first of these three equations balances the flow into state $(1, 1, 1)$ due to the arrival of a customer to station 3 with that out of the same state due to the departure of a customer from station 3 again. In a similar manner the other two equations refer to arrivals and departures from stations 2 and 1, respectively. As one can see, these equations are individually simpler than the global balance equation (3.48). Moreover, they often provide ways of constructing their solution in a relatively straightforward manner.

Splitting the global balance equation (3.48) into the local balance equations (3.49) amounts thus to the construction of a larger system of linear equations that is usually easier to solve. Moreover, it is not difficult to show that if such a system is compatible, so that a solution exists, then this solution has a product form.

3.6 Computational Aspects of the Solution of BCMP Queuing Networks

When QN are used as models of computing systems, the characterization of the behavior of the system is usually expressed in terms of average performance indices such as utilization of each station (the fraction of time during which the server is busy); throughput (the number of services completed per unit of time by each station); mean queue length (the average number of customers present at each station); and mean waiting time (the average amount of time spent by a customer before departing from a given station). All these average performance indices can be derived from the knowledge of the distribution of the number of customers present at a station. These distributions are thus the actual quantities to be computed during the solution of the model. They can be expressed as marginal distributions of the product form solution discussed in the previous sections.

In the case of open networks (those in which *all* customer classes receive inputs from the outside world) these marginal distributions are exactly the factors of the product form solution; therefore the solution of these networks is comparable to the solution of M service stations in isolation.

In the case of closed networks the computational problem is made much harder by the necessity of evaluating the normalization constant. Using the extended notation in which the state of the QN is represented by the double vector $\underline{N}$ and the state of the ith station by the vector $\mathbf{N}_i$ introduced in the statement of the BCMP theorem in section 3.5.5, the formal expression of the normalization constant becomes relatively simple,

$$G = \sum_{\underline{N}} \prod_{i=1}^{M} h_i(\mathbf{N}_i), \qquad (3.50)$$

but the number of terms involved in the summation is usually so large as to make a direct computation of G infeasible.

The state space of closed QN is in most practical cases quite large. Indeed, the presence of several classes of customers makes the size of the state space explode dramatically. A good understanding of the computational problems that one faces when solving a closed product form QN can be obtained by analyzing the details of the solution of single class product form closed QN; this will be thus discussed next.

In this simplified case the size of the state space is provided by the following binomial coefficient,

$$D = \binom{\hat{N} + M - 1}{M - 1}, \tag{3.51}$$

and is thus exponential in the number of stations and of customers in the network.

3.6.1 The Convolution Method

The key to an efficient computation of the normalizing constant is a recursive expression of the function (3.50) that in the simplified case of single class queuing networks becomes

$$G = \sum_{\mathbf{N}} \prod_{i=1}^{M} h_i(N_i). \tag{3.52}$$

One way of obtaining the desired recursive expression is partitioning the state space of the network in subsets characterized by a constant number of customers at a given station [BUZE73]. By so doing it is possible to define the following function,

$$g(n, m) = \begin{cases} h_m(n), & m = 1 \\ \sum_{k=0}^{n} h_m(k) g(n - k, m - 1), & m > 1, \end{cases} \tag{3.53}$$

so that the desired normalization constant G is obtained by evaluating this function with parameters $\hat{N}$ and M:

$$G = g(\hat{N}, M). \tag{3.54}$$

Using the recursive expression (3.53), the computation of the normalization constant requires on the order of $\hat{N}^2 M$ arithmetic operations and N memory locations. The reduction of the computational complexity provided by this recursive approach is amazing, and is made even more remarkable by observing that simpler computations are required when the QN are of particular types (e.g., when some stations have service speeds independent of the lengths of their queues).

Once an efficient method for the computation of the normalization constant has been devised [notice that expression (3.53) can be easily converted into an algorithm], it is possible to observe that most of the interesting average performance indices can be obtained as by-products of the same computation. Indeed, considering first the performance of the Mth station embedded into a QN in which circulate $\hat{N}$ customers, and starting from the distribution of the number of customers at this station $\pi_M(k|\hat{N})$, we can observe

$$\pi_M(k|\hat{N}) = \sum_{\mathbf{N}:N_M=k} \frac{1}{G} \prod_{i=1}^{M} h_i(N_i)$$
$$= h_M(k) \frac{g(\hat{N}-k, M-1)}{G}. \quad (3.55)$$

Equation (3.55) states that by saving intermediate results, computed just before the last step of the recursion, the desired distribution can be readily obtained with little extra cost.

From this expression it is easy to observe that the following equations for utilization $U_M(\hat{N})$ and throughput $X_M(\hat{N})$ of the Mth station hold:

$$U_M(\hat{N}) = 1 - \frac{g(\hat{N}, M-1)}{G} \quad (3.56)$$

and

$$X_M(\hat{N}) = \lambda_M \frac{g(\hat{N}-1, M)}{G}, \quad (3.57)$$

where we recall that λ_M represents the unnormalized arrival rate at the Mth station obtained as the solution of the flow balance equations (3.43).

When the mean number of customers at the station is required, we cannot avoid doing the extra computation required by the following expression,

$$E[N_M(\hat{N})] = \sum_{k=1}^{\hat{N}} k \pi_M(k|\hat{N})$$
$$= \frac{1}{G} \sum_{k=1}^{\hat{N}} k h_M(k) g(\hat{N}-k, M-1), \quad (3.58)$$

which can be conveniently computed in parallel with the last step of the recursion for the evaluation of the normalization constant. Little's formula is then used to obtain the average waiting time.

Because of the limited cost of the evaluation of the performance indices of the Mth station, it is often advisable to compute the performance indices of the other stations of the network in a straightforward manner involving a reindexing of the stations and a repeated evaluation of the normalization constant.

From this brief discussion, we can conclude that a problem that originally appeared of exponential complexity has been reduced to polynomial complexity by a proper formulation of the expressions yielding the performance indices of the network. These considerations extend directly to the multiclass networks of the BCMP theorem. The difficulty of proving them for this more general class of networks usually resides in the necessity of handling a more complex notation that often hides the intrinsically simple aspects of these results.

3.6.2 The Mean Value Analysis Method

An alternative approach to the computation of the average performance indices of a product form QN is that of formulating the recursive computation not in terms of results obtained with one less station in the network, but in terms of results computed for the original network visited by one less customer [REIS80].

Again to simplify matters, we consider single-class closed product form QN with the understanding that the ideas behind the computational techniques that we discuss extend in a straightforward manner to the solution of the whole class of networks defined by the BCMP theorem.

To simplify the discussion further, assume that all stations are single server queues, that they have negative exponential service time distribution, that their service discipline is FCFS, and that their service speed is independent of the length of the queue,

Consider first a customer arriving at the ith station for service. The time W_i this (tagged) customer spends at the station can be divided into two components: $W_i^{[a]}$ and σ_i, representing, respectively, the service time required to complete the service of all the customers present at the station at the time of the arrival of the tagged customer, and the time that it takes the server to satisfy the request of the tagged customer. Upon joining the queue of the station, the tagged customer finds $N_i^{[a]}$ customers already there. Because of the exponential distribution of the service time, $W_i^{[a]}$ is the sum of $N_i^{[a]}$ identically distributed random variables with individual means $1/\mu_i$. The mean waiting time of the arriving customer can thus be computed using the following expression:

$$E[W_i] = \frac{1}{\mu_i}(1 + E[N_i^{[a]}]). \tag{3.59}$$

When the station is embedded in a closed product form QN with a population of $\hat{N}$ customers, an interesting property of these networks is that the tagged customer

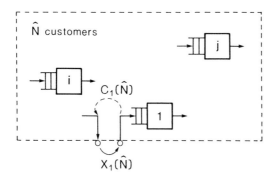

Figure 3.7
Cycle of a customer through the network.

sees the queue at the station as a random observer; thus

$$E[W_i(\hat{N})] = \frac{1}{\mu_i}(1 + E[N_i^{[a]}(\hat{N})])$$
$$= \frac{1}{\mu_i}(1 + E[N_i(\hat{N} - 1)]). \tag{3.60}$$

This equation is interesting because it expresses a quantity concerning a population of $\hat{N}$ customers in terms of another quantity concerning a population of $(\hat{N} - 1)$ customers.

In order to complete the recursive scheme needed for the solution of the whole network, assume that the flow balance equations of the network have been solved with respect to station 1 (see section 3.5.4) so that V_i represents the mean number of visits to station i per each visit to station 1; then

$$C_1(\hat{N}) = \sum_{i=1}^{M} V_i E[W_i(\hat{N})] \tag{3.61}$$

represents the mean time taken by customers to cycle through the network and to return to join the queue of station 1. By referring to figure 3.7, Little's formula yields the throughput of the first station,

$$X_1(\hat{N}) = \frac{\hat{N}}{C_1(\hat{N})}, \tag{3.62}$$

from which

Chapter 3   65

$$X_i(\hat{N}) = V_i \frac{\hat{N}}{\sum_{j=1}^{M} V_j E[W_j(\hat{N})]}. \tag{3.63}$$

Once the throughput of each station is known, the utilization is easily obtained as

$$U_i(\hat{N}) = \frac{X_i(\hat{N})}{\mu_i}, \tag{3.64}$$

and another application of Little's formula provides the final results:

$$E[N_i(\hat{N})] = X_i(\hat{N})E[W_i(\hat{N})] = U_i(\hat{N})(1 + E[N_i(\hat{N} - 1)]). \tag{3.65}$$

The solution of the whole network is thus computed by a cyclic evaluation of equations (3.60) and (3.63)–(3.65) initialized by

$$E[N_i(0)] = 0, \quad i = 1, 2, \ldots, M. \tag{3.66}$$

The computational space and time complexities of this method are comparable to those of the normalization constant approach discussed before. In most cases the choice of which of the two methods is to be used to solve a product form QN is simply a matter of taste.

3.7 The CHW Theorem

The nature of the product form solution discussed in the previous sections is reflected in the recursive expression of the normalization constant provided by (3.53). As we observed before, this recursion is done in terms of stations of the network that are accounted for one at a time. The operation of considering a new station in this recursive procedure is a convolution performed over a discrete and finite state space.

The nice properties of the convolution operator (associativity, commutativity, etc.) can be exploited to show that the order in which the different stations are considered is not essential for the final result. Moreover, the same value of the normalizing constant is obtained if the stations of the network are subdivided in groups, and intermediate values of the normalizing constant are computed considering each group individually. By assuming, for example, that two groups of stations are identified (group 1 comprising stations $1, \ldots, K$, and group 2 comprising stations $K + 1, \ldots, M$), the normalizing constant can be obtained in the following way:

$$g(\hat{N}, M) = \sum_{n=0}^{\hat{N}} H_1(n) H_2(\hat{N} - n), \tag{3.67}$$

where the function $H_1(n)$ is obtained by accounting for the stations in the first group, and $H_2(n)$ for those in the second group. Formally $H_1(n)$ can be obtained from the following auxiliary function,

$$\gamma(n,m) = \begin{cases} h_m(n), & m = 1 \\ \sum_{k=0}^{n} h_m(k)\gamma(n-k, m-1), & 1 < m \leq K, \end{cases} \quad (3.68a)$$

defining

$$H_1(n) = \gamma(n, K). \quad (3.68b)$$

In a similar manner it is possible to construct $H_2(n)$.

The result represented by (3.67) shows that for the behavior of the first group of stations of the model, the second group can be replaced by an equivalent server as long as its unnormalized queue length distribution has the values provided by $H_2(n)$. This observation represents the essence of the CHW theorem (named after the initials of the authors Chandy, Herzog, and Woo [CHAN75]), which can be stated in the following form:

CHW THEOREM   In any product form QN, a group of stations can be replaced by a (load-dependent) equivalent server without affecting the behavior of the other stations of the network as long as the unnormalized distribution of customers in the composite server is computed as indicated by (3.68).

In the special case of a subnetwork connected to the rest of the network by a single input and single output path, the QN obtained after the replacement of the subnetwork with the composite server can still be treated as a BCMP QN in which the load-dependent service rate of the composite server is the throughput of the subnetwork in isolation computed assuming that the input and output paths are short-circuited and a *controlled experiment* is performed, meaning that the model is solved for all possible population values. Figure 3.8 represents in a schematic way such an aggregation procedure.

3.8 Approximation Methods

The use of QN models for the analysis of real systems often leads to models whose features do not satisfy the restrictions of the BCMP theorem. Typical examples are the necessity of modeling servers with general service time distributions and FCFS queuing disciplines; the existence of service stations with finite waiting rooms that, once filled, force other stations to stop working (blocking); and the existence of passive

Chapter 3

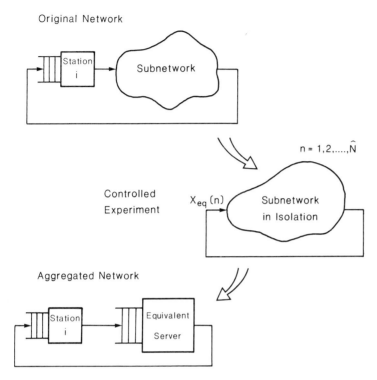

Figure 3.8
Application of the CHW theorem.

resources that are available in limited quantities and that are held by customers for periods of time that depend on the degree of congestion of some station of the network.

The fact that queuing systems with these features do not fit into the class of the BCMP networks does not always mean that they are not amenable to an analytic solution. Indeed, in many cases an underlying Markov process can be recognized and standard Markov chain techniques can be applied to their analysis. However, the lack of a product form solution always corresponds to a dramatic increase in the computational complexity of the analysis. Because of this observation, much effort has been made to extend in an approximate fashion the range of applicability of the solution techniques devised for product form networks.

3.8.1 Nearly Decomposable Systems

The main justification of the extensions mentioned before relies on the observation that often these generalizations concern only parts of the whole system whose interaction with the rest of the system is weak relative to the strong interactions observed within the subsystem itself.

The study of these models results, then, in a decomposition of the system into subsystems that are first studied in isolation and whose overall behavior is later used to account for the influences that each subsystem has on the performance of the others. A mathematical study of the impact that such a method of system analysis has on the accuracy of the final results was performed by Courtois [COUR77] within the framework of the computation of the steady state solution of large Markov chains in which states are aggregated into macrostates to reduce the computational complexity of the solution (as mentioned in section 2.5).

In this case the states of the subsystems are used to identify macrostates of the underlying Markov chain and the state transition rate matrix **Q** is partitioned by recognizing that the elements corresponding to interactions between subsystems are relatively small. Using this idea, we can decompose such a matrix in the following way,

$$\mathbf{Q} = \mathbf{Q}^* + \varepsilon \mathbf{C}, \tag{3.69}$$

such that **Q*** is block diagonal, ε is an error term, and **C** is a matrix representing the redistribution of elements of **Q** that is needed to make **Q*** block diagonal and such that the elements of each row sum to zero. The matrix **Q*** is such that the solution of the eigenvalue problem

$$\mathbf{v}^* = \mathbf{v}^* \mathbf{Q}^* \tag{3.70}$$

corresponds exactly to the computation of the steady state probability distributions of the subsystems considered in isolation. These results can also be interpreted as estimates of the conditional probabilities of finding the system in a particular state given that it is in the corresponding macrostate, and used in (2.105a) for the construction of an approximate high-level transition matrix between macrostates. Courtois was able to show that the accuracy of the approximate solution obtained using this decomposition approach is of the order of ε.

Systems composed of weakly interacting subsystems allow a decomposition with small ε and are thus amenable to such a stepwise solution. The definition of the aggregates is often driven by physical characteristics of the system modeled by such a Markov chain. When the Markov chain represents the behaviour of a QN, aggregates are often defined in terms of groups of stations in the QN. Courtois was able to show that whenever the QN has a product form solution, this method yields exact results with a reduced computational effort.

Even though this method is not guaranteed to work when the original model

Chapter 3   69

represents a non-BCMP QN, practical experience shows that using this technique for the solution of non-BCMP networks made up of subsystems that, taken in isolation, satisfy the condition of the BCMP theorem often yields quite acceptable results.

It is because of this observation that, in these cases, practitioners often extend the application of the CHW theorem beyond the limits of its validity, identifying in non-BCMP models subsystems of the type just mentioned, and replacing them with flow equivalent servers to obtain an aggregated network whose analysis is then completed by solving the underlying Markov chain defined over the space of the macrostates.

The efficient computational algorithms used for the characterization of the equivalent servers and the limited number of (macro)states deriving from the high-level model can make the computational complexity of this approach acceptable when the direct solution of the original model would have been practically impossible.

3.8.2 Passive Resources

One of the most typical uses of the decomposition method for the approximate solution of non-BCMP networks is the analysis of systems including passive resources.

A passive resource is a modeling construct useful for describing the fact that access to servers is granted to customers only upon the availability of a resource taken from a pool [KELL76].

The number of resources in the pool is limited, so that is limited the number of customers simultaneously receiving service from the subsystem. Customers trying to access the subsystem when the pool is empty are delayed outside the subsystem until a resource becomes available. A QN containing passive resources does not satisfy the conditions of the BCMP theorem, since the queue of customers waiting to enter the subsystem is not associated to a server, whereas the service time of the customers at the head of the queue (i.e., the residence time of customers in the subsystem) depends on the behavior of other servers in the network. To provide the reader with an idea of how these types of networks are analyzed, let us suppose that, apart from the passive resource, all stations of the network satisfy the conditions of the BCMP theorem. Figure 3.9 provides a rather abstract representation of such a network.

Let $\hat{N}$ denote (as usual) the number of customers circulating in the network, and K the number of items originally available in the passive resource pool. The number of customers simultaneously present in the subsystem is controlled by the number of passive resources and cannot exceed K. The parameters of the flow equivalent server intended to represent the subsystem in the higher level model can thus be determined

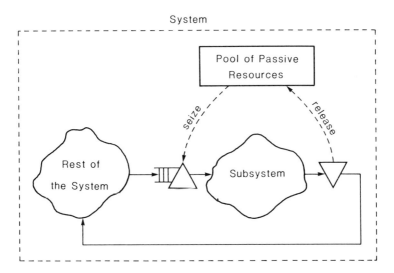

Figure 3.9
A queuing network with a subsystem controlled by passive resources.

by computing the mean response time of the subsystem under different loading conditions ranging from 1 up K customers. Let $C_{eq}(n)$, $n = 1, 2, \ldots, K$, denote this quantity. When n customers load the subsystem, they leave (and reenter) the subsystem every

$$S_{eq}(n) = \frac{C_{eq}(n)}{n}, \qquad n = 1, 2, \ldots, K, \tag{3.71}$$

time units in the average. $S_{eq}(n)$ can thus be considered as the mean service time of the flow equivalent server conditional on n being the number of customers accessing the subsystem. When $n > K$, only K customers are allowed in the subsystem, while the other $n - K$ are kept outside in the passive resource queue. It follows that the level of congestion of the subsystem never exceeds that observed when K customers are using it. Thus it seems reasonable to assume that the mean response time of the subsystem is in this case always $C_{eq}(K)$, independent of the number of customers waiting in the passive resource queue. The behavior of the subsystem controlled by the passive resources is thus approximately represented by a flow equivalent server with an FCFS queuing discipline with the following service function (mean service time conditional on the queue length):

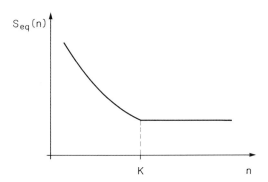

Figure 3.10
Qualitative behavior of the load-dependent service rate of the equivalent service station replacing a subsystem controlled by passive resources.

$$S_{eq}(n) = \begin{cases} \dfrac{C_{eq}(n)}{n}, & n \leq K \\ \dfrac{C_{eq}(K)}{K}, & n > K. \end{cases} \qquad (3.72)$$

Figure 3.10 shows the qualitative behavior of this service function.

When the subsystem and the passive resources are replaced by the flow equivalent server in the higher-level model of the system, the resulting QN appears to satisfy the BCMP conditions once again. It is at this point that the approximation is introduced, and the exact product form solution of the aggregated model is an approximation of the solution of the original non-BCMP model.

A discussion of the accuracy of this method must take into account that the best case for the method is represented by $K = \hat{N}$. In this case the results one obtains are exact. The worst case for the method corresponds to $K = 1$. In this case no queue can form at the stations controlled by the passive resource. If all these stations have exponential distribution of the service times, the subsystem corresponds to a server characterized by an overall service time distribution made up of a complex combination of exponential stages (thus of the Coxian type). Because of the nature of the method, higher moments of this distribution are neglected, and only its mean ($1/C_{eq}(1)$) is reflected in the approximate solution. For any other intermediate values of K the method provides results whose accuracy lies between these two extremes.

In chapter 8 we will show, however, that special types of subsystems controlled by passive resources exist that, in spite of admitting new customers in a manner dependent on their level of congestion, preserve, under special conditions, the product form of the model.

References

[BASK75] Baskett, F., Chandy, K.M., Muntz, R. R., and Palacios, F., "Open, Closed and Mixed Networks of Queues with Different Classes of Customers," *Journal ACM* 22(2) (April 1975), 248–260.

[BURK56] Burke, P. J., "The Output of a Queueing System," *Operations Research* 4(6) (December 1956), 699–704.

[BUZE73] Buzen, J. P., "Computational Algorithms for Closed Queueing Networks with Exponential Servers," *Communications ACM* 16(9) (September 1973), 527–531.

[CHAN75] Chandy, K. M., Herzog, U., and Woo, L., "Parametric Analysis of Queueing Networks," *IBM Journal of R. and D.* 19(1) (January 1975), 36–42.

[COHE69] Cohen, J. W., *The Single Server Queue*, American Elsevier, New York, 1969.

[COOP72] Cooper, R. B., *Introduction to Queueing Theory*, MacMillan, New York, 1972.

[COUR77] Courtois, P. J., *Decomposability: Queueing and Computer System Applications*, Academic Press, New York, 1977.

[DENN78] Denning, P. J., and Buzen, J. P., "The Operational Analysis of Queuing Network Models," *Computing Surveys* 10(3) (September 1978), 225, 261.

[GELE80] Gelenbe, E., and Mitrani, I., *Analysis and Synthesis of Computer Systems*, Academic Press, New York, 1980.

[GORD67] Gordon, W. J., and Newell, G. F., "Closed Queueing Systems with Exponential Servers," *Operations Research* 15(2) (April 1967), 245–255.

[JACK63] Jackson, J. R., "Jobshop-like Queueing Systems," *Management Science* 10(1) (October 1963), 131–142.

[KELL76] Keller, T. W., "Computer System Models with Passive Resources," Ph. D. Thesis, University of Texas at Austin, 1976.

[KEND51] Kendall, D. G., "Some Problems in the Theory of Queues," *J. Roy. Statist. Soc. Ser. B* 13(2) (1951), 151–185.

[KLEI75] Kleinrock, L., *Queueing Systems*, Vol. I: *Theory*, Wiley, New York, 1975.

[KOBA78] Kobayashi, H., *Modeling and Analysis: An Introduction to System Performance Evaluation Methodology*, Addison-Wesley, Reading, MA, 1978.

[LAVE83] Lavenberg, S. S. (ed.), *Computer Performance Modeling Handbook*, Academic Press, New York, 1983.

[LAZO84] Lazowska, E. D., Zahorjan, J., Graham, G. S., and Sevcik, K. C., *Quantitative System Performance*, Prentice-Hall, Englewood Cliffs, NJ, 1984.

[LITT61] Little, J. D. C., "A Proof of the Queueing Formula $L = \lambda W$," *Operations Research* 9(3) (May 1961), 383–387.

[REIS80] Reiser, M., and Lavenberg, S. S., "Mean Value Analysis of Closed Multichain Queueing Networks," *Journal ACM* 27(2) (April 1980), 313–322.

[SAUE81] Sauer, C. H., and Chandy, K. M., *Computer System Performance Evaluation*, Prentice-Hall, Englewood Cliffs, NJ, 1981.

4 Stochastic Petri Nets

Petri nets (PN) are an effective modeling tool for the description and the analysis of concurrency and synchronization in parallel systems exhibiting the cooperative actions of different entities. PN were introduced by C. A. Petri in 1962 [PETR66]. The theoretical problems associated with PN have been deeply investigated during the last twenty years (see, for example, [PETE81, BRAM83, REIS82]). Today PN can be regarded as a formal structure for which a well-assessed theory has been developed and a wide range of application fields have been identified.

The success of PN is mainly due to the simplicity of the basic mechanism of the model, which is, however, paid for with the complexity of the description of large systems. Many extensions have been added to the basic PN model by several authors in order to facilitate the use of PN in different application fields. Many authors extended PN models by introducing the notion of time; timed PN models can be used for the quantitative performance analysis of systems. When random variables are used to specify the time behavior of the model, timed PN are called stochastic PN (SPN). It can be shown that SPN are, under certain conditions, isomorphic to homogeneous Markov chains (MC).

The use of SPN as a modeling tool for multiprocessor systems evaluation is extremely attractive. The SPN capability of describing simultaneously both parallelism and synchronization seems very interesting when the needed level of detail makes queuing network models inadequate. Moreover, it is possible to obtain the state transition rate diagram of the associated MC automatically from the SPN description of the system. The latter can often be derived from a simple analysis of the system behavior, whereas the direct characterization of the system in terms of an MC can be by far more complex.

In the following section, a definition of what is generally intended for standard PN is given, and the basic PN properties are presented. The notation is taken from [AGER79]; for a more detailed analysis and discussions of PN the reader can refer to [PETE81], [BRAM83], and [REIS82]. Timed PN are introduced in a later section, and SPN models are then discussed in some detail. A further extension introduced by the authors to SPN models is then presented and deeply analyzed.

4.1 Standard Petri Nets

The structure of a *standard PN* is a bipartite graph that comprises a set of *places P*, a set of *transitions T*, and a set of *directed arcs A*. In the graphical representation of PN, places are drawn as circles and transitions as bars. Arcs connect transitions to places and places to transitions. A place is an *input* to a transition if an arc exists from the

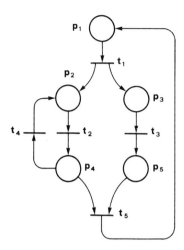

Figure 4.1
Example of graphical representation of a Petri net.

place to the transition. A place is an *output* of a transition if an arc exists from the transition to the place. The set of arcs can be partitioned into the sets of transition input arcs A_i and transition output arcs A_o.

A formal definition of such a structure is thus the following:

$$PN = (P, T, A),$$

$$P = \{p_1, p_2, \ldots, p_n\},$$

$$T = \{t_1, t_2, \ldots, t_m\},$$

$$A_i \subset (P \times T),$$

$$A_o \subset (T \times P),$$

$$A = (A_i \cup A_o).$$

(4.1)

An example of graphical representation of a PN is shown in figure 4.1. The PN depicted in figure 4.1 comprises five places and five transitions.

4.1.1 Petri Net Marking

PN places may contain *tokens* (a primitive concept for PN) graphically drawn as black dots. A PN with tokens is called *marked PN*. The state of a marked PN is defined by the number m_i of tokens contained in each place p_i. The PN state is usually called the PN *marking* and is denoted by $M = \{m_1, m_2, \ldots, m_n\}$.

A formal definition of a marked PN is thus the following:

$$\text{PN} = (P, T, A, M_0),$$

$$P = \{p_1, p_2, \ldots, p_n\},$$

$$T = \{t_1, t_2, \ldots, t_m\},$$

$$A_i \subset (P \times T), \tag{4.2}$$

$$A_o \subset (T \times P),$$

$$A = (A_i \cup A_o),$$

$$M_0 = \{m_{01}, m_{02}, \ldots, m_{0n}\},$$

where m_{0i} denotes the number of tokens in place p_i in the initial marking M_0.

It is then possible to define the *execution* of a marked PN. A PN executes according to the following rules.

1. A transition is *enabled* when all of its input places contain at least one token.
2. An enabled transition can *fire*, thus removing one token from each input place and placing one token in each output place.
3. Each firing of a transition modifies the distribution of tokens on places and thus produces a new marking for the PN.

In the following m_{p_i} denotes the number of tokens in place p_i, $\#(p_a, t_b)$ is equal to 1 if an arc from place p_a to transition t_b exists (and to 0 otherwise); similarly $\#(t_a, p_b)$ is equal to 1 if an arc from transition t_a to place p_b exists (and to 0 otherwise). A transition t_b is enabled if

$$m_{p_i} \geq \#(p_i, t_b) \qquad \forall p_i \in P, \tag{4.3}$$

and the result of the firing of t_b is a new marking $M' = \{m'_1, \ldots, m'_n\}$ defined as

$$m'_{p_i} = m_{p_i} - \#(p_i, t_b) + \#(t_b, p_i) \qquad \forall p_i \in P. \tag{4.4}$$

Tokens are atomic entities; i.e., the firing of a transition may disable other transitions by removing tokens from shared input places. Disabled transitions are said to be in conflict with the one that fires.

In the marked PN in figure 4.2 the initial marking $M_0 = \{1, 0, 0, 0, 0\}$ enables only transition t_1. After the firing of t_1 the marking becomes $M' = \{0, 1, 1, 0, 0\}$. In this case,

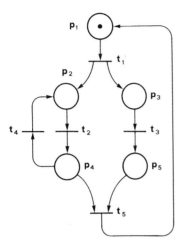

Figure 4.2
Example of a marked PN.

both transitions t_2 and t_3 are enabled and can fire independently. The firing of t_2 enables transition t_4; the firing of t_3 puts a token in p_5. The reached marking $M'' = \{0, 0, 0, 1, 1\}$ enables both t_4 and t_5. Only one of these two transitions can fire; the selection is non-deterministic, and the firing of one transition automatically disables the other. If t_5 fires, the system returns to the initial marking.

4.1.2 Some Extensions to Standard Petri Nets

Many extensions to the standard PN described in the previous section were introduced to increase the modeling power of the tool. The extensions considered in this section are the definition of *multiple arcs* and *inhibitor arcs*.

As shown in figure 4.3a, more than one arc is allowed to connect a place to a transition and a transition to a place. In the first case, the two arcs from p_1 to t_1 mean that only the presence of two or more tokens in p_1 enables transition t_1. In the second case, the three arcs from t_1 to p_3 mean that, when t_1 fires, three tokens are put in p_3. Equations (4.3) and (4.4), which define the transition enabling condition and the execution rules, are still valid as long as $\#(p_a, t_b)$ denotes the number of arcs from place p_a to transition t_b, and $\#(t_a, p_b)$ denotes the number of arcs from transition t_a to place p_b. Figure 4.3b shows a more compact representation of multiple arcs, which is used in the following to simplify the drawing of intricate PN.

The other extension to PN considered here is the introduction of inhibitor arcs. An

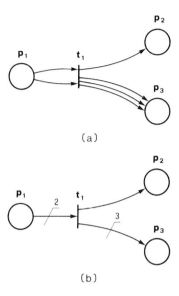

Figure 4.3
(a) Example of a portion of a PN with multiple arcs. (b) Compact representation of multiple arcs.

inhibitor arc connects a place to a transition and is represented by a line terminating with a circle rather than with an arrowhead at the transition, as shown in figure 4.4. The firing condition of a transition can thus be generalized by saying that a transition is enabled when all of its normal input places contain at least one token and no token is contained in the transition inhibitor input places. The firing of the transition removes a token from each of its normal input places.

The two extensions considered here are very different in their theoretical nature and consequences. The introduction of multiple input and output arcs is essentially a convention that allows one to draw, in some cases, graphically simpler PN. On the other hand, the zero testing ability introduced by inhibitor arcs effectively increases the modeling power of PN, as we shall see in the following.

PN with multiple and inhibitor arcs will be considered as standard in the rest of the book.

4.1.3 Some Petri Net Properties

We introduce in this section some of the basic concepts and most common terms normally used in PN analysis.

A marking M' is said to be *immediately reachable* from M if M' can be obtained by

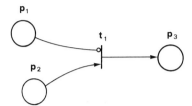

Figure 4.4
Example of a portion of a PN with inhibitor arcs.

firing a transition enabled in M. The PN execution allows a sequence of markings $\{M_0, M_1, M_2, \ldots\}$ and a sequence of transitions $\{t_1, t_2, \ldots\}$ to be defined. The firing of t_1, enabled in M_0, changes the PN state from M_0 to M_1 and so on. A marking M'' is said to be *reachable* from M if there exists a sequence of transition firings that moves the PN state from M to M''.

We define the reachability set $R(M_0)$ of a PN as the set of all markings that are reachable from M_0. The reachability set of a PN can be represented by a tree. It can be shown that the tree in figure 4.5 represents the reachability set of the PN in figure 4.2. The reachability tree can be constructed by starting from the initial marking M_0 and considering the markings immediately reachable from it (in this case only M_1). The same procedure must be followed considering this new marking, from which two new markings M_2 and M_3 are immediately reachable. The immediately reachable markings from M_2 are now M_1 and M_4, where M_4 is a new marking and M_1 was already considered. From M_1 we could repeat the same operation done before, and this would obviously engender an infinite structure.

To represent this infinite structure with a finite tree, we stop to expand the tree when we reach an already considered marking. We shall call such markings duplicate nodes. During the construction of the reachability tree we can also find *dead* markings, i.e., markings in which no transition is enabled. Dead and duplicate markings constitute the frontier markings (leaves) of the tree.

A marked PN is said to be *safe* if the number of tokens in each place is ≤ 1 for all markings in $R(M_0)$. The PN in figure 4.2 is safe. A PN is said to be *k-bounded* if the number of tokens in each place is $\leq k$ for all markings in $R(M_0)$. A k-bounded PN with multiple and inhibitor arcs has a finite reachability set and can therefore be represented by a finite state machine. It can then be shown to be equivalent to a "not extended" PN, being the first representation, only more convenient. On the other hand, adding the zero testing ability (inhibitor arcs) to PN that are not k-bounded gives the model

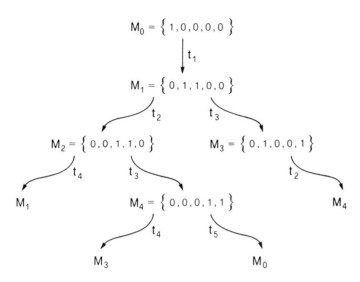

Figure 4.5
The reachability tree of the marked PN in figure 4.2.

the computational power of a Turing machine, thus allowing any computable system to be modeled [PETE81].

A PN is said to be *strictly conservative* if, for all markings in $R(M_0)$, the sum of the tokens in the net is constant, i.e., if tokens move only around the net and every transition firing does not destroy or create tokens; that is, for all $M \in R(M_0)$,

$$\sum_{i=1}^{n} m_i = \text{constant}. \qquad (4.5)$$

This implies that for each transition the number of input arcs equals the number of output arcs.

A PN is said to be *conservative* with respect to a vector of nonnegative components $W = \{w_1, w_2, \ldots, w_n\}$ if, for all markings in $R(M_0)$,

$$\sum_{i=1}^{n} w_i m_i = \text{constant}. \qquad (4.6)$$

When a PN is used to model real systems, the concept of conservation is very important. For example, in a PN model of a computer system, a token can be associated with a resource (e.g., a processor in a multiprocessor system). It is obvious that in general the number of resources cannot increase or decrease, and as a consequence the number of tokens representing physical resources cannot change.

A transition $t_i \in T$ is said to be *live* if, for all $M \in R(M_0)$, there is a marking M', reachable from M, that enables transition t_i. A PN is said to be *live* if all $t_i \in T$ are live. The concept of liveness is very significant in the modeling of computer systems, and it is usually associated with the absence of deadlock states.

A special subclass of PN can be obtained if for all $t_1, t_2 \in T$, $t_2 \neq t_1$, and for any reachable marking, the firing of t_1 cannot disable the firing of t_2. These nets are called *persistent* [LAND78].

4.2 Timed Petri Nets

Standard PN do not include any time concept. Therefore with standard PN it is possible to describe only the logical structure of systems, and not their time evolution. Timing, on the other hand, usually plays a fundamental role in the description of the behavior of any system.

The introduction of time into standard PN models allows the description of the dynamic behavior of systems, taking into account both the state evolution and the duration of each action performed by the system. Many of the most interesting parameters of system design, such as delay and throughput, and in general any time-dependent behavior, can in this way be modeled. There are, however, different ways to introduce time into a standard PN.

A first possibility consists in associating with each transition a number that indicates, in some time unit, the delay between the enabling and the firing of the transition. This is the approach that was used, for example, in [MERL76] and [ZUBE80], as well as in [NOEN73] where higher level constructs are also proposed. In a more formal way we can say that a timed Petri net (TPN) is defined as

$$\text{TPN} = \{P, T, A, M_0, \Theta\}, \tag{4.7}$$

where P, T, A, and M_0 are as in (4.2) and $\Theta = (\theta_1, \theta_2, \ldots, \theta_m)$ is the set of delays associated with PN transitions.

As a simple example of the modeling capabilities of a TPN, consider the net shown in figure 4.6. This net models the behavior of a processing unit that, in order to perform some action, needs the possession of a resource. A token in p_3 means that the resource is available, and a token in p_1 represents the processing unit when it does not need it. The initial marking $M_0 = \{1, 0, 1, 0\}$ enables only t_1, whose associated delay θ_1 represents the time interval during which the processing unit does not need the

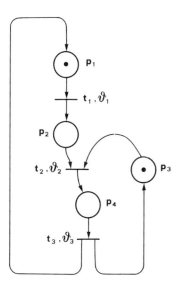

Figure 4.6
Example of timed PN. Delays are associated with transitions.

resource. The TPN stays then in M_0 until the firing of t_1. The system reaches then the marking $M_1 = \{0, 1, 1, 0\}$, which enables only t_2. The delay θ_2 associated with t_2 models the time needed by the computing unit to obtain the resource. The TPN, after the firing of t_2, reaches marking $M_2 = \{0, 0, 0, 1\}$, which models the state of the system in which the resource is used. The TPN will return to its initial state M_0 after a delay θ_3.

As a second possibility of introducing the concept of time, assume, for instance, that a token that reaches a new place becomes *available* only after a delay θ. So every token can be in one of the two states *available* and *unavailable*, and only available tokens can enable a transition. The unavailability of a token models the time spent performing an activity. The time is here associated with places. This approach was followed, for example, in [SIFA77].

Consider in this case the TPN in figure 4.7, which models a system behaving like the one modeled by the TPN in figure 4.6. When a token reaches p_1 it remains unavailable for a time interval θ_1, thus modeling the state of the system when the resource is not needed. When the token becomes available, transition t_1 fires; a token moves then into p_2, where it remains unavailable for a time θ_2, to model the time needed to get the resource. When the token becomes available, t_2 fires and the token is moved to p_4. Again, the token remains unavailable for a time θ_4, to model the time

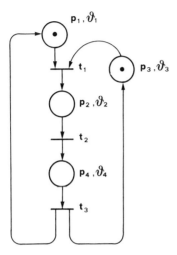

Figure 4.7
Example of timed PN. Delays are associated with places.

needed to use the resource; then, when it becomes available, t_3 fires, and the system returns to its initial state.

It must be observed that the TPN in figures 4.6 and 4.7 do not model exactly the same system. Consider the TPN in figure 4.6; in this case, during the time interval needed to get the resource, the latter is still unused (p_2 contains a token). Instead, in the TPN in figure 4.7, during the same time interval, the resource is already busy. This different behavior may be not significant for modeling a system with a single processing unit, but can become relevant if the system to be modeled is more complex—for instance, when the resource is shared among many processing units.

The introduction of time into PN is a very critical process, and great attention must be paid to understanding completely the semantics of the model as well as the details of its behavior.

4.3 Stochastic Petri Nets

Probabilistic performance models try to represent the behavior of complex deterministic systems by means of stochastic processes. In this way it is possible to avoid a detailed deterministic description of the system operations by trying, instead, to capture the essence of the system behavior through probabilistic assumptions. The possibility of merging the capability of PN to describe synchronization and concurrency with a stochastic model seems a very attractive way to obtain performance estimates of complex computing systems.

Several authors suggested the introduction of random firing times in PN ([MOLL81, SYMO78, NATK80]). In this section we refer mainly to the work of M. Molloy, and we introduce stochastic Petri nets (SPN).

SPN are obtained by associating with each transition in a PN an exponentially distributed random variable that expresses the delay from the enabling to the firing of the transition, as explained in the previous section. On the other hand, given an SPN, the associated PN is obtained by disregarding the transition timing.

Consider an SPN with a marking M in which several transitions are simultaneously enabled. The transition with which is associated the shortest delay will fire first. The SPN reaches then a new marking M' in which transitions that were already enabled in the previous marking, but did not fire, may be still enabled. Because of the memoryless property of the exponential distribution that yields a residual life distribution equal to the distribution of the firing delay itself, it can be assumed that the activity associated with each transition is restarted in any new marking. This assumption is valid even if the semantics of the model implies that activities are continued; indeed the restarting of the activity associated with a transition is not "felt" by the model.

A formal definition of an SPN is thus the following:

$$\text{SPN} = (P, T, A, M_0, L), \tag{4.8}$$

where P, T, A, and M_0 are as in (4.2) and

$$L = \{l_1, l_2, \ldots, l_m\} \tag{4.9}$$

is the set of possibly *marking-dependent* firing rates associated with the PN transitions. When necessary the dependence upon a given marking M of the firing rate of transition j will be denoted $l_j(M)$.

Molloy [MOLL81] showed that, due to the memoryless property of the exponential distribution of firing delays, SPN are isomorphic to continuous-time Markov chains. In particular a k-bounded SPN can be shown to be isomorphic to a finite MC. The MC associated with a given SPN can be obtained following these rules:

1. The MC state space S corresponds to the reachability set $R(M_0)$ of the PN associated with the SPN ($M_i \leftrightarrow i$).
2. The transition rate from state i (corresponding to marking M_i) to state j (M_j) is

$$q_{ij} = \sum_{k \in H_{ij}} l_k, \qquad (4.10)$$

where H_{ij} is the set of transitions enabled by marking M_i, whose firing generates marking M_j.

By using these rules, it is possible to devise an algorithm that automatically derives from the SPN description the state transition rate matrix of the isomorphic CTMC. Molloy has also shown that, in some cases, with appropriate series and parallel expansions, using the method of stages, it is possible to model transitions with generally distributed firing times, provided that these distributions have rational Laplace transforms. In any case the extension from exponentially (memoryless) distributed firing times to generally distributed firing times must be done with great care.

In this book we consider only SPN that originate ergodic CTMC. An SPN is said to be ergodic if it generates an ergodic CTMC. It is possible to show that an SPN is ergodic if M_0, the initial marking, is reachable from any $M_i \in R(M_0)$. If the SPN is ergodic, it is possible to compute the steady state probability distribution of markings solving the usual matrix equation

$$\pi \mathbf{Q} = 0 \qquad (4.11\text{a})$$

with the additional constraint

$$\sum_i \pi_i = 1, \qquad (4.11\text{b})$$

where $\mathbf{Q}$ is the infinitesimal generator whose elements are obtained as explained in (4.10) and π is the vector of the steady state probabilities.

From the steady state distribution π it is possible to obtain quantitative estimates of the behavior of the SPN. For example:

1. The *probability of a particular condition* of the SPN. If in the subset A of $R(M_0)$ the particular condition is satisfied, the required probability is given by

$$P\{A\} = \sum_{i \in A} \pi_i. \qquad (4.12)$$

2. The *expected value of the number of tokens in a given place*. If $A(i, x)$ is the subset of $R(M_0)$ for which the number of tokens in place p_i is x, and the place is k-bounded, then the expected value of the number of tokens in p_i is given by

$$E[m_i] = \sum_{n=1}^{k} [n P\{A(i, n)\}]. \qquad (4.13)$$

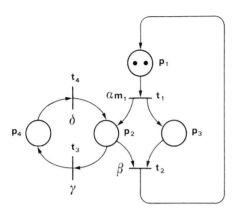

Figure 4.8
Example of a stochastic Petri net.

3. The *mean number of firings in unit time*. If A_j is the subset of $R(M_0)$ in which a given transition t_j is enabled, then the mean number of firings of t_j in the unit time is given by

$$f_j = \sum_{M_i \in A_j} \left[\pi_i \left(l_j \Big/ \sum_{\forall t_k \text{ enabled in } M_i} l_k \right) \right]. \tag{4.14}$$

4.3.1 An Example of a Stochastic Petri Net

Consider, for example, the SPN in figure 4.8, comprising four places and four transitions. Transition t_1 fires at a marking-dependent rate equal to αm_1, where m_1 is the number of tokens in p_1. The other transition rates (β, γ, δ) are indicated close to the corresponding transitions. The reachability tree of the marked SPN in figure 4.8 is depicted in figure 4.9. The corresponding CTMC state transition rate diagram is shown in figure 4.10.

Assuming $\alpha = \beta = \gamma = \delta = 1$, we can write the system of equations whose solution yields the steady state distribution on the CTMC states:

$$\pi \begin{bmatrix} -2 & 2 & 0 & 0 & 0 & 0 \\ 1 & -3 & 1 & 1 & 0 & 0 \\ 0 & 1 & -2 & 0 & 1 & 0 \\ 0 & 1 & 0 & -2 & 1 & 0 \\ 0 & 0 & 1 & 1 & -3 & 1 \\ 0 & 0 & 0 & 0 & 1 & -1 \end{bmatrix} = 0$$

and

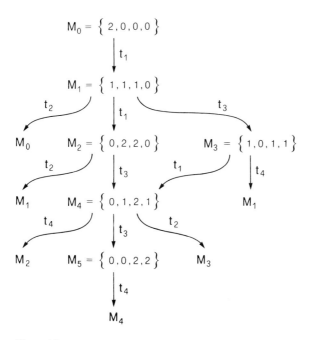

Figure 4.9
The reachability tree of the SPN in figure 4.8.

$$\sum_{i=0}^{5} \pi_i = 1.$$

By solving the system we obtain

$$\pi_0 = \frac{1}{11}, \quad \pi_1 = \pi_2 = \pi_3 = \pi_4 = \pi_5 = \frac{2}{11}.$$

As an example, we can now compute the average number of tokens in p_1. Since in M_0 there are two tokens in p_1, and in M_1 and M_3 there is one token in p_1, we have

$$E[m_1] = 2\pi_0 + \pi_1 + \pi_3 = \frac{6}{11}$$

and the absolute firing rate of t_2 is

$$f_2 = \frac{1}{3}\pi_1 + \frac{1}{2}\pi_2 + \frac{1}{3}\pi_4 = \frac{7}{33},$$

since t_2 is enabled only in M_1, M_2, and M_4.

Chapter 4

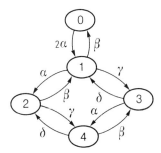

Figure 4.10
The MC state transition rate diagram of the SPN in figure 4.8.

4.4 Generalized Stochastic Petri Nets

4.4.1 Basic Motivations

Often it is not desirable to associate a random time with each transition, since one would rather associate times only with the events that are believed to have the largest impact on system performance.

A typical example might be the case in which the operating sequence of a system comprises activities whose durations differ by orders of magnitude. It is then conceivable that the short activities be modeled only from the logical point of view, whereas time is associated with the longer ones. This choice becomes particularly convenient if, by so doing, the number of states of the associated MC model is reduced, hence reducing the solution complexity. Moreover, the availability of a logical structure that can be used in conjunction with the timed one allows the construction, by using some ingenuity, of compact models of complex systems.

Generalized stochastic Petri nets (GSPN) [AJMO84] are obtained by allowing transitions to belong to two different classes: *immediate* transitions and *timed* transitions. Immediate transitions fire in zero time once they are enabled. Timed transitions fire after a random, exponentially distributed, enabling time. We adopt the convention of drawing timed transitions as thick bars, and immediate transitions as thin bars. Firing rates are obviously associated only with timed transitions, and they may depend on the GSPN marking.

A formal definition of a GSPN is thus as in (4.8), where now the array L contains only m' elements, m' being the number of timed transitions in the GSPN.

Several transitions may be simultaneously enabled in a marking. If the set of enabled transition H comprises only timed transitions, then transition t_i ($i \in H$) fires with probability

$$\frac{l_i}{\sum_{k \in H} l_k}, \tag{4.15}$$

exactly as in the case of SPN. If H comprises both immediate and timed transitions, then only immediate transitions can fire. If H comprises zero or more timed transitions and only one immediate transition, then this is the one that fires. When H comprises several immediate transitions, it is necessary to specify a probability density function on the set of enabled immediate transitions according to which the firing transition is selected. The subset of H comprising all enabled immediate transitions, together with the associated probability distribution, is called a *random switch*. In the following this associated probability distribution is called a *switching distribution*. Different markings may engender a single random switch whenever they enable the same set of immediate transitions upon which a single (possibly marking-dependent) switching distribution can be defined.

4.4.2 An Example of a Generalized Stochastic Petri Net

Consider the GSPN in figure 4.11, comprising seven places and seven transitions. Three of the transitions are timed: t_1, t_4, and t_5. Transition t_1 fires at a marking-dependent rate equal to α times the number of tokens in place p_1. Transitions t_4 and t_5 fire at fixed rates β and γ, respectively. t_6 and t_7 are two conflicting immediate transitions: they are always enabled simultaneously, so that it is necessary to define a switching distribution for each marking in which m_7 is larger than zero. The immediate transitions t_2 and t_3 may be simultaneously enabled if p_3 and p_4 contain tokens. Hence a switching distribution must be defined for each marking in which m_2, m_3, and m_4 are greater than zero. Note that no more than two immediate transitions can be simultaneously enabled. Two random switches can thus be identified in this GSPN. A possible switching distribution definition is the one given in table 4.1.

Starting from the initial marking shown in figure 4.11, a possible evolution of the GSPN state may be the following: after an exponentially distributed random time with average $1/(2\alpha)$, transition t_1 fires, and one of the two tokens contained in p_1 moves to p_2. Now in zero time either t_2 or t_3 fires. The firing transition is selected according to the switching distribution defined in table 4.1 that in this case assigns equal probabilities to the two transitions. Assume that t_2 fires, removing a token from p_2 and p_3, and placing one token in p_5. The two timed transitions t_1 and t_4 are now enabled. Transition t_1 fires with probability

$$P\{t_1\} = \frac{\alpha}{\alpha + \beta}, \tag{4.16}$$

whereas transition t_4 fires with probability

$$P\{t_4\} = \frac{\beta}{\alpha + \beta}. \tag{4.17}$$

If t_1 fires first, one token moves from p_1 to p_2, thus enabling the immediate transition t_3. This transition fires immediately, being the only enabled transition of this type, moving one token from p_2 to p_6 and removing one token from p_4. The resulting GSPN marking is such that one token exists in places p_5 and p_6. The enabled transitions are t_4 and t_5, each one of which can fire first with the following probabilities:

$$P\{t_4\} = \frac{\beta}{\beta + \gamma}, \qquad P\{t_5\} = \frac{\gamma}{\beta + \gamma}. \tag{4.18}$$

Assume t_4 fires, so that a token is moved from p_5 to p_7, and a token is put in p_1. The two immediate transitions t_6 and t_7 are now simultaneously enabled, and, as specified by the switching distribution defined in table 4.1, each one of them can fire with probability 1/2, so that the token in p_7 can move either to p_3 or to p_4. Now transitions t_1 and t_5 are enabled, and the PN evolution continues.

Table 4.2 shows the reachability set of the GSPN in figure 4.11. It comprises 17 markings, whereas the reachability set of the associated PN comprises 33 states. It must be pointed out that in general the reachability set of a GSPN is a subset of the reachability set of the associated PN, because precedence rules introduced with immediate transitions do not allow some states to be reached. The reachability set of an SPN is, instead, the same as for the associated PN. Moreover, the reachability set of the GSPN can be divided in two disjoint subsets, one of which comprises markings that enable timed transitions only, while the other one comprises markings that enable immediate transitions.

The definition of random switches in a GSPN may sometimes require ingenuity and insight in the system operations. Consider, for instance, the GSPN in figure 4.11, with the marking $\{1, 1, 1, 1, 0, 0, 0\}$. The semantics of the enabled random switch (will t_2 or t_3 fire first?) is implicit in some well-defined local property of the system. So it is easy to identify the probabilities associated with the two events. Consider now the portion of GSPN drawn in figure 4.12. Assume t_1 (t_2) fires first, so that a token moves to place p_1 (p_2), thus enabling the immediate transitions t_4 and t_5 (t_6 and t_7). The switching distribution on the two enabled transitions can be easily defined because it depends

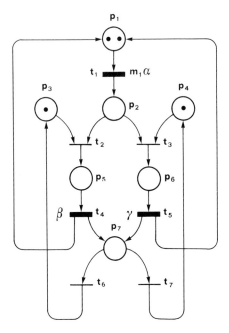

Figure 4.11
Example of a generalized stochastic Petri net.

Table 4.1
Switching probabilities of the GSPN in figure 4.11

$$\begin{cases} p\{t_2\} = \dfrac{m_3}{m_3 + m_4} \\ p\{t_3\} = \dfrac{m_4}{m_3 + m_4} \end{cases}$$

$$\left.\begin{cases} p\{t_6\} = \dfrac{m_4}{m_3 + m_4} \\ p\{t_7\} = \dfrac{m_3}{m_3 + m_4} \end{cases}\right\} \quad \text{if } m_3 \neq 0 \text{ or } m_4 \neq 0$$

$$p\{t_6\} = p\{t_7\} = 1/2 \quad \text{if } m_3 = m_4 = 0$$

Table 4.2
Reachability set of the GSPN in figure 4.11

	m_1	m_2	m_3	m_4	m_5	m_6	m_7
Markings that enable only timed transitions	2	0	1	1	0	0	0
	1	0	0	1	1	0	0
	1	0	1	0	0	1	0
	0	0	0	0	1	1	0
	1	0	0	1	0	1	0
	1	0	1	0	1	0	0
	0	0	0	0	0	2	0
	0	0	0	0	2	0	0
Markings that enable immediate transitions	1	1	1	1	0	0	0
	0	1	0	1	1	0	0
	2	0	0	1	0	0	1
	0	1	1	0	0	1	0
	2	0	1	0	0	0	1
	1	0	0	0	0	1	1
	1	0	0	0	1	0	1
	0	1	0	1	0	1	0
	0	1	1	0	1	0	0

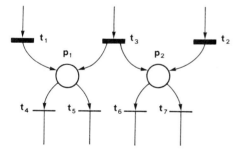

Figure 4.12
Portion of a GSPN model with multiple random switches.

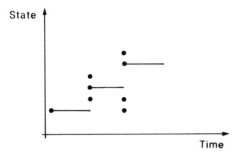

Figure 4.13
Possible sample path of the stochastic process underlying a GSPN and presenting "multiple discontinuities."

on some local and already identified behavior of the system. Assume now that t_3 fires first, so that a token is placed in both p_1 and p_2, thus simultaneously enabling the four immediate transitions t_4, t_5, t_6, and t_7. In this case the random switch accounts for the (possibly unclear) relations existing between the local behaviors of two separate parts of the system. A crucial aspect of the definition of a GSPN is the identification of all random switches and the definition of the "correct" switching distributions in all markings.

4.4.3 Evaluation of the Generalized Stochastic Petri Net Steady State Probability Distribution

By examining the GSPN behavior as a function of time we can easily realize that it is equivalent to the time behavior of a stochastic process $\{X(t), t \geq 0\}$ with a finite state space. A one-to-one correspondence exists between GSPN markings and stochastic process states. In the following the terms *marking* and *state* will be used equivalently. Sample functions, such as the one depicted in figure 4.13, representing a possible behavior sequence of the stochastic process, may present "multiple discontinuities" due to the sequential firing of one or more immediate transitions. The process is observed to spend a nonnegative amount of time in markings enabling timed transitions only, while it transits in zero time through markings enabling immediate transitions. We call *tangible* a state (or marking) of the former type and *vanishing* a state (or marking) of the latter type.

The GSPN application purposes that are considered in this book allow the following assumptions to be made:

1. The reachability set is finite.
2. Firing rates do not depend on time parameters.
3. The initial marking is reachable with a nonzero probability from any marking in the reachability set. No marking (or group of markings) exists that "absorbs" the process.

These assumptions further specify the nature of the stochastic process, which can thus be classified as a finite state space, stationary (homogeneous), irreducible, and continuous-time stochastic process.

Disregarding, for the time being, the concept of time and focusing our attention on the set of states that the process enters because of a transition (note that the word *transition* in this context indicates a change of state) out of a given state, we can observe that an embedded Markov chain (EMC) can be recognized within the stochastic process. The behavior specifications listed previously are sufficient for the computation of the transition probabilities.

Let S indicate the state space of the EMC (and of the stochastic process as well), and distinguish tangible and vanishing states within S so that it can be partitioned in the following way:

S = state space of stochastic process; $\quad |S| = K_s$;

T = set of tangible states in stochastic process; $\quad |T| = K_t$;

V = set of vanishing states in stochastic process; $\quad |V| = K_v$;

$S = T \cup V, \quad T \cap V = 0, \quad K_s = K_t + K_v.$

The transition probability matrix $\mathbf{U}$ of the EMC can be written as follows:

$$\mathbf{U} = \mathbf{A} + \mathbf{B} = \begin{bmatrix} \mathbf{C} & \mathbf{D} \\ \mathbf{0} & \mathbf{0} \end{bmatrix} + \begin{bmatrix} \mathbf{0} & \mathbf{0} \\ \mathbf{E} & \mathbf{F} \end{bmatrix} \qquad (4.19)$$

where the top block has K_v rows and the bottom block has K_t rows, and the columns are partitioned into K_v and K_t.

The elements of the matrix $\mathbf{A}$ can be obtained using the characteristics of random switches, and the elements of the matrix $\mathbf{B}$ can be obtained using the firing rates of timed transitions.

The solution of the system of linear equations

$$\pi = \pi \mathbf{U}, \tag{4.20}$$

in which π is a row vector representing the stationary probability distribution of the EMC, can be interpreted in terms of numbers of transitions performed by the EMC. Indeed, $1/\pi_i$ is the mean recurrence time for state i measured by the number of transitions [see (2.26)].

By selecting one of the states of the EMC as a reference state for the chain, and assuming, without loss of generality, that it is a tangible state (say state i), the mean number of visits to state j between two subsequent visits to state i is obtained from (2.29), which is repeated here for convenience:

$$v_{ji} = \frac{\pi_j}{\pi_i}. \tag{4.21}$$

The computation of the steady state probability distribution of the stochastic process can be obtained by reintroducing the concept of time by means of the average sojourn time in each state ($E[W_i], i \in S$). Using the definition of immediate transitions, or equivalently that of vanishing states, we can write

$$E[W_i] = 0, \quad i \in V. \tag{4.22}$$

The computation of the average sojourn times in tangible states requires the definition of the set

$$H_i = \{(\text{timed}) \text{ transition enabled by tangible state } i\}, \quad i \in T,$$

so that

$$E[W_i] = \frac{1}{\sum_{f \in H_i} l_f}, \quad i \in T. \tag{4.23}$$

The mean amount of time spent by the stochastic process in returning to the reference state i (mean cycle time) is thus given by [see (2.129)]

$$C_i = \sum_{j \in S} v_{ji} E[W_j] = \sum_{j \in T} v_{ji} E[W_j], \tag{4.24}$$

where $v_{ji} E[W_j]$ is the mean time spent by the stochastic process in state j during a cycle. The average fraction of time spent by the stochastic process in each of its states can be computed using (2.126):

$$\pi_j = \frac{v_{ji} E[W_j]}{C_i}, \quad j \in S. \tag{4.25}$$

The steady state probability distribution of the stochastic process can finally be written as

$$\pi_j = \begin{cases} 0, & j \in V \\ v_{ji} E[W_j]/C_i, & j \in T. \end{cases} \qquad (4.26)$$

Given the conditions specified at the beginning of this section, it can be shown that this solution method is equivalent to a simple extension of the method originally proposed by Molloy to handle similar cases. Let us assume that all immediate transitions are replaced by timed transitions characterized by very high firing rates proportional to an arbitrary value x. Under this assumption all states are tangible, so that the GSPN reduces to a standard SPN and Molloy's solution method applies. If an explicit solution expression for the probability distribution of this standard SPN (expressed in terms of x) is obtained, the stationary probability distribution of the original GSPN can be obtained by taking the limit with x going to infinity. Since most practical cases involve GSPN with a large state space, an explicit expression of the solution in terms of x is usually not easy to obtain, and the practical approach suggested by Molloy of numerically solving the problem by assuming x to be very large and arbitrarily setting to zero those probabilities that appear exceptionally small is prone to numerical problems.

4.4.4 A Computationally More Efficient Solution Method

The solution method proposed in the previous section is computationally acceptable whenever the size of the set of vanishing states is small (compared with the size of the set of tangible states, i.e., $K_v \ll K_t$). However, this method requires the computation of the mean number of visits to each vanishing state, which, as we know a priori, does not increase the information content of the solution. Moreover, vanishing states not only require useless computations, but, by enlarging the size of the transition probability matrix **U**, make the computation of the visits expensive and in some cases even impossible to obtain.

In order to remove vanishing states from the EMC introduced in the previous section, and to define a reduced embedded Markov chain (REMC) over tangible states only, we must compute the total transition probabilities among tangible states only. For the purpose of the derivation of a method for accomplishing this task, let i and j represent arbitrary tangible states ($i, j \in T$), while r and s represent arbitrary vanishing states ($r, s \in V$). By using c_{rs}, d_{rj}, e_{is}, and f_{ij} to represent elements of the submatrix blocks **C**, **D**, **E**, and **F** of the transition probability matrix **U** of the original EMC, the total transition probability matrix between any two tangible states i and j (u'_{ij}) can be computed in the following way:

$$u'_{ij} = f_{ij} + \sum_{r \in V} e_{ir} P\{r \to j\}, \tag{4.27}$$

where $P\{r \to j\}$ represents the probability that the stochastic process moves from vanishing state r to tangible state j in an arbitrary number of steps, following a path through vanishing states only.

In order to provide a general and more efficient method for the computation of the state transition probability matrix $\mathbf{U}'$ of the REMC, we must refer to (4.19). Recalling the interpretation of the partition of the transition probability matrix of the EMC (U), we focus our attention on the matrix $\mathbf{A}$ whose elements represent transition probabilities out of vanishing states only. The lth power of such a matrix can be written as

$$\mathbf{A}^l = \begin{bmatrix} \mathbf{C}^l & \mathbf{C}^{l-1}\mathbf{D} \\ \mathbf{0} & \mathbf{0} \end{bmatrix}.$$

Each component of the upper portion of the matrix $\mathbf{A}^l$ represents the probability of moving from any state $r \in V$ to any other state of the original stochastic process in exactly l steps, in such a way that intermediate states can be of the vanishing type only. The matrix $\mathbf{G}^l$ defined as

$$\mathbf{G}^l = \sum_{h=0}^{l-1} \mathbf{C}^h \mathbf{D},$$

provides the probability of reaching any tangible state $i \in T$, moving from any vanishing state $r \in V$ in no more than l steps, visiting intermediate states of the vanishing type only.

The irreducibility property of the stochastic process ensures that the spectral radius of the submatrix $\mathbf{C}$ is smaller than one [VARG62]. This implies that

$$\lim_{l \to \infty} \mathbf{C}^l = \mathbf{0}.$$

Having obtained this result, we can state that a limit for the sum

$$\lim_{l \to \infty} \sum_{h=0}^{l} \mathbf{C}^h$$

exists and is finite.

Whenever loops among vanishing states do not exist, a suitable ordering of these states can be found that allows writing $\mathbf{C}$ as an upper triangular matrix, so that there exists a value $l_0 \leq K_v$ such that

$$\mathbf{C}^l = \mathbf{0} \qquad \forall l > l_0$$

and the previous infinite sum reduces to a sum of a finite number of terms. If, instead, such loops among vanishing states exist, the infinite sum has the asymptotic value

$$\sum_{h=0}^{\infty} \mathbf{C}^h = [\mathbf{I} - \mathbf{C}]^{-1}.$$

These two possible forms of the same infinite sum can be used to provide an explicit expression for the matrix $\mathbf{G}^{\infty}$,

$$\mathbf{G}^{\infty} = \begin{cases} [\sum_{h=0}^{l_0} \mathbf{C}^h]\mathbf{D}, & \text{no loops among vanishing states} \\ [\mathbf{I} - \mathbf{C}]^{-1}\mathbf{D}, & \text{loops among vanishing states,} \end{cases}$$

whose elements represent the probabilities that the stochastic process reach for the first time a given tangible state, moving out of a given vanishing state in no matter how many steps. We can thus conclude that an explicit expression for the desired total transition probability among any two tangible states is

$$u'_{ij} = f_{ij} + \sum_{r \in V} e_{ir} g^{\infty}_{rj} \qquad \text{for any} \quad i, j \in T.$$

The transition probability matrix of the REMC can thus be expressed as

$$\mathbf{U}' = \mathbf{F} + \mathbf{E}\mathbf{G}^{\infty}, \tag{4.28}$$

where each component of $\mathbf{G}^{\infty}$ is the explicit expression of the above-mentioned $P\{r \to j\}$.

The solution of the problem

$$\boldsymbol{\pi}' = \boldsymbol{\pi}'\mathbf{U}', \tag{4.29}$$

in which $\boldsymbol{\pi}'$ is a row vector representing the stationary probability distribution of the REMC, allows the direct computation of the mean number of visits performed by the stochastic process to tangible states only between two subsequent visits to a reference state. The steady state probability distribution associated with the set of tangible states is thus readily obtained by means of their average sojourn times, as discussed in the previous section.

The advantage of this method of solution is twofold. First, the time and space complexity of the solution is reduced, since instead of solving a system of K_s linear equations, we must now (in the worst case) compute the inverse of a $K_v \times K_v$ matrix and then solve a system of K_t linear equations. Recalling that the complexity of the Gauss elimination solution method of systems of K linear equations is $O(K^3)$, the proposed approach reduces the complexity of the solution of the GSPN from $O(K_s^3)$ to $O(K_t^3) + O(K_v^3)$. Second, by decreasing the impact of the size of the set of vanishing states on the complexity of the solution method, we are allowed greater freedom in the explicit specification of the logical conditions of the original GSPN, making it easier to understand.

References

[AGER79] Agerwala, T., "Putting Petri Nets to Work," *IEEE Computer* 12(12), (December 1979), 85–94.

[AJMO84] Ajmone Marsan, M., Balbo, G., and Conte, G., "A Class of Generalized Stochastic Petri Nets for the Performance Evaluation of Multiprocessor Systems," *ACM Trans. on Computer Systems*, 2(2), (May 1984), 93–122.

[BRAM83] Brams, G. W., *Reseaux de Petri: Theorie et Pratique*, Masson, Paris, 1983.

[LAND78] Landweber, L. H., and Robertson, E. L., "Properties of Conflict-Free and Persistent Nets," *Journal of the ACM*, 25(3) (July 1978), 352–364.

[MERL76] Merlin, J. A., and Farber, D. J., "Recoverability of Communication Protocols—Implications of a Theoretical Study," *IEEE Trans. on Commun.* COM-24(9) (September 1976), 1036–1043.

[MOLL81] Molloy, M. K., "On the Integration of Delay and Throughput Measures in Distributed Processing Models," Ph. D. Thesis, University of California, Los Angeles, 1981.

[NATK80] Natkin, S., "Reseaux de Petri Stochastiques," Thèse de Docteur-Ingegneur, CNAM-Paris, June 1980.

[NOEN73] Noe, J. D., and Nutt, G. J., "Macro E-Nets Representation of Parallel Systems," *IEEE Trans. on Computers* C-22(8) (August 1973), 718–727.

[PETE81] Peterson, J. L., *Petri Net Theory and the Modeling of Systems*, Prentice-Hall, Englewood Cliffs, NJ, 1981.

[PETR66] Petri, C. A., "Communication with Automata," Ph. D. Thesis, Technical Report RADC-TR-65-377, New York, January 1966.

[REIS82] Reisig, W., *Petri-Netze, eine Einfuhrung*, Springer-Verlag, Berlin, 1982.

[SIFA77] Sifakis, J., "Use of Petri Nets for Performance Evaluation," Third Intl. Workshop on Modeling and Performance Evaluation of Computer Systems, Amsterdam, 1977.

[SYMO78] Symons, F. J. W. "Modelling and Analysis of Communication Protocols Using Numerical Petri Nets," Ph. D. Thesis, University of Essex, (1978).

[VARG62] Varga, R. S., *Matrix Iterative Analysis*, Prentice-Hall, Englewood Cliffs, NJ, 1962.

[ZUBE80] Zuberek, W. M., "Timed Petri Nets and Preliminary Performance Evaluation," Proc. of the 7th Annual Symposium on Computer Architecture, La Baule, France 1980.

II

5 Multiprocessor Architectures

Distributed computing systems, ranging from computer networks to multiple processors and highly parallel systems, have come to play a major role in computer science today, both in the application and research fields. The objective of this chapter is briefly to overview the main features of distributed computing architectures, focusing on multiprocessor systems, since they represent the architecture of main interest in the rest of the book.

A classification of distributed systems is presented first, and the most common taxonomies are discussed. Multiprocessor architectures are then discussed along with their motivations, advantages, and possible disadvantages. Some methods for the description and analysis of multiprocessor systems and of their workload are introduced. Finally, the basic modeling assumptions that are used throughout the book for the construction of stochastic models of multiprocessor systems are presented.

5.1 Distributed Systems

Many classifications and taxonomies of distributed computing systems were published in the last decade (see, for example, [ANDE75, ENSL78, FLYN72]), but different views still exist, together with disagreements, on what can be considered a distributed computing system.

A first classification of the different types of distributed systems takes into account the "granularity" [JONE80] of the interaction among the activities that are executed in parallel. It is possible to consider, on one side, systems in which the cooperation (data exchange and/or synchronization) among the elements occurs very seldom and involves large blocks of structured data at a time, and, on the other side, systems in which the data exchange is frequent and the synchronization occurs, for example, at the instruction level.

Using these guidelines, we can identify three major areas: computer networks, multiprocessors, and special parallel machines.

5.1.1 Computer Networks

Computer networks are the oldest class of distributed computing systems; they originated in the interconnection of large mainframes through a packet-switched communication subnetwork. Each processor in a computer network retains a strong local autonomy and devotes a very limited part of its processing power to common activities. For this reason there is not, in general, agreement on considering large geographic computer networks as a part of distributed processing. The rapid spread of mini/

microcomputer systems and the availability, at low cost, of personal computers have created new interest in the field, with the introduction of local area networks (LAN), which generally comprise many small computers. LAN have changed to some extent the scenario of the computer network field. The main characteristics of the network are still maintained, since processors are stand-alone computers that perform independent processing activities. On the other hand, global policies for handling common resources that can be both physical, like high-cost peripherals, or logical, like distributed data bases, are introduced, and processors cooperate in their management.

It must be pointed out that the increased interdependence among units moves to the forefront the role of the physical and the logical structure of the communication network that allows the different resources of the system to communicate.

5.1.2 Multiprocessor Systems

The second class of distributed computing systems comprises multiprocessors in which each processor is a fully programmable unit capable of executing its own program. The key issue distinguishing computer networks from multiple processor systems is the fact that in the latter case all system resources are coordinated toward a common goal under the control of a single (centralized or distributed) mechanism, and the set of processors forms a single entity. The amount of information exchange among the basic processing units can now be significantly greater than in the previous case. The interconnection topology and the communication strategy among processing units become in this case the crucial elements of the system, and a more detailed classification must be based on the structure of the interconnection network.

5.1.3 Special Purpose Machines

The third class of distributed computing systems comprises special purpose machines, i.e., processing systems built for the solution of either specific applications or a set of applications. These structures often are stand-alone machines, but they can also be connected, as peripherals, to some high-power computing system such as a mainframe, in order to speed up the execution of some specific, frequently needed computation. In this class we can find

1. *Highly parallel structures.* Highly parallel structures are composed of a large number of identical hardware units, each one able to perform a fixed basic operation. These units are interconnected, and work in parallel for the fast solution of CPU-bound algorithms, such as matrix operations and discrete Fourier transforms. An example of a highly parallel computing structure is provided by systolic arrays, whose architec-

tural properties appear to be very well suited to VLSI implementation [MEAD80]. A systolic array consists of a set of identical computing cells interconnected according to a regular topology in which the flow of information is allowed only among adjacent units in a pipelined style. The I/O needs of the single unit are hence very limited, and the short distance that must be covered by the interconnection allows a significant speed up of the internal operations. Doing so satisfies one of the major constraints of VLSI elements, in which the computing capabilities depend on the number of active elements, and therefore on the silicon area, whereas the number of I/O interconnections is limited by the length of the border. The programmability of these structures is very limited because each one is specifically designed and optimized to perform efficiently only a well-defined algorithm.

2. *Array processors.* Array processors perform in lockstep the same operation on many different data, typically vectors or matrices. These machines have a degree of programmability higher than the previous ones, but their use is restricted to the solution of problems that require the efficient manipulation of large arrays of data. Extensions to high-level languages were proposed for some commercially available array processors in order to allow the programmer to exploit the parallel features of the machine without being involved in the peculiarities of the architecture.

3. *Non-von Neumann machines.* Von Neumann machines are characterized by the presence of a processing unit that executes instructions (stored in a memory) in sequence, under the control of a program counter. The sequential program execution does not allow the parallelism that can be inherent in the program to be efficiently exploited. Among the architectures proposed for overcoming this problem are data flow computers. In this case the execution of an instruction is allowed as soon as the requested operands (and the hardware resources) become available. This type of architecture is also called data-driven, whereas von Neumann machines are termed control-driven systems. It must be pointed out, however, that usually non-von Neumann machines are obtained by connecting together in some peculiar way, elements that are basically von Neumann. This is the reason why they are included here in the large family of distributed systems.

5.1.4 Other Classifications of Distributed Systems

The classification just described is based on the granularity of the interaction among the units that compose the systems. Different classifications can be found in the literature. Among them the most significant ones were proposed by Flynn [FLYN72] and by Enslow [ENSL78]. Flynn introduced the following three classes of computer organizations:

- the single-instruction-stream-single-data-stream (SISD) class, which comprises conventional uniprocessor computer systems;
- the single-instruction-stream-multiple-data-stream (SIMD) class, which includes array processors;
- the multiple-instruction-stream-multiple-data-stream (MIMD) class, which includes most of the multiprocessor systems.

Enslow proposed, instead, the use of a three-dimensional space to characterize distributed systems. The three Cartesian axes represent, respectively,

- the distribution of processing units—this corresponds to the physical organization of the hardware structure that can go from a single central processor unit up to a geographically distributed multiple computer system;
- the organization of the control—the span is from a system with a centralized control to a distributed system composed of a set of fully cooperating and homogeneous processing units;
- the distribution of the data—from this point of view it is possible to have systems with a centralized data structure and systems with a completely partitioned data base.

It is very difficult, in general, to classify a real system using one of the previous schemes. For instance, in a multiprocessor system the level of cooperation among activities is not only defined by the system architecture, but also by the operating system, possibly distributed, as well as by the application program itself. Processors can run, for example, tasks that are executed independently and very seldom need data exchanges: when necessary, they use a message-passing scheme, as in an LAN structure, even if they have access to shared memory areas. The same system can, on the other hand, support pipelined operations on a single data stream with very frequent exchanges of intermediate results, as in an SIMD structure operating synchronously on vectors or arrays. In conclusion, the aim of these classifications is not to offer a precise scheme in which to insert a known architecture, but to offer a global view of the design space and of the possible different solutions in the framework of the large area of distributed computing systems.

5.2 Multiprocessor Systems

In this section we briefly review multiprocessor architectures in order to point out the main advantages of these structures and to try a further classification ([BOWE80, PARK83, HWAN84, CONT85]).

Chapter 5

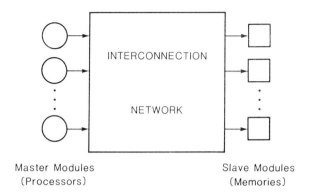

Master Modules
(Processors)

Slave Modules
(Memories)

Figure 5.1
General structure of a multiprocessor system.

The most general structure of a multiprocessor system is depicted in figure 5.1; a multiprocessor consists of a set of master modules (processors) and of a set of slave units (memories and/or I/O modules) linked together by means of an interconnection structure. More generally, master units are the system elements allowed to issue access requests to the interconnection structure for the transfer of data; slave units receive access requests from master units and can accept and honor them. It must be pointed out that the actual direction of the information transfer can be either the same as the access request (write operation) or the opposite (read operation). Master units other than processors can be, for example, I/O modules with a DMA unit, but for the sake of clarity we always use the term processor instead of master unit, as well as memory instead of slave unit. In figure 5.1, and in the following, processors are represented by circles and memories by rectangles. The interconnection structure is a very important part of the system because it allows communication among processors and memories, and therefore data exchange among processors. No generally accepted standard solution for the interconnection network exists, and for this reason, whereas processors and memories are available at low cost as integrated circuits, the interconnection network is always designed according to the requirements of the specific application.

It is therefore of great interest to estimate the ability of a specific interconnection network to support efficiently a given application, and/or to compare the different architectural solutions.

5.2.1 Multiprocessor Topology

The multiprocessor design space can be divided into two main areas: loosely coupled and tightly coupled systems. The first class comprises systems with autonomous units connected by I/O links. The architecture, in this case, may be, except for the system size, similar to that of either a geographically distributed computer network or a LAN. The interconnection network can be implemented using either parallel or serial links, and data transmission rates can range from few Kbps up to tens of Mbps. A thorough analysis of this kind of architecture is beyond the scope of this book.

The second area comprises systems in which a number of processors can access a common memory area. It must be observed that the minimal functional unit that can execute a program is formed by a processor and a memory. The purpose of the interconnection network is thus that of linking at a given instant of time each processor with the requested memory module. There are two main reasons why the satisfaction of processor requests may be hindered:

1. Two or more processors simultaneously request the same memory unit.
2. Two or more processors simultaneously request the same communication link to access different memory units.

In both cases, processors that cannot access the requested memory unit must wait. The structure of the interconnection network must keep as low as possible the time lost by processors waiting for nonfree memories and nonfree communication resources. The complete (or almost complete) elimination of any sort of contention for common resources usually requires the availability of a very expensive and complex interconnection structure. The design trade-off is thus reduction in the complexity and cost of the interconnection network without significantly affecting the performance of the multiprocessor system.

One of the first design alternatives, from the architectural point of view, is the choice between a homogeneous set of memory modules and a hierarchy of specialized memory elements. The second alternative is more effective, but it reduces the regularity of the system and may require (from either the user's or the programmer's point of view) a good knowledge of the operations the system must perform. One of the most effective solutions is the partition of the set of memory modules into two main groups. The first one comprises a set of independent memory modules, each one associated with a processor and only accessible from it (private memory). These memories can, for example, contain the programs each processor must execute. The second group comprises a set of memory modules containing the common memory cells that every processor in the system can access (with the same or different accessing rights). The general structure of a multiprocessor system with this architecture is shown in figure 5.2.

From the point of view of the interconnection network, many different solutions exist. In the following subsections we examine crossbar switches, shared bus systems, and multistage networks.

Chapter 5

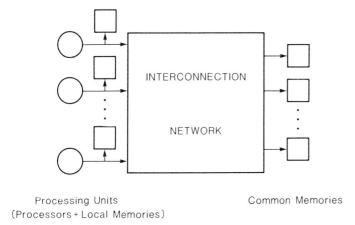

Processing Units
(Processors + Local Memories)

Common Memories

Figure 5.2
Structure of a multiprocessor system in which processing units are composed of a processor and a memory module.

5.2.1.1 Crossbar Switches

In these systems one path is connected to each memory bank and another one to each processor, as shown in figure 5.3. A set of switches may connect any processor path to any memory path. The system supports simultaneous accesses to all memory units. Contention may arise only when the same memory bank is simultaneously requested by more than one processor. The cost of the interconnection network grows proportionally to the number of switches (which equals $p \times m$, where p is the number of processors and m is the number of memories). Each processing unit comprises a CPU and possibly a private memory. A crossbar interconnection among several PDP11 minicomputers was implemented in C.mmp, one of the earliest multiprocessor systems [WULF72]. However, the complexity of the interconnection network prevented further use of this structure. Recent proposals suggest the use of VLSI elements to implement this interconnection network [MCFA82].

5.2.1.2 Shared Bus Systems

From the logical point of view this is the simplest interconnection structure between processors and memory modules. A shared bus is a single communication path to which all functional units (such as memories and processors) are connected, as shown in figure 5.4. If only one processor unit is connected to the bus, no contention problems arise. When two or more processors are connected to the same bus, some policy must be used to establish the connections: fixed time slots can be assigned to each processor,

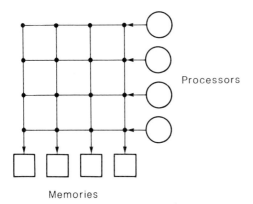

Figure 5.3
Structure of a crossbar multiprocessor system.

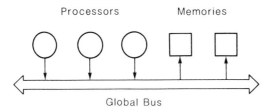

Figure 5.4
Structure of a single global bus multiprocessor system.

or, alternatively, the system must be able to resolve contention arising from unconstrained request sequences. In the latter case processors issue their memory access requests, and then an arbiter handles simultaneous requests. It is obvious that this interconnection network allows no simultaneous transfer between different processor/memory pairs, so that the single bus structure may easily become the bottleneck of the whole system. To achieve better performance, the single global bus can be replaced by a set of parallel buses.

This approach is far more complex, and a careful trade-off must be made between cost, complexity, and the resulting functional upgrading obtained with the redundancy.

The general scheme of a multiple bus structure is shown in figure 5.5. This network can also be viewed as a generalization of the crossbar switch, since it comprises two sets of elementary switches, the first one being the links between processors and buses, the second set representing the links between buses and memory modules. In the

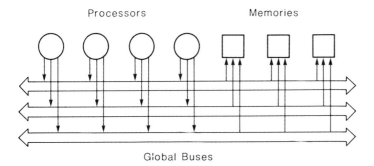

Figure 5.5
Structure of a multiple global bus multiprocessor system.

Figure 5.6
The two settings of the basic 2×2 switching element.

general case the number of switches is $(m + p) \times b$, where b is the number of buses.

From a functional point of view global buses can be divided into two classes, depending on whether they allow information exchange on a circuit-switching or on a packet-switching basis. Circuit-switched buses establish a fixed connection between processor and memory for all the time in which the data exchange occurs. On a packet-switching bus, instead, a data request (a request packet) is transmitted from the processor to the memory, and the requested data are transmitted back to the processor using a data packet when it is available. This mode of operation can be convenient when the bus is much faster than the memories connected to it, so that it is possible to transmit on the bus several request and data packets while memories assemble new data packets.

5.2.1.3 Multistage Interconnection Networks

The multiprocessor system interconnection network can be implemented using an array of identical building blocks [SIEG85]. Each element must be able to perform a very simple switching function. Consider, for example, the basic 2×2 switching element shown in figure 5.6. The switch can be set in two configurations, yielding either a direct or a crossed connection. An array of N 2×2 switches yields a single-stage

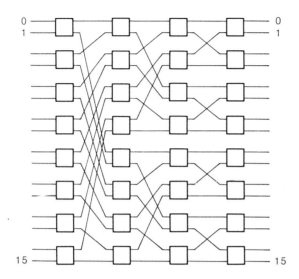

Figure 5.7
Structure of a multistage "baseline" network.

interconnection network. A matrix of $N/2(\log_2 N)$ basic switches forms a multistage network that can interconnect a set of N input elements to a set of N output elements. Different interconnection strategies between the stages generate different types of interconnection networks. In all cases a proper setting of the elementary switches can connect any input to any output. Figure 5.7 shows, as an example, a special case of multistage interconnection network known as "baseline" [FENG81].

In the case of multiprocessor systems, inputs are processors (possibly with the associated local memory) and outputs are common memory banks. If more than one input-output pair must be simultaneously connected, conflicts can occur in the communication path. From this point of view multistage interconnection networks can be divided into three classes: blocking, rearrangeable, and nonblocking. Networks are referred to as blocking if unresolvable conflicts may occur. A network is said to be rearrangeable if, by properly rearranging the existing connections, it is always possible to establish a new interconnection path between a processor and a free memory. A network in which all possible interconnections can be established without conflicts is called nonblocking.

From a functional point of view also these networks can be divided into two classes, depending on whether they allow information exchange on a circuit-switching or on a packet-switching basis. The former establish a fixed connection between the input and the output port for all the time in which the data exchange occurs. In a packet-switching network, instead, packets are transmitted through the network, and stored at intermediate points along the path, where they can wait if the path to the final address is not free.

As noted for crossbar structures, these interconnection networks will become really effective only when the basic switching elements are available as VLSI chips.

5.3 The Advantages of a Multiprocessor System

The potential advantages of multiple processor systems and the motivations for their development have been expressed for a long time by the following key words: performance, reliability, and availability. As already noted, the most recent progress in VLSI technology makes available, at low cost, high-performance microprocessor units; 32-bit microprocessors have been available since 1984 with performance comparable to ten-year-old superminis.

The first design objective of a multiprocessor system is obviously performance increase. The basic idea is that doubling the number of processing units should almost double performance, but should not double the cost of the system, since the most expensive system components are the peripherals. Extrapolating, if a system with ten times the performance of a single processor is needed, it should be sufficient to assemble something more than ten processing units.

The performance advantages of multiple processor systems over high-speed and high-power monoprocessor computers can be exploited, however, only if some conditions hold:

- The activity that must be performed can be *partitioned* into smaller tasks that can be executed in parallel. To achieve this goal it is necessary to find, for the activity to be performed, an algorithm with an intrinsic parallelism. The algorithm must then be subdivided into tasks that can be executed in parallel by different processors.
- The tasks can be conveniently *allocated* to processors so as to keep low the system overhead due to processor cooperation. In other words tasks must be allocated to processors with the aim of ensuring coordination and synchronization and minimizing the data exchange.
- The system is modularly designed, so that the addition of new elements is possible and cost effective. Modularity can be obtained only with proper design choices at the architectural level in the earliest stages of the project (the interconnection structure is a key point of this problem).

The first two requirements imply that the computational problem must be decomposed according to the distributed nature of the multiprocessor system in order to profit from its parallelism.

Focusing our attention on system overhead, we can identify three main factors that contribute to the reduction in overall system efficiency:

- Processor cooperation is managed by an executive program that uses processing power doing no "useful" work.
- The presence of synchronization constraints among concurrent processes forces some process to wait for the end of activities allocated to other units.
- Contention for the use of common resources (memories) may cause processors to queue, so that time is lost waiting.

In this book we focus mainly on the third factor, which has been the concern of most works on multiprocessor performance analysis.

From the reliability point of view the basic idea is that duplicating the hardware leads to a system that is more resistant to failures. It is obvious that the replication of hardware is not sufficient to obtain a system with higher reliability, but it is necessary to add special hardware and software elements that can locate errors, restart the system from some secure point, and possibly reconfigure the system in order to exploit as efficiently as possible those units that are operating correctly.

5.4 Modeling Assumptions

As we said in chapter 1, estimating the performance of a system with either simulation or analytical tools requires the definition of a model that captures the relevant features of the actual system. A model should contain a definition of the set of building blocks that compose the system, a description of the functional relationships among these components, and the characterization of the workload that applies to the system itself.

5.4.1 Level of Abstraction of the Analysis

In order to define a proper system model, we must first clearly define the objectives of the analysis and then decide the level of abstraction of the representation. The definition of the level of abstraction drives the choice of the level of detail of the description of each subsystem, as well as the functional relationships and the rules of communication among building blocks. The level of abstraction should be chosen bearing in mind the parameters that significantly describe system performance. The evaluation (or the estimation) of such parameters is the actual goal of the analysis and must be performed as efficiently as possible. The model must contain all elements relevant to the analysis, whereas all the details that are not significant at that level of abstraction must be eliminated.

In the performance evaluation of a computing system, we can identify several possible levels of detail. Starting from the lowest level of abstraction (maximum level of detail) we have

1. *Hardware level*: This corresponds to the objective of verifying the correctness of the design from a logical point of view. Basic building blocks of these models are the representations of integrated circuits. The functional description of the model can be given in terms of either simple gates or the behavior of basic integrated circuits. Specialized programming languages are available for this description.
2. *Functional level*: This corresponds to the objective of evaluating the behavior of basic hardware units, such as processors, memory modules, and buses, while they cooperate (or interfere) in performing simple operations, such as task execution. The description of the model can be given in terms of speed, capacity, and delay of each unit.
3. *System level*: This corresponds to the objective of verifying the efficiency of the global system, identifying the functions of each subsystem unit. Basic building blocks are the representation of complex hardware/software units, such as processing units, I/O units, and communication units. The description of the model is again given in terms of speed and capacity of each unit.

These three levels correspond also to steps in the hierarchical design of computing systems. The selection of the most convenient abstraction level derives, of course, from a trade-off between the accuracy of the model and the cost of its analysis. Implementation details, such as the behavior at the integrated circuit level, may not be relevant in the architecture design phase, while, on the other hand, during the design of a general purpose multiprocessor machine a precise knowledge of the system activity in its actual environment may not be known precisely. An intermediate level such as (2) seems therefore the most appropriate for multiprocessor system analysis. Indeed, note that such a level corresponds to the one already used in section 5.2 to describe multiprocessor systems.

We summarize here the basic assumptions made to obtain the models of multiprocessor systems that will be presented in the following:

- The basic elements of a multiprocessor system are processors, memories, and the interconnection structure.
- A processor can issue access requests directed to memories.

- A memory may accept and serve requests issued by processors. Most often memories are assumed to be capable of serving requests one at a time, and to stress the presence of a memory arbiter we draw a memory bus in those cases in which several interfaces are connected to the memory. In a few cases we consider memories capable of serving several simultaneous access requests. Memories of this type are referred to as multiport memories, and they are drawn with several direct connections to the interconnection network.
- The interconnection network links processors and memories. The topology of the interconnection network and the policy of the arbitration logic are specified case by case. Unless otherwise stated the time delays introduced by the interconnection network are assumed to be zero.

5.4.2 Formulation of the Workload Model

The second, but no less important, part of the performance evaluation model is the characterization of the workload applied to the system. The experience acquired in the modeling of large computer systems has proved the difficulty of properly defining this part of the model.

Different models to study the performance degradation of multiple processor systems due to memory interference have been proposed. In some of these, the system is considered at the instruction level; instructions are thus represented as synchronous operations. Time is divided into slots. At the beginning of each slot processors can issue access requests; then the arbitration mechanism selects the requests that can be honored, and connects processors to memories. The connection is maintained for the entire duration of the time slot.

In other cases a more abstract view of the system is used and asynchronous operations are assumed corresponding to the execution of program segments and to memory accesses for transferring data. Processors are assumed to execute programs stored in their own private memories. The execution of a program is interleaved with accesses to common memories where the data common to the system are assumed to be stored. One can thus identify processor activities as sequences of accesses to the different memory modules of the system for moving variable quantities of data. Contention may arise for the use of the interconnection network and for accessing common memory modules.

From a less abstract point of view this kind of processor activity can be the result of very different behavior patterns at the system level.

We can assume, for a first example, that processors execute tasks that cooperate by passing messages. Tasks can communicate either with other tasks allocated to the same

Chapter 5   115

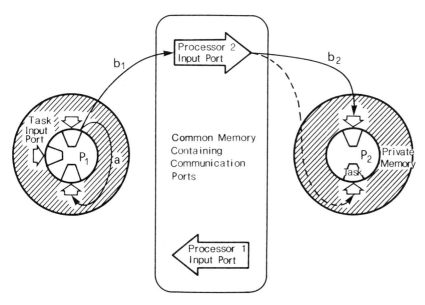

Figure 5.8
Logical structure of the communication between tasks. (a) A task allocated to P_1 puts a message into the input port of another task allocated to the same processor. (b) A task allocated to P_1 sends a message to a task allocated to P_2 with a two-step action: (b_1) the message is put into the input port of P_2; (b_2) the message is moved to the input port of the destination task.

processor or with tasks allocated to other processors. Associated with each task is an "input port" stored in the private memory of the processor to which the task is allocated. Every message issued by the task is directed to the input port of the destination task. Communication between tasks allocated to the same processor takes places through private memory only. No common resources (common memories and interconnection network) are involved in the message exchange operation. Communication between task allocated to different processors must use a "communication port" residing in common memory. One communication port is associated with each processor as its input port. A pictorial view of the logical structure of the communication between tasks is shown in figure 5.8.

The execution of tasks cooperating in message-passing fashion therefore amounts to executing repeatedly a "CPU burst-transfer period" cycle. Contention for the use of shared resources, such as global bus and common memory modules, can add a queuing component to the execution cycle. The assumption of a continuous flow of instruction being executed by each processor implies that idle periods due to task synchronization are negligible, and that the number of tasks allocated to processors is very large with respect to the number of processors itself.

Consider now, as a second example, a system in which each processor executes only one task. Processor instruction code and local data are stored in local memory, whereas data that need to be referenced by different processors are stored in global memories. An execution of a program therefore is a sequence of accesses to different memory modules. In detail, a sequence of accesses to local memories is followed by accesses to external memories (where global data are stored), and at the end of the cycle processors access again local memories.

As a third example, consider the multiprocessor organization that was recently proposed for the implementation of a billion-instructions-per-second computer system [GOYA84]. In this case processors are directly connected to very-high-speed private cache memories, which they access as long as the required information is found. When the needed data are not found in the private cache memory, they must be retrieved from a large common memory that is connected to all processors through an interconnection network. Thus again we can identify sequences of accesses to the private caches, intermixed with accesses to common memories for retrieving blocks of data.

It is important to note that the three examples just described correspond to multi-processors that behave quite differently at the system level; but at the functional level the workload models for the three systems are identical, and correspond, from the processor point of view, to the repeated execution of the following sequence:

- an access, or a sequence of accesses, to the local memory,
- an access, or a sequence of accesses, to common memory.

We can thus classify the states of a processor as follows:

- ACTIVE: The processor executes in its private memory.
- ACCESSING: The processor exchanges information with other cooperating processors by writing into (or reading from) common memory areas.
- QUEUED: The processor queues waiting to access common memory areas.

In order to obtain quantitative performance indices from the multiprocessor model it is necessary to assign quantitative values to the model parameters, which in the examples we have presented are the durations of the sequences of accesses to local and common memories. These two quantities completely specify the cyclical workload for each processor, and the model must be able to combine the parameters of each processor and the architecture description in order to provide the estimates of the processor queuing times and the desired performance indices.

Obviously, the selection of the workload parameters is very important, since the performance indices obtained from the model may be meaningless if the parameters (or the workload model in general) are not correct.

Essentially two types of approach can be followed to define the workload model, using either a deterministic approach or a probabilistic view of the system operations.

Consider first the deterministic case, and hence assume that the workload of each single processor is completely known. It is then possible to derive a precise trace of the operations performed by the different processing units (time duration of the single activities, destination of each access request, etc.), and to use them to study the behavior of the complete system. Parameters such as the time needed by the multiprocessor to complete some well-defined activity can be evaluated via simulation, and the presence of bottlenecks can be detected using the same tool.

This approach suffers from at least three drawbacks:

1. An exact knowledge of the system workload is required. This cannot be obtained in the early design stages, when the architectural choices are made, since the application may not yet be precisely defined.
2. A discrete event digital simulator is necessary to replicate on a computer the history of the system evolution through its state space.
3. The results obtained by this technique are limited to the specific case under test, and functional relationships between input parameters and output results cannot be easily obtained.

Using, instead, a probabilistic view of the system, it is possible to develop a stochastic model, in which the many details of the system workload are not individually represented. A stochastic model tries to capture the essence of the system operations by defining the workload parameters to be random variables with appropriate probability distributions. In the examples given earlier, the duration of the access sequence both in local memory and in common memory must be described through probability distributions. A probabilistic model is, of course, less powerful than a deterministic one with respect to a precisely known workload, but it offers the advantage of providing results in the form of functional relationships between system parameters and performance, and may thus be very useful for understanding better the actual behavior of a complex multiprocessor system. Moreover, a stochastic model can be constructed in the very early stages of the system design, and it can be used to test different architectural choices with respect to given performance objectives.

In the rest of the book we construct and solve stochastic models of multiprocessor systems, considering crossbar as well as bus-oriented interconnection networks.

References

[ANDE75] Anderson, G. A., and Jensen, E. D., "Computer Interconnection Structures: Taxonomy, Characteristics, and Examples," *Computing Surveys* 7(4) (December 1975), 197–213.

[BOWE80] Bowen, B. A., and Buhr, R. J. A., *The Logical Design of Multiple-microprocessor systems*, Prentice-Hall, Englewoods Cliffs, NJ, 1980.

[CONT85] Conte, G., and Del Corso, D., editors, *Multi-Microprocessors Systems for Real-Time Applications*, Reidel, Dordrecht (Holland), 1985.

[ENSL78] Enslow P. H., "What Is a Distributed Data Processing System?" *IEEE Computer* 11(1) (January 1978), 13–21.

[[FENG81] Feng, T. Y., "A Survey of Interconnection Networks," *IEEE Computer* 14(12) (December 1981), 12–27.

[FLYN72] Flynn, M. J., "Some Computer Organizations and Their Effectiveness," *IEEE Trans. on Computers* C-21(9) (September 1972), 948–960.

[GOYA84] Goyal, A., and Agerwala, T., "Performance Analysis of Future Shared Storage Systems," *IBM J. Res. Develop.* 28(1) (January 1984), 95–108.

[HWAN84] Hwang, K., and Briggs, F. A., *Computer Architecture and Parallel Processing*, McGraw-Hill, New York, 1984.

[JONE80] Jones, A. K., and Schwarz, P., "Experiences Using Multiprocessor Systems—A Status Report," *Computing Surveys* 12(2) (June 1980), 121–165.

[MEAD80] Mead, C. A., and Conway, L. A., "*Introduction to VLSI Systems*, Addison-Wesley, Reading, MA, 1980.

[MCFA82] McFarling, S., Turney, J., and Mudge, T., "VLSI Crossbar Design Version Two," CRL-TR-8-82, University of Michigan, February 1982, 18 pp.

[PARK83] Parker, Y., "*Multi-microprocessor System*, Academic Press, London, 1983.

[SIEG85] Siegel, H. J., *Interconnection Networks for Large Scale Parallel Processing. Theory and Case Studies*, Lexington Books, Lexington, MA, 1985.

[WULF72] Wulf W. A., and Bell, C. G., "C.mmp—a Multi-miniprocessor," Proc. AFIPS Fall Joint Computer Conf., N.J., Vol. 41, 1972, pp. 765–777.

6 Analysis of Crossbar Multiprocessor Architectures

The main characteristic affecting the performance of most multiprocessor systems is their sharing of primary memory. Memory conflicts occur whenever two or more processors attempt to access the same memory module simultaneously. In some cases the additional contention due to the use of the switch that connects processors to memory modules heavily influences the performance of the multiprocessor system. As we pointed out in the previous chapter, a *crossbar* switch is an interconnection structure that gives to any processor the possibility of accessing any memory module at any time without interfering with other processors, provided that the memory module is free. No contention for the use of the switch thus exists in this case.

Multiprocessor systems with crossbar interconnection structure have been quite common in the past and have been the subject of extensive studies directed to the characterization of memory interference. For this purpose, several researchers proposed different Markovian models of memory interference, each model corresponding to an abstract representation of a quite complex real system. It is not surprising that the simplifying assumptions introduced by the different authors to ease the model solution are often slightly different, so that results are seldom directly comparable.

In this chapter we present a unified discussion of the most important models of crossbar multiprocessor systems that have appeared in the literature, and particular attention is paid to the comparison of their underlying assumptions as well as to their solution methods. In these models the performance of a crossbar multiprocessor is measured in terms of successful memory accesses per unit of time. Because of the level of detail considered in the analysis, time is divided into *slots* and processors are assumed to issue their memory access requests at the beginning of each slot. A probability α is introduced to represent the fact that in some cases at the beginning of each time slot the processor has a chance of not issuing a memory access request (see figure 5.2), and to account for the fact that processors may skip one or several slots between two subsequent requests. Figure 6.1 provides an example of the timing of a typical processor execution cycle. The case $\alpha = 1$ corresponds to architectures similar to that depicted in figure 5.1 for which no local processing is possible.

Traditionally, the processor execution cycle considered in the development of these models has been centered on the possible overlapping between the processor *active time* (t_p) and the memory *rewrite time* (t_w) [BHAN75]. Using our slotted time approach, a value of α equal to 1 corresponds to a complete overlapping between the above two times, while a value of α smaller than 1 corresponds to geometrically distributed active times.

Under these assumptions, the problem of memory interference is analyzed with a discrete time queuing model in which p processors are represented as p delay stations,

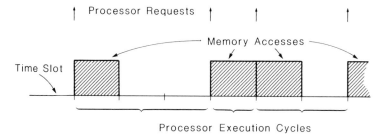

Figure 6.1
Timing of typical processor execution cycles.

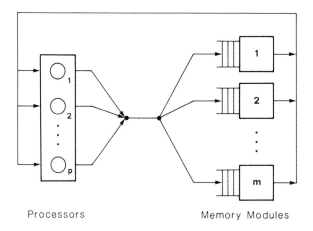

Figure 6.2
Queuing model of a crossbar multiprocessor system.

and *m* memory modules are represented as *m* service stations. Queuing may arise only in front of the (memory) service stations. Figure 6.2 provides a general representation of such a queuing model.

Memory modules are assumed to be synchronized. At the beginning of each time slot every module with a nonempty queue starts serving the first request in the queue. At most one request is served by each memory module during a time slot. The request issued by a processor is directed to a memory module chosen at random. Several requests may be simultaneously directed to the same memory module. Processors can issue new requests only after their previous ones have been satisfied.

Unless otherwise specified, all processors and all memories are assumed to behave similarly. This allows the state of the multiprocessor model to be represented by a vector describing the sizes of the various queues without having to represent explicitly the identity of the processors waiting or accessing the memory modules.

The mathematical models used to evaluate this class of multiprocessor systems are based on the theory of Markov chains. In most cases discrete-time Markov chains are used. The construction of their state transition probability matrix is the critical part of the analysis, as will be discussed in the following. The steady state solution of these Markov chains can be used to assess the performance of the multiprocessor systems. In this chapter we always use the average number of busy memory modules as an index of the efficiency of the system. Other performance indices can be obtained either from the steady state solution or as functions of the average number of executing processors and busy memories.

6.1 Model Classification

As we already pointed out, several authors investigated the problem of memory interference in crossbar multiprocessors, proposing many alternative models capable of capturing the main features of this class of systems with different degrees of accuracy.

A classification of these models can be attempted using as criteria the assumptions introduced by the authors. The model representation of three basic features of the system will be considered.

1. *Active times.* Several models assume $\alpha = 1$, making the whole system synchronized with the memory cycle (a time slot). At the beginning of each time slot, every processor whose previous request has been served by one of the memory modules issues a new request. From the point of view of the memory modules, processors behave as *zero-delay* service stations; the *effective* active time of processors is thus null. Other models assume $\alpha < 1$, allowing a geometric distribution of the active time. From the point of view of memory modules, in this case processors behave as *delay* service stations. In some models the constraint of synchronized accesses is released and generally distributed active times are allowed.

2. *Memory reference pattern.* Most models assume that processors select memory modules according to a uniform distribution. In a few cases nonuniform memory references are considered to represent either systems in which each processor may have a different memory reference pattern or the locality phenomenon that can be observed in most computations.

3. *Lost independent requests.* To simplify the construction and the solution of the models, many authors assume that when several requests are addressed to the same

Table 6.1
Model classification

	Uniform memory reference		Nonuniform memory reference	
	$\alpha = 1$	$\alpha < 1$	$\alpha = 1$	$\alpha < 1$
Queued requests	SKIN69a BHAN75a BASK76a BASK76b BASK76c RAU79a	BHAN75c	SETH79a	
Lost requests	STRE70a BHAN75b	BHAN75d YEN82a YEN82b YEN82c	HOOG77a	HOOG77b MUDG82a

memory module, only one is actually served while all others are lost. At the beginning of the subsequent time slot all the processors whose requests were lost issue new independent requests that can be directed to different memory modules. In these models the existence of a queue of requests waiting in front of a specific memory model is neglected. This assumption simplifies considerably the complexity of the model construction and solution, but yields an underestimate of the memory interference.

Table 6.1 visualizes the classification of the models considered in this chapter according to the above criteria. Models are named with the acronyms used to reference the papers in which they were first discussed. Letters a, b, c, ... are used to identify the different models that were presented in the same paper.

6.2 Model Discussion

In this section we discuss the main features of the models proposed in the literature, with particular attention to the methods that were used for their construction and solution. The results obtained with the different models will be illustrated and compared whenever possible. The model presentation follows the classification introduced in the previous section. The models proposed by Bhandarkar in his pioneering work [BHAN75], and motivated by the necessity of evaluating the C.mmp system built at Carnegie-Mellon University [WULF72], will be discussed in some detail because of their importance as reference elements on which the other authors improved.

6.2.1 Uniform Memory Reference Pattern

We first consider models in which memory modules are selected according to a uniform distribution. Every time a processor issues a request, it selects a specific memory module with probability $1/m$.

6.2.1.1 Zero-Delay Models—Queued Requests

The first class of models that we consider in detail is that in which $\alpha = 1$. With $\alpha = 1$ the analysis is much simpler than in the case of $\alpha < 1$, and it provides results that are bounds for those of the other case. Hence, assuming $\alpha = 1$ provides an interesting case for a preliminary comparison of different modeling techniques, even though in practice this equality is quite uncommon. Assuming that all processors have similar behaviors, the queuing network in figure 6.2 comprises only a set of parallel servers operating in a perfectly synchronous way.

A rigorous analysis of this queuing model was first attempted by Skinner and Asher [SKIN69] (model SKIN69a). They proposed a discrete time Markov chain for small multiprocessor systems with no more than two processors. The complexity of the problem deterred the authors from pursuing the analysis of larger systems.

Bhandarkar [BHAN75] overcame the enormous complexity of this analysis by first observing that the behavior of the system can be completely described without keeping track of the identity of individual processors waiting or being served by the memory modules (model BHAN75a). The state of the system is thus represented with an m-component vector $\mathbf{K} = (k_1, k_2, \ldots, k_m)$ where all entries are nonnegative integers and $\sum_{i=1}^{m} k_i = p$. The number of distinct states of the system is given by the binomial

$$\binom{p + m - 1}{m - 1}.$$

However, since all memory modules have identical behavior, a partition of the state space can be made that groups equally likely states together. In particular, all states that have the same occupancy distribution (i.e., the same number of queues of identical length) are equally likely. For instance, states (1, 2, 1), (2, 1, 1), and (1, 1, 2) of a multiprocessor system with 4 processors and 3 memory modules belong to the same equivalence class, characterized by the vector (2, 1, 1) in which the components are listed in decreasing order. State (2, 1, 1) is called the *representative* state of the equivalence class. The number of equivalence classes defined in this way is asymptotically given (for $p \leq m$) by

$$\frac{1}{4\pi\sqrt{3}} \exp\left(\frac{\pi\sqrt{2p}}{3}\right). \tag{6.1}$$

Let S_i be the representative state of equivalence class i, S_j that of equivalence class j, S_{jk} a state of equivalence class j, and q_{ij} the probability that at the beginning of the next time slot, the system transits from a state in equivalence class i to a state in equivalence class j. Due to the symmetry of the problem this transition probability can be expressed as

$$q_{ij} = \sum_{S_{jk} \in S_j} P\{\text{transition from } S_i \text{ to } S_{jk}\}. \tag{6.2}$$

Denoting by n the number of nonzero components in the representative state S_i, at the end of the time slot n new requests are reassigned to memory modules. The change of state of the Markov chain [from $\mathbf{H} = (h_1, h_2, \ldots, h_m)$ to $\mathbf{K} = (k_1, k_2, \ldots, k_m)$] then happens via an intermediate partial state $\mathbf{J} = (j_1, j_2, \ldots, j_m)$ characterized by the following relation:

$$j_i = \max(0, h_i - 1). \tag{6.3}$$

A new state is reachable from $\mathbf{J}$ if $k_i \geq j_i$ for $1 \leq i \leq m$. In these conditions the state transition probability is given by

$$\frac{n!}{d_1! d_2! \cdots d_m!} \left(\frac{1}{m}\right)^n, \tag{6.4}$$

where $d_i = k_i - j_i$ and $\sum_{i=1}^{m} d_i = n$.

Due to the symmetry of the problem, it suffices to generate the transition probabilities for the representative states of the equivalence classes. The large amount of states that still plague this model suggested to Bhandarkar using an algorithmic approach that, given an initial representative state, enumerates all other representative states that are reachable from it and computes the corresponding transition probabilities.

The amount of computations involved in this method is such that only relatively small multiprocessor systems ($m \leq 16$) can actually be analyzed and results cannot be expressed in closed form. In a later work, Willis [WILL78] reported the same algorithmic approach and evaluated the average number of busy memory modules (β) in closed form for the cases of 2 and 3 processors, obtaining

$$\beta = \frac{2m - 1}{m}, \quad p = 2, \tag{6.5}$$

$$\beta = \frac{3m^3 - 6m^2 + 6m - 2}{m^3 - m^2 + m}, \quad p = 3. \tag{6.6}$$

Despite the impossibility of using this discrete Markov chain method for the evaluation of large multiprocessor systems, the results obtained by Bhandarkar were very important for the assessment of the accuracy of many approximations proposed in the literature (and that will be discussed in later sections). Moreover, from the numerical data, Bhandarkar observed that the behavior of crossbar multiprocessor systems is almost symmetrical with respect to the configuration of processors and memory modules. Indeed the value of β computed for a system comprising $p = n_1$ processors and $m = n_2$ memory modules is very close to that computed for a system comprising $p = n_2$ processors and $m = n_1$ memory modules.

In an effort to overcome the limitations of the exact approach proposed by Bhandarkar, Baskett and Smith [BASK76] devised a set of alternative approximate models, all relying on the same basic assumptions introduced at the beginning of this subsection.

As the number of processors and of memory modules tends to infinity while keeping the ratio between the two parameters constant ($p/m = L$), the model described admits a closed form solution (model BASK76a). In this asymptotic environment we can decompose the original model into a set of separate single-server queues operating in discrete time. At the end of each time slot one service is completed by the server if there exists a processor accessing the corresponding memory module; at the same time zero or more requests arrive. Let π_i be the equilibrium probability of finding i requests in queue, and let p_{ij} be the probability of having j requests in queue at the beginning of a time slot given that i requests were enqueued at the beginning of the previous time slot. Then in equilibrium we have

$$\pi_j = \sum_{i=0}^{j+1} \pi_i p_{ij}. \tag{6.7}$$

For very large values of p and m, p_{ij} becomes a function of $j - i$, so that denoting by A_k the pobability of k requests arriving at the beginning of a time slot at a given memory module, we obtain

$$p_{0j} = A_j \tag{6.8}$$

and

$$p_{ij} = \begin{cases} A_{j-i+1}, & j \geq i - 1 \\ 0, & j < i - 1 \end{cases} \quad i \geq 1. \tag{6.9}$$

When p and m grow to infinity, the number of new requests arriving to a memory module at the beginning of a time slot tends to have a Poisson distribution, so that the Pollaczek-Khintchin mean value formula (3.35) discussed in chapter 3 can be used to express the average number of queued requests per memory module $E[N]$:

$$E[N] = \rho + \frac{\rho^2}{2(1-\rho)}, \quad (6.10)$$

where ρ represents the utilization of the memory module. In this system, however, the value of $E[N]$ is known ($E[N] = p/m = L$), so that the following expression for the average number of busy memory modules ($\beta = \rho m$) can be obtained:

$$\beta = (m+p) - \sqrt{p^2 + m^2}. \quad (6.11)$$

This result, which was observed to be quite accurate for very large systems, was further improved by the same two authors observing that the distribution of the number of arrivals at the beginning of a time slot in the case of large but finite values of p and m is better approximated by a binomial distribution (model BASK76b). The distribution involves the uniform probability of selecting a specific memory module and the average number n of requests issued at the beginning of each time slot in the following way:

$$P\{i \text{ arrivals}\} = \binom{n}{i} \left(\frac{1}{m}\right)^i \left(1 - \frac{1}{m}\right)^{n-i}. \quad (6.12)$$

Using this distribution, the same derivation employed to obtain the previous result can be repeated to yield

$$\beta = \frac{2(p+m) - 1 - \sqrt{[2(p+m)-1]^2 - 8pm}}{2}. \quad (6.13)$$

Another variation of the previous two models was also proposed by Baskett and Smith (model BASK76c). They observed that the queuing model in figure 6.2 can be viewed as a queuing network in which customers (processors) are served from a service station (memory module) and then branch with equal probability to one of the other servers. This model can be solved efficiently (and exactly) in two special cases: either the service times are exponentially distributed or they are constant, but the queuing discipline is of the type Last Come First Served (LCFS) with preemptive service [BASK75]. Under these hypotheses the solution has a product form and the average number of busy memory modules assumes the form

$$\beta = \frac{pm}{p+m-1}. \quad (6.14)$$

The solution method that they propose to use is valid for continuous-time models. The first special case that they consider represents a considerable variation of the hypotheses usually introduced for these models since it amounts to assuming access times of variable (and continuous) length. The second case is instead treated assuming that deterministic memory access times are asymptotically represented with random variables having Erlang distributions with an infinite number of stages.

An idea originally proposed by Baskett and Smith, but then discarded because considered marginally convenient, was later used by Rau [RAU79] (model RAU79a), who was able to obtain a very accurate closed form expression for the average number of busy memory modules under the assumptions considered in this subsection. The decomposition approximation suggested by Rau assumes that the steady state probability distribution of the model in which requests are queued in front of some memory modules, while other memory modules are idle, is identical to that obtained by solving a reduced model in which the idle memory modules are removed. In a formal manner, using $p_{p,m}(\mathbf{K})$ to denote the probability that a distribution of requests represented by vector $\mathbf{K}$ is found in a multiprocessor with p processors and m memory modules, the above decomposition idea can be described by the following equality:

$$p_{p,m}(k_1, k_2, \ldots, k_{m-1} | k_m = p - K) = p_{K,m-1}(k_1, k_2, \ldots, k_{m-1}), \qquad (6.15)$$

where $K = \sum_{i=1}^{m-1} k_i$.

Under this hypothesis the analysis of the system can be decomposed, solving first a multiprocessor system model comprising only 1 processor, and then constructing on this result the (approximate) solution of a system with 2 processors, and so on, until the solution of the original problem is obtained.

The closed form expression of the average number of busy memory modules derived by Rau is the following:

$$\beta = \frac{\sum_{i=0}^{b-1} 2^i \binom{m-1}{i}\binom{p-1}{i}}{\sum_{i=0}^{b-1} \frac{2^i}{i+1}\binom{m-1}{i}\binom{p-1}{i}}, \qquad (6.16)$$

where $b = \min(p, m)$.

This formula is symmetrical with respect to the number of processors and memory modules, and thus agrees with the observation originally made by Bhandarkar. Another interesting aspect of this result is also the possibility of writing it in a recursive form:

$$\beta(m, p) = m \frac{2p - \beta(m-1, p)}{2p + m - 1 - \beta(m-1, p)}. \qquad (6.17)$$

This last expression immediately suggests that for large values of m we can assume that $\beta(m-1,p)$ is approximately equal to $\beta(m,p)$. Interestingly enough, introducing this further approximation on the expression, we obtain the same result derived by Baskett and Smith using their "binomial approximation."

6.2.1.2 Delay Models—Queued Requests

The algorithmic approach originally proposed by Bhandarkar for the case of a null effective active time was extended by the same author to the case in which the effective active time has a geometric distribution (model BHAN75c). The distribution assumed for this model is the following:

$$P\{\text{delay} = i \text{ time slots}\} = (1-\alpha)\alpha^i. \tag{6.18}$$

This model is quite general since it allows one to accommodate any (positive) average delay value. Again the representative state of an exact Markov chain model is given by a vector $\mathbf{H} = (h_0, h_1, h_2, \ldots, h_m)$, where the component h_0 is added to represent the number of active processors. A partial state reached by the Markov chain at the end of a time slot is given by the vector $\mathbf{J} = (0, j_1, j_2, \ldots, j_m)$, whose components are defined, as in (6.3), by the following relation:

$$j_i = \max(0, h_i - 1), \quad 1 \leq i \leq m. \tag{6.19}$$

The next state is obtained distributing $h_0 + n$ requests over the $m + 1$ locations of the state vector in addition to the occupancy represented by the partial state $\mathbf{J}$. The expression of the state transition probability for this new case is a relatively simple extension of that obtained for the zero effective processing time case given by (6.4). The transition probability matrix of the corresponding discrete-time Markov chain is constructed using an enumeration algorithm similar to that proposed for the previous simpler case, but requiring a very large amount of computation.

Bhandarkar evaluated this case for a multiprocessor configuration comprising $p=2$ processors and $m=2$ memory modules, obtaining the following closed form expression for the average number of busy memory modules:

$$\beta = (1-\alpha)\frac{\alpha^2 + 1}{\alpha^2 - \alpha + 2}. \tag{6.20}$$

An approximate solution for the more general case of an effective active time with arbitrary distribution is provided by Baskett and Smith as an extension of their binomial approximation model discussed before. Measuring the effective active time in terms of time slots, the execution cycle of a processor is now assumed to be the result of the sum of three components,

$$F(N) + 1 + T, \tag{6.21}$$

which correspond, respectively, to the time spent waiting in queue, the time needed for serving the request, and the "think" (active) time of the processor. $F(N)$ represents the queue length observed by an incoming request and is not necessarily equal to the equilibrium mean queue length $E[N]$. An estimate of the average number of busy memory modules is obtained also in this case using a derivation similar to the one employed for the binomial approximation. The derivation is now more complex because of the necessity of first estimating a value for $F(N)$. The closed formula obtained by Baskett and Smith is the following:

$$\beta = \frac{(1 - 2Lm - 2m) - \sqrt{(1 - 2Lm - 2m)^2 - 8Lm^2}}{2}, \tag{6.22}$$

where

$$L = \frac{-\{1 + T - [(p-1)/m]\} + \sqrt{\{1 + T - [(p-1)/m]\}^2 + 4[(p-1)/m]}}{2[(p-1)/p]}. \tag{6.23}$$

6.2.1.3 Zero-Delay Models—Lost Requests

An easy way of simplifying the formidable task of computing the exact solution of the detailed model of a crossbar multiprocessor system was initially proposed by Strecker [STRE70] (model STRE70a). His idea was that of disregarding the queues that may form in front of busy memory modules, assuming that at the end of a time slot the requests that were not served are resubmitted by the corresponding processors with a new random selection of the destination memory modules.

The advantage of this approach is that, besides making the derivation of the discrete time Markov chain transition probability matrix simple, it also provides a closed form expression for the average number of busy memory modules β. With this method the state of the system at the beginning of each time slot is independent of that observed at the beginning of the previous time slot. Using this assumpton, the number of processors N queued in front of a given memory module after the requests have been issued follows the binomial distribution

$$P\{N = i\} = \binom{p}{i} \left(\frac{1}{m}\right)^i \left(1 - \frac{1}{m}\right)^{p-i}. \tag{6.24}$$

Under these hypotheses the result can be expressed in the following closed form:

$$\beta = m\left[1 - \left(1 - \frac{1}{m}\right)^p\right]. \tag{6.25}$$

During his analysis of crossbar architectures, Bhandarkar observed that this formula provided a better approximation of the exact results when the number of memory modules m exceeded the number of processors p. He also observed that (6.25) is not symmetrical with respect to the parameters m and p, while his exact analysis of relatively small systems indicated such a symmetry. He thus empirically improved this result, proposing the following expression for the average number of busy memory modules (model BHAN75b):

$$\beta = r\left[1 - \left(1 - \frac{1}{r}\right)^s\right], \tag{6.26}$$

where

$$r = \max(m, p) \quad \text{and} \quad s = \min(m, p).$$

6.2.1.4 Delay Models—Lost Requests

The idea introduced by Strecker to derive his approximation for the case of $\alpha = 1$ was used by Bhandarkar to reduce the number of states characterizing a multiprocessor system with a geometric distribution of the processor active times (model BHAN75d). At the end of a time slot the requests that were queued at the memory modules during the cycle, but that were not served, are removed from the queues so that the corresponding processors are allowed to issue new requests with a new (independent) random selection of the destination modules. Under this assumption, the state of the system is characterized by the number of processors that actually issue a request at the beginning of a new time slot. The number of states of the Markov chain is thus reduced to $p + 1$. The only aspect of the problem that makes the computation of transition probabilities slightly complex is the necessity of accounting for the fact that if in a given state, n requests were left unserved at the end of a time slot, at least n processors issue a request at the beginning of the subsequent memory cycle. The resulting expression for such a transition probability is moderately complex and is omitted since it does not lead to a closed form result for the average number of busy memory modules. The interested reader is referred to the original paper for the explanation of the details of the derivation.

This same problem was also studied by Yen, Patel, and Davidson. The first model presented in [YEN82] is a simple extension of the original Strecker formula (6.25) to account for the possibility that an executing processor has of not issuing a request at the beginning of a time slot (model YEN82a):

$$\beta = m\left[1 - \left(1 - \frac{\alpha}{m}\right)^p\right]. \tag{6.27}$$

Chapter 6

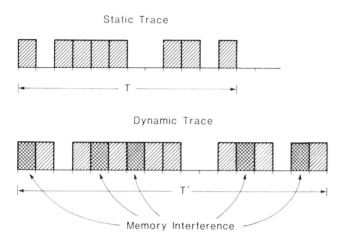

Figure 6.3
Memory access traces of a processor.

The explanation of this extension is that if $(1 - 1/m)^p$ represented (in the case of $\alpha = 1$) the probability that none of the p processors selected a given memory module, in this new case the same probability can be espressed by $(1 - \alpha/m)^p$.

An improvement on this formula was proposed by the same authors after having observed that the major drawback of the approximations based on Strecker's idea is that of neglecting the additional interference that is due to the presence of memory queues upon the arrival of new requests (model YEN82b). The approach suggested by Yen was that of adjusting the rate at which processors issue requests at the beginning of a time slot in order to account for the unnatural request replication due to the necessity of resubmitting those requests that were not served. Figure 6.3 depicts two sample traces in which this forced request replication is explicitly represented. The first trace of length T contains shaded slots, representing memory cycles during which an access request was issued, and blank slots, corresponding to time slots characterized by pure execution. Over a long trace of this type, the number of blank slots is (asymptotically) given by $T(1 - \alpha)$. The second trace (called *dynamic* trace) has a length $T' > T$, and is characterized by cross-shaded slots corresponding to time slots in which memory interference arises, making a memory access request to be resubmitted to the memory modules. The two traces contain an identical number of blank slots, which in this second case is given by $T'(1 - \delta)$, where δ is the dynamic request rate.

The improvement proposed by Yen et al. is simply that of including the dynamic rate δ in place of the static rate α in (6.27). The real problem is that of finding a way of expressing δ in terms of α and of the other parameters of the model.

Letting P_A be the probability that a request is accepted, then the expected number of submissions of a request is given by $1/P_A$. It then follows that

$$T' = \left[(1-\alpha) + \frac{\alpha}{P_A}\right] T, \qquad (6.28)$$

from which the expression of δ becomes

$$\delta = \frac{1}{1 + P_A[(1/\alpha) - 1]}. \qquad (6.29)$$

The solution of this model is obtained by iteration, observing that an expression for P_A is the following:

$$P_A = \frac{\beta}{p\delta}. \qquad (6.30)$$

The iteration is initialized assuming $\delta = \alpha$.

This result is further improved in the same paper on trying to cope with the fact that it is too optimistic, since it assumes that rejected requests are, on the subsequent time slot, uniformly distributed over the whole set of memory modules (model YEN82c). These authors found empirical evidence that a more accurate result could be obtained modifying the formulas to let rejected requests be distributed only over p of the m queues of the system. The technique of finding the dynamic request rate via iteration is maintained also in this new model, and we refer the interested reader to the original paper for the details of the formulas concerning the solution of this variation of the model.

6.3 Nonuniform Memory Reference Pattern

In this section we consider two different cases of nonuniform memory reference patterns used to represent the locality of actual computations and the possibility that different programs running on different processors have a nonuniform view of the memory.

The first model is due to Sethi and Deo [SETH79] and considers a multiprocessor system with $\alpha = 1$ and such that a high probability of repeatedly referring to the same memory module exists (model SETH79a). If the kth request of a processor is for memory module i, then the $(k + 1)$th request is for module i with probability γ and for module j ($j \neq i$) with probability $(1 - \gamma)/(m - 1)$. Probability γ is constant and is equal for all processors.

The general approach used by Sethi and Deo follows closely that of Bhandarkar discussed in subsection 6.1.1, since the main idea is that of constructing the state transition probability matrix introducing the equivalence classes and the representative states used by Bhandarkar. Considering this a formidable task, the authors address two simple cases (2 processors and m memory modules and p processors and 2 memory modules) whose closed form solutions provide some insight into the general behavior of the model.

The first model ($2 \times m$ system) has a quite simple reduced state space comprising only two states: $(2, 0)$ and $(1, 1)$. The transition probability matrix for this system is very easy to construct, and the exact solution of the Markov chain provides the following closed form result for the average number of busy memory modules:

$$\beta = \frac{m(2m + \gamma - 3)}{m(m + \gamma - 1) - 1}. \tag{6.31}$$

The second model ($p \times 2$ system) has a reduced state space comprising $\lfloor p/2 \rfloor + 1$ states:

$$(p, 0), (p - 1, 1), \ldots, (\lfloor (p + 1)/2 \rfloor, \lfloor p/2 \rfloor). \tag{6.32}$$

Also in this case the transition probability matrix of the discrete time Markov chain can be easily computed and the following closed form expression derived:

$$\beta = \frac{2(p + \gamma - 1)}{p + 2\gamma - 1}. \tag{6.33}$$

A general expression for the average number of busy memory modules was not found by these authors, who, however, noticed that in practice values of γ relatively close to 1 are quite common. They observed that the estimates provided by the previous two formulas evaluated at $\gamma = 1$ are quite accurate whenever the actual value of γ is larger than 0.75. Assuming $\gamma = 1$, they derived a general expression for the solution of the Markov chain just given that, not surprisingly, is exactly the same as obtained by Baskett and Smith with their queuing network approximation model (BASK76c).

The second type of model was proposed by Hoogendoorn, and assumes that processors issue requests to different memory modules following different reference patterns. As in a previous case, the idea behind this model is that of distinguishing between the static memory reference pattern characterizing the "program" running on the processor and the actual (dynamic) reference pattern that is affected by the memory interference. Using η_{ij} to represent the static probability that a request issued by processor i is directed to memory j, Hoogendoorn [HOOG77] uses simple probabilistic arguments to derive the dynamic reference rates $\{\delta_{ij}\}$ from any processor to any memory module. Indeed the probability p_{ij} that during a given time slot processor i successfully accesses memory module j can be expressed in terms of the dynamic reference rates in the following way:

$p_{ij} = P\{\text{processor } i \text{ references module } j \text{ alone}\}$

$\quad + P\{\text{processor } i \text{ and another processor reference module } j\}/2$

$\quad + \cdots$

$\quad + P\{\text{all processors reference module } j\}/p$

$$= \delta_{ij} \prod_{i \neq k} (1 - \delta_{kj}) \tag{6.34}$$

$$+ \delta_{ij} \left[\sum_{k \neq i} \delta_{kj} \prod_{h \neq i, k} (1 - \delta_{hj}) \right] \Big/ 2$$

$$+ \cdots$$

$$+ \delta_{ij} \left(\prod_{k \neq i} \delta_{kj} \right) \Big/ p.$$

Letting p_i represent the probability of a successful access of processor i, we have

$$p_i = \sum_{j=1}^{m} p_{ij} \tag{6.35}$$

and

$$\frac{p_{ij}}{p_i} = \eta_{ij}. \tag{6.36}$$

Also in this case the resubmission of requests due to memory interference makes the time interval needed to complete successfully a series of memory accesses longer. Using the same idea expressed for a previous model in figure 6.3, and defining $q = (1/\alpha) - 1$, it is possible to write

$$\sum_{j=1}^{m} \delta_{ij} + q p_i = 1. \tag{6.37}$$

An iterative scheme based on (6.34)–(6.37) [HOOG77] provides the values of the dynamic access rates $\{\delta_{ij}\}$, from which it is possible to obtain the expression of the average number of busy memory modules:

$$\beta = \sum_{i=1}^{p} p_i. \tag{6.38}$$

This derivation heavily relies on the hypothesis that the individual values of the $\{\eta_{ij}\}$ are independent of each other. This assumption is in general not satisfied in the actual model, so that the results provided by this analysis must be considered as approximations. When the memory access patterns are uniform, the results obtained using this method are identical to those provided by Strecker's formula (model STRE70a). In the more general case of nonuniform memory access patterns, we call this model HOOG77a when evaluated under the hypothesis of $\alpha = 1$, i.e., of $q = 0$. The model is called HOOG77b when, on the other hand, it considers processors with nonzero effective active times.

The implicit result of Hoogendorn can be expressed in an explicit form when the nonuniform reference pattern is such that a processor refers more often to a specific "favorite" memory module. Restricting further the problem to the symmetrical case of a crossbar multiprocessor system with the same number of processors and memory modules ($p = m$), Mudge and Makrucki [MUDG82] derive an explicit expression for the probability of a successful access of processor i to memory module j, p_{ij} (model MUDG82a).

The special kind of memory reference pattern used in this model can be characterized by the following relations:

$$\begin{aligned} \eta_{ii} &= \phi \quad \text{for any } i, \\ \eta_{ij} &= \psi \quad \text{for any } i \neq j. \end{aligned} \tag{6.39}$$

Using relatively simple arguments based on (6.34) for p_{ij}, they show that this probability can be computed by the following formulas:

$$p_{ii} = \frac{\phi}{p\psi}[1 - (1 - \psi)^p] \tag{6.40}$$

and

$$p_{ij} = \frac{\phi}{p\psi}[1 - (1 - \psi)^p] + \frac{(\psi - \phi)}{(p-1)\psi}[1 - (1 - \psi)^{p-1}]. \tag{6.41}$$

The value of the average number of busy memory modules is then obtained using (6.35) and (6.38). Using these results, they found that the average number of busy memories obtained in this case is larger than that observed when processors reference memories in a uniform manner.

References

[BASK75] Baskett, F., Chandy, K. M., Muntz, R. R., and Palacios, F., "Open, Closed and Mixed Networks of Queues with Different Classes of Customers," *Journal ACM* 22(2) (April 1975), 248–260.

[BASK76] Baskett, F., and Smith. A. J., "Interference in Multiprocessor Computer Systems with Interleaved Memory," *Communications of the ACM* 19(6) (June 1976), 327–334.

[BHAN75] Bhandarkar, D. P., "Analysis of Memory Interference in Multiprocessors," *IEEE Transactions on Computers* C-24(9) (September 1975), 897–908.

[HOOG77] Hoogendoorn, C. H., "A General Model for Memory Interference in Multiprocessors," *IEEE Transactions on Computers* C-26(10) (October 1977), 998–1005.

[MUDG82] Mudge, T. N., and Makrucki, B. A., "Probabilistic Analysis of a Crossbar-Switch," Proc. 9th Annual Symposium on Computer Architecture, Austin, Texas, April 1982.

[RAU79] Rau, B. R., "Interleaved Memory Bandwidth in a Model of a Multiprocessor Computer System," *IEEE Transactions on Computers* C-28(9) (September 1979), 678–681.

[SETH79] Sethi, A. S., and Deo, N., "Interference in Multiprocessor Systems with Localized Memory Access Probabilities," *IEEE Transactions on Computers* C-28(2) (February 1979), 157–163.

[SKIN69] Skinner, C., and Asher, J., "Effect of Storage Contention on System Performance," *IBM System Journal* 8(4) (1969), 319–333.

[STRE70] Strecker, W. D., "Analysis of the Instruction Execution Rate in Certain Computer Structures," Ph.D. Dissertation, Carnegie-Mellon University, Pittsburgh, Pensylvania, 1970.

[WILL78] Willis, P. J., "Derivation and Comparison of Multiprocessor Contention Measures," *IEE Journal of Computers and Digital Techniques* 1(3) (August 1978), 93–98.

[WULF72] Wulff, W., and Bell, C. G., "C.mmp, a Multi-Mini-Processor," *AFIPS Conf. Proc.*, Vol. 41, Part II, 1972 FJCC, AFIPS Press, Montvale, NJ, 1972, pp. 765–777.

[YEN82] Yen, D. W. L., Patel, Y. H., and Davidson, E. S., "Memory Interference in Synchronous Multiprocessor Systems," *IEEE Transactions on Computers* C-31(11) (November 1982), 1116–1121.

7 Single-Bus Multiprocessors with External Common Memory

We begin our presentation of performance models of bus-oriented multiprocessor systems by considering the single global bus multiprocessor architecture, already described in chapter 5 and sketched in figure 5.4. It consists of a set of p processing units (or processors for short), composed of a CPU and a private memory connected to a set of shared resources by means of a single (circuit switched) global bus. A three-processor system with this architecture is depicted in more detail in figure 7.1. Shared resources (such as I/O devices, common memory modules, and mass memory devices) can be accessed by any processor through the global bus. Private memories can, instead, only be accessed by the CPU to which they are local. Since shared resources are not tied to any processor (as happens with other architectures that will be considered in later chapters), they are said to be external. For simplicity we use the term common memory whenever referencing a system shared resource.

This architecture was used in the implementation of many multiprocessor systems (see, for example, [INTE81, HART84, KIRR84]). Its main advantages lie in the simplicity of implementation, the modularity, the possibility of an easy upgrading of the system, and the low cost of the interconnection network (the bus), which can be completely passive.

The assumptions on the multiprocessor system workload closely reflect the hypotheses outlined in chapter 5; in this case, however, we take a different approach from that of the previous chapter, and use a continuous-time stochastic model rather than a discrete-time one. The workload assumptions are precisely described by the GSPN (see chapter 4) model in figure 7.2, in which a two-processor system is considered. Processors are initially active (i.e., they execute segments of programs that require accesses to their private memory modules only). After a random active time, processors issue a bus request in order to access the system common memory. If the bus is not available, processors must wait until they are granted access to the bus, and hence to the common memory. The memory is used for the random time needed to complete the access; then the bus is released, and processors return to the active state. In more detail, the key modeling assumptions are the following:

1. The durations of active and access periods are assumed to be random variables.
2. When a processor requires access to common memory, a path is immediately established (with no delay) between the processor and the referenced memory module, provided that the bus is free.
3. If a path cannot be established, the processor idles, waiting for the bus.
4. Upon common memory access completion, memory and bus are immediately released (with no delay) and the processor returns to its active state.

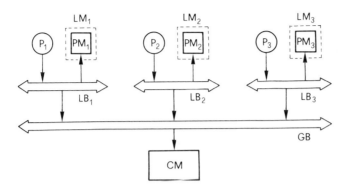

Figure 7.1
Structure of the multiprocessor architecture, with three processors composed of CPU (P_i) and private memory (PM_i) connected by a local bus (LB_i). The global bus (GB) connects processors to the common memory (CM).

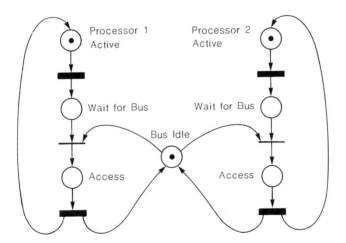

Figure 7.2
GSPN model of the multiprocessor workload in the case of two processors.

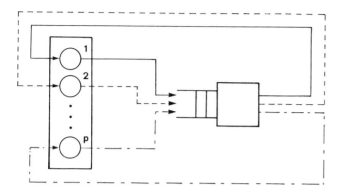

Figure 7.3
Queuing network model of the multiprocessor behavior.

Assumptions 2 and 4 imply that we neglect the times needed for the bus arbitration and release.

The presence of only one bus in the system masks the contention for common memory modules that was observed and analyzed in the case of crossbar multiprocessors.

Since contention for the bus is the only source of performance degradation that we consider, it is possible to model the system using the queuing network in figure 7.3, which is usually referred to as a machine repairman model. The network comprises two service stations: the first one models active processors. This station comprises as many servers as there are processors in the system, and the service time is a random variable describing the processor active time. The second station comprises only one server (the bus), and the service time is a random variable describing the common memory access time. In order to complete the specification of this multiprocessor system model, it is necessary to specify the number of processors, p; the distributions of the random variables comprised in the random vector $\varepsilon = \{\varepsilon_1, \varepsilon_2, \ldots, \varepsilon_p\}$, representing the active times for each processor; the distributions of the random variables comprised in the random vector $\sigma = \{\sigma_1, \sigma_2, \ldots, \sigma_p\}$, representing the common memory access times for each processor; as well as the bus arbitration policy.

In most of the cases that we analyze in this chapter, we assume that the vector ε contains exponentially distributed random variables, whose parameters are entries of the vector of scalars $\lambda = \{\lambda_1, \lambda_2, \ldots, \lambda_p\}$. Sometimes we make the further simplification of letting $\lambda_i = \lambda$, for all i. In a few cases we assume that the entries of ε have general distributions.

Associating a distribution to the random variables in σ requires some further assumption on the number, and on the type of common memory modules available in the system. If there is either only one module or if all modules are equal, it can be reasonable to assume that all random variables have the same distribution. If, instead, the system comprises several different common memory modules, we must consider the probability distribution according to which each processor chooses the module to be accessed, and use it together with the distributions of the access duration to each module in order to determine the distribution of the entries of σ. Different distributions for the different entries are thus likely to be found in multiprocessor systems comprising several different common memory modules in which processors choose the module to be accessed according to different probability distributions. In this chapter we analyze systems in which the distributions of the entries of σ are either equal for all processors or different, and in the two cases we consider the exponential distribution as well as the general case. In the case of exponential distributions we assume that the random vector σ contains random variables whose parameters are entries of the vector of scalars $\mu = \{\mu_1, \mu_2, \ldots, \mu_p\}$.

Finally, in order to complete the definition of the multiprocessor model, we must specify the bus arbitration policy used in the case of multiple access requests. This is equivalent to defining the queuing discipline to be used in the closed queuing network at the single-server station. Three policies are considered in the analysis: the FCFS (first come first served) discipline, the FP (fixed priority) discipline, also known as head-of-the-line priority discipline, and the PS (processor sharing) discipline. This last discipline is useful in modeling the case in which the bus is granted in a round robin fashion to queued processors for fixed time slices. Indeed, the PS discipline is the limit of the round robin discipline when the time slice goes to zero.

Before considering each model separately, let us introduce some notation for a compact description of the system features. For what concerns the distributions of the entries of ε and the distributions of the entries of σ we use a notation that is very similar to Kendall's notation for queuing systems (see chapter 3). Thus the letter *M* indicates an exponential distribution, and the letter *G* indicates a general distribution. Furthermore, the subscript e (equal) tells that all random variables have the same distribution, whereas the subscript d (different) indicates that the distributions are not identical. The two letters are separated by a slash. Another slash followed by the acronym of the bus arbitration policy completes the description of the system. The averages of the entries of ε are always denoted by

$$\left\{\frac{1}{\lambda_1}, \frac{1}{\lambda_2}, \ldots, \frac{1}{\lambda_p}\right\}$$

and the averages of the entries of **σ** by

$$\left\{\frac{1}{\mu_1}, \frac{1}{\mu_2}, \ldots, \frac{1}{\mu_p},\right\}.$$

As an example, the notation $M_e/M_e/\text{FCFS}$ denotes a system with exponential distribution for all the entries of **ε**, with the same parameter λ, as well as for all the entries of **σ**, with the same parameter μ, and an FCFS bus arbitration policy.

Due to space limitations, not all cases ($4 \times 4 \times 3 = 48$) are explicitly considered in this chapter, but the more general cases provide results also for some of the models that are not explicitly solved. Moreover, in some cases, we resort to approximations, because no exact solution is known for the corresponding models.

7.1 Performance Indices

The performance index used in this book to describe how well a bus-oriented multiprocessor system behaves is the average number of active processors, called processing power and denoted by P.

Processing power is not the most appropriate performance index for all applications. Other parameters better describe the quality of the system in some cases. Fortunately, however, many different performance indices can be simply derived from processing power, as we show in this section for an $M_e/M_e/\text{FCFS}$ multiprocessor model.

Define γ to be the rate at which customers cycle through the queuing network in figure 7.3. From Little's result we have

$$\gamma = P\lambda. \tag{7.1}$$

Applying again Little's result to the entire memory system, including queues and servers, we find the average customer delay $E[D]$:

$$E[D] = \frac{p - P}{P\lambda}. \tag{7.2}$$

Finally, subtracting from $E[D]$ the average service time $1/\mu$, we have the average queuing time $E[W]$:

$$E[W] = \frac{p - P(1 + \rho)}{P\lambda}, \tag{7.3}$$

where $\rho = \lambda/\mu$.

The average number of queued processors is

$$E[N_q] = E[W]P\lambda = p - P(1 + \rho); \tag{7.4}$$

therefore the average number of processors accessing common memory modules is

$$E[N_s] = \frac{E[D] - E[W]}{P\lambda} = P\rho. \tag{7.5}$$

The average cycle time is then

$$E[C] = E[W] + \frac{1}{\lambda} + \frac{1}{\mu} = \frac{p}{P\lambda}. \tag{7.6}$$

From the values of average cycle time, average queuing time, average active time, and average service time we can now construct many different performance indices, choosing the one that best suits the particular multiprocessor application.

If processors are updating a database, a reasonable performance index could be the ratio of the memory access time to the sum of the access time plus the waiting time. Using the previous results, this performance index is expressed as follows:

$$I_{db} = \frac{(1/\mu)}{(1/\mu) + E[W]} = \frac{P\lambda}{p\mu + P(\lambda + \mu)}. \tag{7.7}$$

If, instead, the multiprocessor system is a packet switch operating under heavy load conditions, where input processors process packets and write them into a common memory, and output processors read them and again process them before queuing them for output, then the active time represents the time necessary to process an incoming (outgoing) packet and the service time represents the time necessary to write (read) a packet from an input (output) processor (note that the exponential read/write time corresponds to exponential packet length distributions). The throughput of the packet switch can then be expressed as

$$I_{ps} = \frac{p}{2E[C]} = \frac{P\lambda}{2}. \tag{7.8}$$

Note that each packet must be processed by an input and an output processor; both operations require one cycle time, and p packets can be processed simultaneously.

Performance indices for other applications can be derived in a similar manner.

Moreover, note that we always derive the steady state distribution of the stochastic model associated with the multiprocessor system, and processing power is only one of the many different aggregate results that can be computed from it.

7.2 Equal Exponentially Distributed Active and Access Times ($M_e/M_e/*$)

This is the simplest model of the single-bus multiprocessor system architecture under consideration. All processors have exponentially distributed active and access times, with the same parameters, λ and μ, respectively. The bus arbitration policy is irrelevant in the computation of the distribution of active processors: due to the equal exponential distributions of active and access times, results are identical for FCFS, PS, and FP, as well as for any other work-conserving discipline [KLEI76].

The model reduces in this case to an $M/M/1$ queuing system with finite population (p customers), and it can be analyzed as a continuous-time birth-and-death (B-D) process with

$$\lambda'_k = \begin{cases} \lambda(p-k), & 0 \leq k \leq p-1 \\ 0, & k \geq p, \end{cases} \tag{7.9a}$$

$$\mu'_k = \begin{cases} \mu, & 1 \leq k \leq p \\ 0, & k = 0, \quad k \geq p+1, \end{cases} \tag{7.9b}$$

where λ'_k and μ'_k [see (2.84)] are the birth and death rates, respectively, when k customers ($0 \leq k \leq p$) are awaiting or receiving service at the single-server station.

The steady state probability distribution at the single-server station, $\boldsymbol{\pi} = \{\pi_0, \pi_1, \ldots, \pi_p\}$, is easily obtained [see (2.90) and (2.91)],

$$\pi_k = \pi_0 \left(\frac{\lambda}{\mu}\right)^k \frac{p!}{(p-k)!}, \qquad 0 \leq k \leq p, \tag{7.10}$$

with

$$\pi_0 = \left[\sum_{k=0}^{p} \left(\frac{\lambda}{\mu}\right)^k \frac{p!}{(p-k)!}\right]^{-1}. \tag{7.11}$$

The processing power P of the multiprocessor system can either be evaluated directly from $\boldsymbol{\pi}$ as

$$P = \sum_{k=0}^{p} (p-k)\pi_k \tag{7.12}$$

or, in a simpler manner, by using Little's result. The rate at which customers cycle through the queuing network in figure 7.3, γ, is found by applying Little's result either to the service facility of the single-server station or to the infinite-server station, obtaining, respectively,

$$\gamma = \mu(1 - \pi_0),\tag{7.13}$$

$$\gamma = \lambda P.$$

Hence

$$P = \frac{\mu}{\lambda}(1 - \pi_0).\tag{7.14}$$

7.3 Equal Exponentially Distributed Active Times and Equal Generally Distributed Access Times—FCFS (M_e/G_e/FCFS)

The model is in this case equivalent to a finite population (p customers) $M/G/1$ queuing system. The underlying stochastic process is not Markovian, but the steady state probability distribution can be found either by using the embedded Markov chain technique or by including in the state definition the information on the amount of service already received by the customer being served at the single-server station; by doing so, the underlying stochastic process is made memoryless, and hence Markovian. The latter method is usually called the supplementary variable technique.

Derivations of the steady state probabilities of the $M/G/1/p/p$ queue using both methods have appeared in the literature ([TAKA62, JAIS68]). We quote here results from [TAKA62]:

$$\pi_k = \sum_{i=p-k}^{p} (-1)^{i+k-p} \binom{i}{p-k} S_i, \qquad 0 \leq k \leq p,\tag{7.15}$$

where

$$S_i = \begin{cases} 1, & i = 0 \\ \dfrac{pC_{i-1}}{i} \dfrac{\sum_{j=i-1}^{p-1} \binom{p-1}{j}(1/C_j)}{1 + [(p\lambda)/\mu]\sum_{j=0}^{p-1} \binom{p-1}{j}(1/C_j)}, & 1 \leq i \leq p, \end{cases}\tag{7.16}$$

and

$$C_j = \begin{cases} 1, & j = 0 \\ \prod_{n=1}^{j} \dfrac{\phi(n\lambda)}{(1 - \phi(n\lambda))}, & j \geq 1, \end{cases}\tag{7.17}$$

and finally $\phi(s)$ is the Laplace-Stieltjes transform of the service time distribution at the single-server station.

Also in this case, the evaluation of the multiprocessor system processing power can be performed either directly, by means of equation (7.12), or by repeated application of Little's result. With the latter method we again obtain the result of equation (7.14).

7.4 Different Generally Distributed Active Times and Equal Exponentially Distributed Access Times—FCFS and PS (G_d/M_e/FCFS and PS)

This model can be solved exactly by applying the BCMP theorem discussed in chapter 3 to the closed queuing network in figure 7.3. Indeed, the network comprises one infinite-server station at which each customer receives a generally distributed amount of service, whose average is different for each customer, and one FCFS single-server station at which all customers receive an exponentially distributed amount of service, with average $1/\mu$. There exist p classes in the network, each class comprising one customer only. The conditions for the applicability of the BCMP theorem hold, provided that the general distributions have rational Laplace transforms. Noting that customers cycle through the network going from one queue to the other, and then back to the previous one, we obtain

$$\pi_k = \frac{1}{G} k! \left[\frac{1}{\mu}\right]^k \sum_{\mathbf{m} \in \mathbf{M}} \prod_{j=1}^{p} \left[\frac{1}{\lambda_j}\right]^{m_j}, \qquad 0 \le k \le N, \tag{7.18}$$

where $\mathbf{M}$ is the set of vectors $\mathbf{m} = (m_1, m_2, \ldots, m_p)$ such that each element m_i can only take the values 0 and 1, and such that $\sum_{i=1}^{p} m_i = p - k$. G is a normalizing constant, and its value is found by solving the equation $\sum_{k=0}^{p} \pi_k = 1$. We find

$$G = \sum_{k=0}^{p} k! \left[\frac{1}{\mu}\right]^k \sum_{\mathbf{m} \in \mathbf{M}} \prod_{j=1}^{p} \left[\frac{1}{\lambda_j}\right]^{m_j}. \tag{7.19}$$

The same result holds also in the case of a PS queuing discipline at the single-server station.

The evaluation of the multiprocessor processing power can either be performed by means of equation (7.12) or by using standard results in the theory of closed queuing networks ([BUZE73, BRUE80]):

$$P = \sum_{i=1}^{p} \frac{1}{\lambda_i} \frac{G^{[-i]}}{G}, \tag{7.20}$$

where $G^{[-i]}$ is the normalizing constant for a system with the ith processor removed.

7.5 Different Generally Distributed Active and Access Times—PS ($G_d/G_d/\text{PS}$)

In order to analyze exactly a system in which both active times and common memory access times are generally distributed random variables, it is necessary to assume that the queuing discipline at the single-server station is PS (or LCFS preempt resume, but we are not considering this queuing policy). The BCMP theorem still holds, and the steady state probabilities can be written in product form as

$$\pi_k = \frac{1}{G} k! \sum_{\mathbf{m} \in \mathbf{M}} \prod_{j=1}^{p} \left[\frac{1}{\mu_j}\right]^{1-m_j} \left[\frac{1}{\lambda_j}\right]^{m_j}, \quad 0 \le k \le p, \tag{7.21}$$

where **m** and **M** are defined as in the previous section.

Note that equations (7.10) and (7.18) can be obtained as special cases of equation (7.21). In both cases all entries of the vector **μ** are equal, and they represent parameters of an exponential service distribution at the single-server station, so that an FCFS queuing discipline can be used. To obtain equation (7.10), we must assume, moreover, that all entries of the vector **λ** are equal. Note that this also implies that equation (7.10) holds independently of the type of the service time distribution at the infinite-server station.

The normalizing constant G in equation (7.21) can be obtained by solving the equation $\sum_{k=0}^{p} \pi_k = 1$:

$$G = \sum_{k=0}^{p} k! \sum_{\mathbf{m} \in \mathbf{M}} \prod_{j=1}^{p} \left[\frac{1}{\mu_j}\right]^{1-m_j} \left[\frac{1}{\lambda_j}\right]^{m_j}. \tag{7.22}$$

Another special case that can be obtained from equations (7.21) and (7.22) is the model for a $G_e/G_d/\text{PS}$ multiprocessor system. In this case we obtain

$$\pi_k = \frac{1}{G} k! \left[\frac{1}{\lambda}\right]^{p-k} \sum_{\mathbf{m} \in \mathbf{M}} \prod_{j=1}^{p} \left[\frac{1}{\mu_j}\right]^{1-m_j}, \quad 0 \le k \le p, \tag{7.23}$$

and

$$G = \sum_{k=0}^{p} k! \left[\frac{1}{\lambda}\right]^{p-k} \sum_{\mathbf{m} \in \mathbf{M}} \prod_{j=1}^{p} \left[\frac{1}{\mu_j}\right]^{1-m_j}. \tag{7.24}$$

It is interesting to note that these results, valid for general distributions, only depend on the averages of the random variables, and not on the distribution type.

In all cases, the system processing power can be obtained from equations (7.12) and (7.20).

Chapter 7

7.6 Different Exponentially Distributed Active Times and Generally Distributed Access Times—FCFS and FP (M_d/G_d/FCFS and FP)

The existence in the queuing network of a single-server station with generally distributed service times and with either a FCFS or a FP queuing discipline violates the hypotheses of the BCMP theorem, so that we cannot directly write the steady state probabilities in closed form. On the other hand, the existence of p customers with different service time distributions at both queues in the network prevents a simple analysis by means of an embedded Markov chain. An approximate technique for the analysis of these models was presented in [FRAN83] in the case of the FP bus arbitration policy. Although it can be very easily extended to the FCFS case, according to our experience this technique exhibits both accuracy and convergence problems. We thus resort to GSPN models for the analysis of some relatively simple cases.

Let us first construct a GSPN model of a two-processor system in which active times are exponentially distributed with rates λ_1 and λ_2, respectively, for the two processors. Moreover, access times for processor 1 have an Erlang-k distribution, whereas access times of processor 2 are hyperexponentially distributed with a given coefficient of variation C_v. The model construction can start from the GSPN in figure 7.2, which was used for the precise description of the workload assumptions in the case of two processors. For what concerns active times, the model requires no modification; it is sufficient to set to λ_1 and to λ_2 the firing rates of the two transitions that correspond to the end of active periods. For what concerns access times, instead, it is necessary to include in the model means for the description of nonexponential distributions. In this case it is possible simply to expand the two transitions that represent the end of access with proper GSPN subnets in order to implement the desired distribution. Note that this technique may not be simple to apply in other cases, where several nonexponential transitions may be in conflict and/or simultaneously enabled and/or enabled by more than one token (see [AJMO85]). The expansion of the Erlang-k distribution is done by cascading k exponential transitions with firing rates equal to k times the firing rate of the desired Erlang-k distribution. The expansion of the hyperexponential distribution can be done by using two parallel transitions, one of which is selected through a random switch whose probabilities (α and $1 - \alpha$) are set according to the desired value of the coefficient of variation. The following formula [SAUE75] can be used to derive the selection probabilities from the given value of C_v:

$$\alpha = \frac{C_v^2 + 1 - \sqrt{C_v^4 - 1}}{2[C_v^2 + 1]}. \tag{7.25}$$

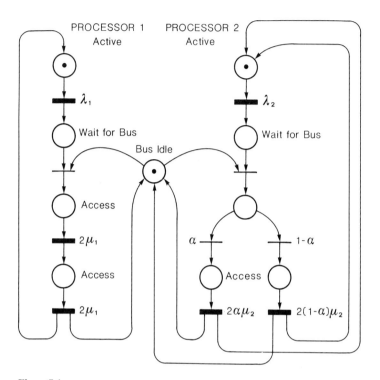

Figure 7.4
GSPN for an M_d/G_d/FCFS model with two processors. Access times of processor 1 have an Erlang-2 distribution; access times of processor 2 are hyperexponentially distributed.

In figure 7.4 is shown the GSPN model of a two-processor system where access times of processor 1 have an Erlang-2 distribution. Note that in the case of two processors it is not necessary to consider the bus arbitration policy; thus the model in figure 7.4 describes the behavior of the FCFS policy as well as of the FP policy. When the number of processors increases, it is instead necessary to model the chosen policy explicitly.

A direct extension of the GSPN model in figure 7.4 to larger numbers of processors rapidly yields unmanageable graphs. More compact models can be constructed, however, when processors can be grouped in a small number of classes whose elements behave in a statistically identical manner. As an example, in figures 7.5 and 7.6 are shown the GSPN models of multiprocessor systems comprising p processors subdivided into two classes. Class 1 comprises one processor, while class 2 comprises all others. Common memory access times have a hyperexponential distribution. Note

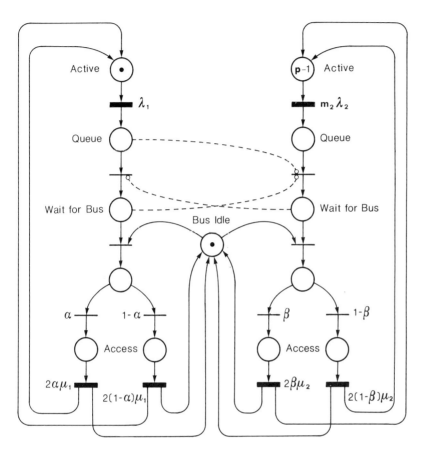

Figure 7.5
GSPN for an $M_d/G_d/$FCFS model with two classes of processors. Class 1 comprises one processor only; all other processors belong to class 2. Access times are hyperexponentially distributed.

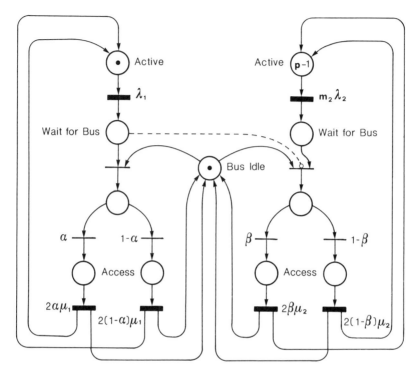

Figure 7.6
GSPN for an $M_d/G_d/FP$ model with two classes of processors. Class 1 comprises one processor only; all other processors belong to class 2. Access times are hyperexponentially distributed.

that two separate circuits exist in the GSPN for the two classes. The parallel activity of processors in class 2 is modeled by a marking-dependent firing rate, taking advantage of the fact that the minimum of k exponentially distributed random variables is still an exponentially distributed random variable whose rate is the sum of the individual rates. Inhibitor arcs are used to implement the FCFS policy in figure 7.5, and the FP policy in figure 7.6, assuming that the only processor in class 1 has priority over all processors in class 2. Unfortunately, the complexity of these GSPN models, both from a graphical viewpoint and from the point of view of the number of states of the associated Markov chain, grows very fast with the number of processor classes and with the number of stages in which the general distributions are expanded. Moreover, notice that the representation of the FCFS policy in the general case requires a detailed description of the waiting line.

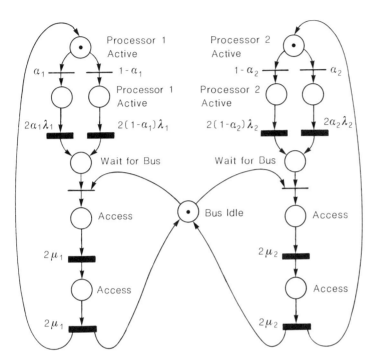

Figure 7.7
GSPN for a G_d/G_d/FCFS model with two processors. Processor active times are hyperexponentially distributed, while memory access times have Erlang-2 distributions.

7.7 Different Generally Distributed Active and Access Times—FCFS (G_d/G_d/FCFS)

The modeling technique described in the previous section can be extended to include generally distributed active times. Both active and access time distributions must be expanded in exponential stages, so that an exact Markovian model can be constructed, and then solved to derive the desired performance indices.

Again, it must be stressed that the expansion of the general distributions at the GSPN level must be done with great attention to the resulting semantics of the model. In particular, when both active and access times are generally distributed, the construction of *compact* GSPN models becomes difficult.

For example, figure 7.7 shows the GSPN model of a two-processor system in which active times are hyperexponentially distributed, and common memory access times

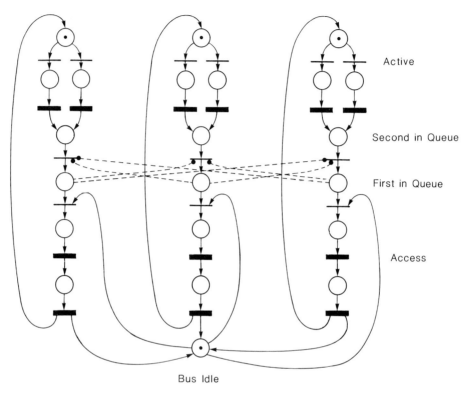

Figure 7.8
Extension of the GSPN model in figure 7.7 to a G_d/G_d/FCFS model with three processors.

have Erlang-2 distributions. As before, in the case of two processors it is not necessary to model the FCFS bus arbitration policy. When the number of processors increases, however, it is necessary to include in the GSPN ways to keep track of the position of requests in the bus queue. An example of how this can be done is shown in figure 7.8, where a G_d/G_d/FCFS GSPN model is shown that extends the one in figure 7.7 to the three-processor case. The construction of a compact GSPN such as the one in figure 7.5 is complex because, even if two processors have identically distributed active times, it is not possible to replace the two subnets modeling processor activity with a single identical subnet in which parameters are marking-dependent. This is due to the fact that the minimum of two random variables with a hyperexponential distribution does not have a hyperexponential distribution.

Chapter 7   153

7.8 Numerical Results

In tables 7.1, 7.2, and 7.3 we present some numerical processing power results obtained using the models described in this chapter.

Three multiprocessor configurations were considered, comprising 2, 5, and 10 processors, respectively. Both active times and common memory access times can be either exponentially or generally distributed. Moreover, we have considered both cases of equal distributions for all processors, and of different distributions. In the latter case we have chosen to unbalance the parameters of the distributions relating to processor 1 only. Thus, when the distributions of active times are different, we set $\lambda_1 = 5\lambda$ and $\lambda_i = \lambda$, for all $i = 2, \ldots, p$. Similarly, when access time distributions are different, we set $\mu_1 = 5\mu$, and $\mu_i = \mu$, for all $i = 2, \ldots, p$. The multiprocessor load ρ is then defined as

$$\rho = \frac{1}{p} \sum_{i=1}^{p} \frac{\lambda_i}{\mu_i}. \tag{7.26}$$

Note that, when both active and access times have either equal or different distributions, all ρ_i ($i = 1, \ldots p$) are equal. Otherwise, ρ_1 is different from all ρ_i ($i = 2, \ldots p$). Results are given for different values of the parameter ρ.

In the tables, the notation C_{ti} is adopted to identify the coefficient of variation of time t (where t can take the two values e = execution time and a = access time) for processor i. For example, $C_{e1} = 5$ means coefficient of variation 5 for the execution time of processor 1.

Table 7.1 shows processing power results in the case of two-processor system models, for several different values of ρ. Results for the $M_e/M_e/*$ model are presented first. The star indicates that results are identical for all work-conserving bus assignment policies. More results in the M_e/M_e/FCFS case are given in chapter 9, where the performance of this architecture is compared with that of different multiprocessor architectures. General distributions for access times are then considered, studying the M_e/G_e/FCFS model, whose solution is reported in the cases of deterministic access times ($C_v = 0$), of Erlang-2 distributed access times ($C_v = 1/\sqrt{2}$), and of hyperexponentially distributed access times ($C_v = 5$). The processing power values are observed to decrease for increasing coefficient of variation of access times, as known from classical queuing theory results.

The G_d/M_e/FCFS–PS models are considered next. No distinction is made between the two queuing policies since they yield the same results. Similarly, the value of the coefficient of variation of the distributions of execution times is not specified, since it

Table 7.1
Processing power for different models in the case of 2 processors versus ρ

ρ	$M_e/M_e/*$	$M_e/G_e/\text{FCFS}$			$G_d/M_e/\text{FCFS-PS}$	$G_d/G_d\left(C_{ci}=5, C_{ai}=\dfrac{1}{\sqrt{2}}\right)$		$M_d/G_d/\text{FCFS}$		
		$C_{ai}=0$	$=\dfrac{1}{\sqrt{2}}$	$=5$		PS	FCFS	$C_{ai}=\dfrac{1}{\sqrt{2}}$	$=1$	$=5$
0.1	1.803	1.810	1.807	1.757	1.817	1.803	1.796	1.794	1.789	1.759
0.2	1.622	1.641	1.631	1.547	1.662	1.622	1.608	1.601	1.593	1.547
0.3	1.461	1.492	1.475	1.377	1.529	1.461	1.445	1.435	1.424	1.374
0.4	1.321	1.360	1.338	1.238	1.416	1.321	1.305	1.293	1.283	1.231
0.5	1.200	1.245	1.220	1.122	1.317	1.200	1.185	1.173	1.163	1.113

Table 7.2
Processing power for different models in the case of 5 processors versus ρ

ρ	$M_e/M_e/*$	$M_e/G_e/\text{FCFS}$			$G_d/M_e/\text{FCFS-PS}$	$M_d/G_d/\text{FCFS}$			$M_d/G_d/\text{FP}$		
		$C_{ai}=0$	$=\dfrac{1}{\sqrt{2}}$	$=5$		$C_{ai}=\dfrac{1}{\sqrt{2}}$	$=1$	$=5$	$C_{ai}=\dfrac{1}{\sqrt{2}}$	$=1$	$=5$
0.1	4.361	4.440	4.398	3.969	4.443	4.346	4.306	3.972	4.356	4.316	3.977
0.2	3.576	3.752	3.653	3.136	3.843	3.570	3.502	3.129	3.594	3.522	3.136
0.3	2.869	3.035	2.940	2.548	3.289	2.878	2.816	2.534	2.901	2.834	2.543
0.4	2.326	2.431	2.374	2.121	2.821	2.338	2.294	2.105	2.354	2.307	2.113
0.5	1.927	1.984	1.956	1.801	2.443	1.937	1.909	1.787	1.946	1.918	1.794

Table 7.3
Processing power for different models in the case of 10 processors versus ρ

ρ	$M_e/M_e/*$	M_e/G_e/FCFS $C_{ai}=0$	M_e/G_e/FCFS $=\frac{1}{\sqrt{2}}$	M_e/G_e/FCFS $=5$	G_d/M_e/FCFS-PS	M_d/G_d/FCFS $C_{ai}=\frac{1}{\sqrt{2}}$	M_d/G_d/FCFS $=1$	M_d/G_d/FCFS $=5$	M_d/G_d/FP $C_{ai}=\frac{1}{\sqrt{2}}$	M_d/G_d/FP $=1$	M_d/G_d/FP $=5$
0.1	7.854	8.210	8.010	6.713	8.203	7.918	7.766	6.710	7.971	7.813	6.725
0.2	4.908	4.988	4.953	4.520	5.707	4.938	4.889	4.506	4.952	4.905	4.524
0.3	3.328	3.333	3.332	3.249	4.064	3.331	3.326	3.241	3.332	3.328	3.256
0.4	2.500	2.500	2.500	2.483	3.110	2.500	2.499	2.480	2.500	2.500	2.484
0.5	2.000	2.000	2.000	1.996	2.511	2.000	2.000	1.995	2.000	2.000	1.996

does not influence the processing power results. Note that this is the only case we have considered in which the ratio λ_1/μ_1 differs from λ_2/μ_2. The only difference in the processor statistical behavior lies in the faster execution time of processor 1. This significantly increases the system processing power; indeed, if we let λ_1 grow indefinitely, processor 1 spends a negligible amount of time executing in its private memory, and hence the other processor must have much longer active times in order to keep fixed the value of ρ as defined by (7.26). This artificially increases the system processing power. Indeed, if we consider a system comprising p processors, and we let the disbalance grow, we force all processors other than processor 1 to spend an increasing fraction of their time being active, and thus we can reach a processing power equal to $p-1$.

The only model that allows general distributions for both active and access times and that can be solved in product form is the $G_d/G_d/PS$. Results for this model are identical to those of the $M_e/M_e/FCFS$ case. They were repeated in table 7.1 to allow a comparison with the results of the $G_d/G_d/FCFS$ model, which were obtained from the GSPN of figure 7.7. With the PS policy, the type of the distribution is irrelevant: only average values appear in the solution. In the case of the GSPN model we used an Erlang-2 distribution for access times, and a hyperexponential distribution with $C_v = 5$ for active times. Processing power results are lower in the FCFS case, in spite of the small coefficient of variation of access times for each processor. The reason of this phenomenon lies in the large difference in speed between the two processors.

The last set of results presented in table 7.1 refers to the $M_d/G_d/FCFS$–FP case (remember that in the case of only two processors the distinction between the FCFS and the FP policy is inessential) for three different values of the access time distribution coefficient of variation. Processing power values are slightly lower than in the case in which both execution and access time distributions are equal for the two processors.

Tables 7.2 and 7.3 report processing power results in the cases of 5 and 10 processors, respectively. The same models already described for the case of 2 processors are considered, with the exception of $G_d/G_d/FCFS$–PS models for which no simple GSPN was presented for more than two processors. The results for the $G_d/G_d/PS$ model are identical to those of the $M_e/M_e/FCFS$.

On the other hand, in the cases of 5 and 10 processors it was necessary to separate the results of the $M_d/G_d/FCFS$ model from those of the $M_d/G_d/FP$, since the bus assignment policy influences the processing power values in these cases. In particular, it is possible to observe that the FP policy yields slightly higher performance. This is due to our choice of giving higher priority to the processor that makes frequent access requests, and that accesses common memory for short periods.

It is interesting to note that a large difference between the results of the simple $M_e/M_e/\text{FCFS}$ model and of the other more complex ones is found when the coefficients of variation of the distributions of the access times are large, and when the queuing discipline is *not* PS. Thus it may be convenient to use the more complex models in those cases only.

Finally, we remark that for multiprocessors with different distributions of the active and access times, the definition of the interesting performance indices, as well as of the significant system load, must be carefully chosen depending on the application.

References

[AJMO85] Ajmone Marsan, M., Balbo, G., Bobbio, A., Chiola, G., Conte, G., and Cumani, A., "On Petri Nets with Stochastic Timing," Proc. International Workshop on Timed Petri Nets, Torino, Italy, July 1985.

[BRUE80] Bruell, S. C., and Balbo, G., *Computational Algorithms for Closed Queueing Networks*, Elsevier, North-Holland, New York, 1980.

[BUZE73] Buzen, J. P., "Computational Algorithms for Closed Queuing Networks with Exponential Servers," *Communications of the ACM*, 16(9) (September 1973), 527–531.

[FRAN83] Franzkowiak, G. H., and Schmid, H., "Efficiency Analysis of Single Bus Multiprocessor Architectures," 1983 Real Time Systems Symposium, Arlington, Virginia, December 1983.

[HART84] Hartwick, P., and Noedel, D., "Ada Machine Delivers High Performance," *Defense Electronics* 16(11) (November 1984), 98–102.

[INTE81] "Introduction to the iAPX432 Architecture," Intel Corporation, 1981.

[JAIS68] Jaiswal, N. K., *Priority Queues*, Academic Press, New York, 1968.

[KIRR84] Kirrman, H. D., and Kaufmann, F., "Poolpo: A Pool of Processors for Process Control Applications," *IEEE Transactions on Computers* C-33(10) (October 1984), 869–878.

[KLEI76] Kleinrock, L., *Queueing Systems*, Vol. 2: *Computer Applications* Wiley, New York, 1976.

[SAUE75] Sauer, C. H., and Chandy, K. M., "Approximate Analysis of Central Server Models," *IBM Journal of Research and Development* 19(3) (May 1975), 301–313.

[TAKA62] Takacs, L., *Introduction to the Theory of Queues*, Oxford University Press, New York, 1962.

8 Multiple-Bus Multiprocessors with External Common Memory

This chapter describes the extension to the multiple-bus case of the performance analysis of the multiprocessor architecture analyzed in chapter 7. Here we study multiprocessor systems in which a set of p processors can access a set of m common memories using a set of b global buses. As an example, in figure 8.1 is shown a 3-processor, 3-memory, 2-bus multiprocessor. The notation $p \times m \times b$ is used to indicate a system with p processors, m common memories, and b global buses.

If the number of global buses is larger than or equal to either the number of processors or the number of common memories, then the interconnection network is equivalent to a crossbar and yields the same performance. We consider here the case in which the number of buses is strictly less than both the number of processors and the number of common memories. Moreover, we pay more attention to the case in which the number of processors is larger than the number of common memories, even if in some cases this complicates the models. In some other cases the distinction is unnecessary.

The system operations and workload are described, as in the previous chapter, by an asynchronous probabilistic model. Each processor is active for some time, while the CPU may be executing a program that only requires access to its own private memory; the duration of these active periods is an exponentially distributed random variable with the same parameter λ for all processors. At the end of an active period, processors generate access requests directed to a specific memory chosen at random among the external common memories; each common memory can be requested with the same probability $1/m$. If a bus is available and the requested memory is free, the processor accesses it for an exponentially distributed random period with parameter μ, the same for all processors and common memories. If either no bus is available or the requested memory is busy, the processor idles waiting. At the end of an access the processor begins a new active period: bus and common memory are released and can be used by other processors. An arbitration policy for the assignment of buses must be defined. We first assume that the policy randomly selects one among the heads of the nonempty queues referencing free common memories. Later in this chapter we shall also consider the FCFS policy. Note that bus arbitration and release times are again neglected in the model.

The system behavior, under these hypotheses, can be represented by a closed queuing network with passive resources ([KELL76, CHAN78]), as shown in figure 8.2.

As we already said, processors can be in one of three possible states: active, accessing, or queued.

Chapter 8

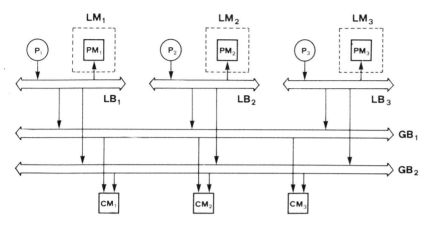

Figure 8.1
Architecture of a 3-processor, 3-memory, 2-bus multiprocessor. Processors are composed of a CPU (P_i) and a private memory (PM_i) [which coincides with the local memory (LM_i)] connected by a local bus (LB_i). Common memories (CM_i) are connected to processors by means of global buses (GB_i).

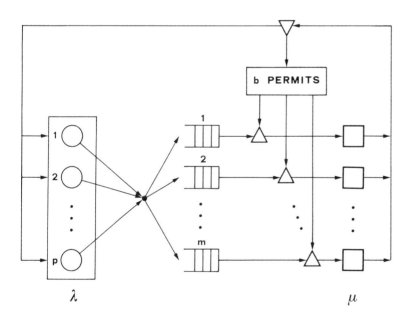

Figure 8.2
Closed queuing network model with passive resources.

8.1 Continuous-Time Markov Chain Models

The behavior of the multiprocessor architecture in figure 8.1 can be modeled using a continuous-time Markov chain whose state is defined by the $2p$-tuple

$$(m_1, s_1, m_2, s_2, \ldots, m_p, s_p), \tag{8.1}$$

where

m_i is the memory referenced by processor i,
s_i is the state of processor i.

m_i can take these values:

0: processor's private memory,
k: kth common memory module.

s_i can take these values:

0: active,
j: queued (jth in queue) for module m_i,
-1: accessing the common memory module m_i.

This state definition, however, is not the most convenient from the computational point of view. Indeed, the continuous-time Markov chain can be lumped, thus obtaining models of substantially smaller size.

The state definition for the lumped (exact) continuous-time Markov chain model is

$$(n_m, q_1, q_2, \ldots, q_b, q_{b+1}, \ldots, q_m), \tag{8.2}$$

where

n_m is the number of processors currently accessing a common memory,
$q_1, \ldots, q_b$ are the numbers of processors queued for the currently accessed common memory modules, arranged in decreasing queue length order,
$q_{b+1}, \ldots, q_m$ are the numbers of processors queued for a free memory, not accessible because no bus is available, arranged in decreasing queue length order.

An example of the state transition rate diagram of the lumped continuous-time Markov chain for a $3 \times 3 \times 2$ system is shown in figure 8.3.

Note that the assumption of a random order bus arbitration allows an important simplification of the state definition of the continuous-time Markov chain model as well as a significant reduction of the dimensions of the state space. Nevertheless, exact

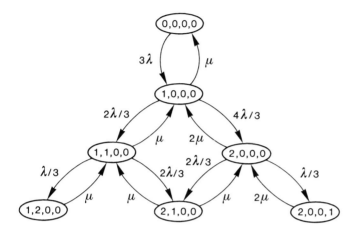

Figure 8.3
State transition rate diagram of the lumped continuous-time Markov chain of a $3 \times 3 \times 2$ multiprocessor system.

continuous-time Markov chain models can be used only to analyze multiprocessor systems of moderate size due to the exponential growth of the number of states with the number of system components.

Approximate models can be derived directly from the lumped continuous-time Markov chain, as explained in [AJMO82]. A few simple approximate models based on queuing networks will be presented in a later section of this chapter.

8.2 Generalized Stochastic Petri Net Models

As we already noted in the previous chapter, the definition of a detailed GSPN model of a multiprocessor system is a relatively easy task. The construction of compact models is, instead, more difficult, and it may require experience and ingenuity. In this section we present different GSPN models of the multiprocessor architecture under study, and we show how compact models can be constructed by cleverly exploiting the modeling power of immediate transitions and of random switches. Key to the success of the model reduction is the abstract probabilistic representation of some features of the model behavior. The construction of a compact model of the system is in principle possible also directly at the level of continuous-time Markov chains, but it surely requires a greater effort, since it is not supported by a graphical, easy-to-use system description.

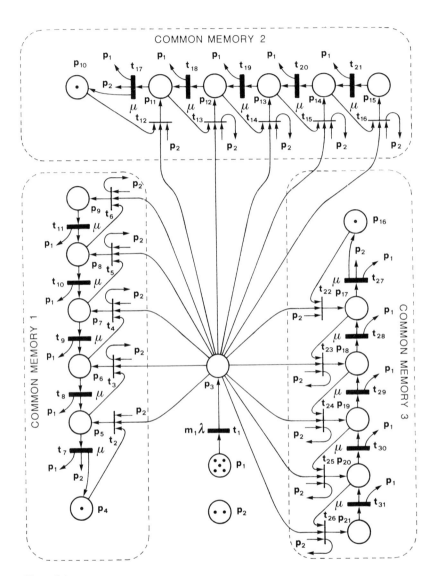

Figure 8.4
GSPN model of the multiprocessor architecture shown in figure 8.1, assuming that the multiprocessor comprises 5 processors, 3 common memories, and 2 buses.

Table 8.1
Legend for the GSPN in figure 8.4

Places	
p_1	Active processors
p_2	Available buses
p_3	Processors waiting for accessing common memories
p_4, p_{10}, p_{16}	Idle common memory
p_5, p_{11}, p_{17}	Processor accessing common memory
p_6, p_{12}, p_{18}	One processor is queued for common memory
p_7, p_{13}, p_{19}	Two processors are queued for common memory
p_8, p_{14}, p_{20}	Three processors are queued for common memory
p_9, p_{15}, p_{21}	Four processors are queued for common memory
Transitions	
t_1	End of a processor activity
t_2, t_{12}, t_{22}	A processor seizes a bus and starts an access
t_3, t_{13}, t_{23}	A processor becomes first in queue for common memory
t_4, t_{14}, t_{24}	A processor becomes second in queue for common memory
t_5, t_{15}, t_{25}	A processor becomes third in queue for common memory
t_6, t_{16}, t_{26}	A processor becomes fourth in queue for common memory
t_7, t_{17}, t_{27}	End of a memory access; common memory and bus are released
t_8, t_{18}, t_{28}	End of a memory access; a processor leaves the queue
t_9, t_{19}, t_{29}	End of a memory access; a processor leaves the queue
t_{10}, t_{20}, t_{30}	End of a memory access; a processor leaves the queue
t_{11}, t_{21}, t_{31}	End of a memory access; a processor leaves the queue

We build GSPN models of the multiprocessor architecture using timed transitions to represent the issuing and the service of requests, and immediate transitions to represent the bus arbitration and release.

An FCFS bus arbitration policy is assumed, with the constraint that a bus can be seized only by processors referencing free common memories. This policy is implemented in the GSPN models in the following way. Processors can choose the common memory to be accessed only when a bus is available; if the chosen memory is free, the access begins; otherwise he processor queues. If a processor, say A, is first in queue for a memory already accessed by another processor, say B, at the end of the access of B the bus is not released, but is immediately given to processor A.

8.2.1 Detailed Model

Figure 8.4 depicts a model of a system with 5 processors, 3 common memories, and 2 buses in which processors and memories are assumed to behave in a statistically equivalent manner. Note that this model can accommodate memories with different characteristics, whereas processors with different behavior patterns induce a substantial modification of the GSPN. The GSPN comprises 21 places, 16 timed transitions, and 15 immediate transitions. The meanings associated with each place and transition are summarized in table 8.1. Tokens in place p_1 represent processors that are executing in their private memory. Tokens in p_2 represent buses available for use. Tokens in places p_4, p_{10}, and p_{16} represent idle common memory modules. Each processor may issue an access request at a rate λ so that t_1 fires at rate $m_1 \lambda$. A token in p_3 represents a processor that needs to select a memory to perform an external access. If no bus is available, the processor waits; if a bus is available, the processor selects a memory according to a uniform distribution. Because of the symmetry of the GSPN, we explain its behavior by focusing our attention on the encased subnet describing the access to the first common memory. Assume that one bus is available and a processor in p_3 decides to access the first common memory. Two cases arise.

The first case corresponds to an access to an idle memory module. Transition t_2 is the only enabled transition that fires, removing tokens from p_2, p_3, and p_4 and placing a token in p_5, meaning that a bus is used by a processor accessing a common memory that becomes busy. Upon firing of transition t_2, the memory access modeled by the timed transition t_7 immediately begins.

The second case corresponds to an access request directed to a busy common memory. Up to 4 processors can be queued in front of each common memory at the time an access request is issued. This is represented in the GSPN in figure 8.4 by a token in places p_5, p_6, p_7, and p_8, respectively. Notice that only one of these places can be occupied by a token at any given time. Let us suppose that a token is in place p_5 to represent that one processor is accessing the common memory and no other processor is waiting in queue for this same common memory. Transition t_3 is enabled and fires, moving a token one step up in the chain of places p_5 to p_9 (from place p_5 to place p_6).

Note that, in order to reduce the number of markings, we assume that processors choose the memory to be accessed only when a bus is available. For this reason all immediate transition connected to p_3 are enabled only when a bus is free (token in p_2). This assumption does not reproduce the actual behavior of the multiprocessor system, where processors request a specific common memory before requesting a bus. However, as long as a processor is not allowed to seize a bus when the requested memory is busy, the assumption does not produce incorrect results. This assumption is reflected in the model by the connections of immediate transitions with p_2, which ensure that a bus is released when the requested common memory is busy. Of course, if a processor can occupy a bus while waiting for a busy memory, the system performance is reduced.

Continuing our description of the GSPN behavior, note that, because of the firing of transition t_3, transition t_7 becomes disabled, while transition t_8 becomes enabled. The two transitions correspond to the same memory access, and are distinct only because of a different queue condition. The memoryless property of the access time distribution ensures that the remaining firing time of t_7 has the same distribution as the firing time of t_8.

Each time one of the transitions t_8 to t_{11} completes its counting, a processor returns to execute in its private memory and the bus is used to allow the processor that is next in the queue to take its turn in accessing the common memory. The bus is released only after the last processor in queue completes its access, i.e., after the firing of transition t_7. The reachability set of the GSPN comprises 64 tangible markings and 22 vanishing markings.

The GSPN in figure 8.4 can be expanded to model a system with a larger number of processors, memories, and buses. A change in the number of buses requires only a modification of the initial marking. A change in the number of processors requires a modification of the initial marking and an expansion of the chains of places p_5 to p_9, p_{11} to p_{15}, and p_{17} to p_{21} to accommodate as many places as there are processors. Finally, a change in the number of common memories calls for a redrawing of the GSPN, since a new subnet must be added for each new common memory.

The detailed system operation description of the GSPN in figure 8.4 makes this model relatively easy to understand at the expense of a nontrivial graphical complexity. A more compact description of the bus and queue management policies can be obtained by avoiding the representation of redundant places and transitions.

8.2.2 Alternative Representation of Memory Subnets

Figure 8.5 depicts a subnet that can be used to replace each of the three subnets in figure 8.4. The meanings associated with each place and transition are in this case summarized in table 8.2. The behavior of the GSPN obtained after having performed this substitution can again be explained by focusing the attention on the accessing of the first common memory. When a bus is available and a processor in p_3 selects a memory to perform an external access, this selection is made according to a uniform distribution. The selection of the first common memory is represented by the firing of the immediate transition t_2, so that a token moves from p_3 to p_4, and a token representing a free bus is absorbed. Then only one of the two transitions t_5 and t_6 can be enabled according to the following rules:

1. Transition t_6 is enabled if another processor is already accessing the same memory and using a bus ($m_7 \geq 1$). In this case the bus is released, meaning that the new accessing

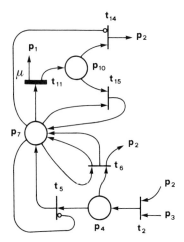

Figure 8.5
Compact representation of the subnets of the GSPN in figure 8.4.

Table 8.2
Legend for the GSPN in figure 8.5

Places	
p_4	A processor wants to access a common memory
p_7	Processors accessing or queued for common memory
p_{10}	The bus selects its next destination
Transitions	
t_2	Selection of a common memory
t_5	A processor selects an idle common memory
t_6	A processor selects a busy common memory
t_{11}	End of a common memory access
t_{14}	The bus is released and the common memory becomes idle
t_{15}	The bus is assigned to the next processor in queue

processor will be waiting for the same memory and for the same bus that is already in use by the processor in p_7.

2. Transition t_5 is enabled if no processor is accessing the selected memory ($m_7 = 0$). In this case the processor keeps the bus and a token moves from p_4 to p_7.

Since $1/\mu$ is the average common memory access time, μ is the firing rate of t_{11}. When t_{11} fires, a token moves to p_1 meaning that the processor is again working on its private memory. At the same time a bus is released (and a token moves to p_2) only if no other processor is queued for the same memory (i.e., $m_7 = 0$). These rules are implemented by the pair of immediate transitions t_{14} and t_{15}. Transition t_{14} is enabled if $m_7 = 0$. If $m_7 \geq 1$, then t_{15} is enabled and the bus is not released. The reachability set of the GSPN comprises 64 tangible states and 199 vanishing states.

Using the subnet in figure 8.5, a change in the number of processors and buses induces only a modification of the initial marking, whereas a change in the number of memories requires the redrawing of the GSPN; 6 transitions and 3 places must be added for each new memory. The complexity of the net is thus observed to grow linearly with the number of memories.

8.2.3 Folding of the Detailed Model

Since we have assumed that the 3 common memories are statistically equivalent, a different GSPN model of the same system can be built, at the expense of a more careful study of the multiprocessor system behavior. Figure 8.6 depicts this new model. The GSPN now comprises 9 places, 6 timed transitions, and 5 immediate transitions. The meanings associated with each place and transition are summarized in table 8.3. The 3 memories are represented by 3 tokens in the same place, p_4. Processors executing in their private memories are represented by tokens in place p_1. Transition t_1 models the issuing of an access request. Requests are put in place p_3, implicitly assuming that, as in the previous case, no choice among memories has yet been made.

Places p_5 to p_9 may contain tokens, each one representing a group of processors requesting the same memory. Only one of the processors in the group is being served. If the group is made of only one processor, the token is in p_5; if the processors are two, the token is in p_6; and so on. If five processors are requesting the same memory, one token is in place p_9. New requests choose memories according to a uniform probability distribution. The choice is described in the model by the five immediate transitions t_2 to t_6, upon which a switching distribution is defined. This GSPN has a lot in common with that in figure 8.4 and can indeed be seen as a straightforward reduction of the GSPN obtained by folding onto each other the subnets representing the common

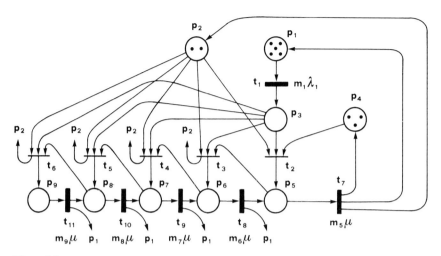

Figure 8.6
Reduced GSPN model of the multiprocessor architecture shown in figure 8.1, in the case of 5 processors, 3 common memories, and 2 buses.

Table 8.3
Legend for the GSPN is figure 8.6

Places

p_1	Active processors
p_2	Available buses
p_3	Processors waiting for accessing common memories
p_4	Idle common memories
p_5	Processors accessing common memory
p_6	Queues for common memories having length one
p_7	Queues for common memories having length two
p_8	Queues for common memories having length three
p_9	Queues for common memories having length four

Transitions

t_1	End of a processor activity
t_2	A processor seizes a bus and starts access
t_3	A processor becomes first in queue for common memory
t_4	A processor becomes second in queue for common memory
t_5	A processor becomes third in queue for common memory
t_6	A processor becomes fourth in queue for common memory
t_7	End of a memory access; common memory and bus are released
t_8, t_9, t_{10}, t_{11}	End of a memory access; a processor leaves the queue

memory accesses. Tokens move along the chain of places p_5 to p_9 following the same rules discussed during the description of the GSPN in figure 8.4. A distinctive characteristic of this new GSPN is that several tokens can now be simultaneously present in the chain of places p_5 to p_9 to represent the queue lengths at the different common memories. Again each token in this chain of places represents a group of processors requesting the same common memory.

The random switches in the GSPN comprise transitions in the set $\{t_2,\ldots,t_6\}$ and switching distributions whose general form is

$$P\{t_2\} = \frac{m_4}{3}, \quad P\{t_3\} = \frac{m_5}{3}, \quad P\{t_4\} = \frac{m_6}{3}, \quad P\{t_5\} = \frac{m_7}{3}, \quad P\{t_6\} = \frac{m_8}{3}. \tag{8.3}$$

Note that this switching distribution is well defined for all random switches, since in every marking enabling more than one immediate transition the sum $m_4 + \cdots + m_8$ equals the number of memories (3 in this case). In fact, all markings of this GSPN are such that $m_4 + \cdots + m_9 = 3$, but whenever $m_9 > 0$ no immediate transition is enabled. The five timed transitions t_7 to t_{11} represent the common memory accesses. The firing of t_7 modifies the marking moving one token from p_5 to p_1 and putting one token in both places p_2 and p_4. Upon firing of transitions t_8 to t_{11}, one token is moved one step to the right in the chain of places p_5 to p_9 and one token is put in place p_1. The policy for the bus arbitration is the same as the one used in the model in figure 8.4.

The development of this GSPN requires more modeling effort than needed for the GSPN in figure 8.4, but results in a much smaller reachability set. Indeed, the number of tangible states reduces from 64 to 16, and that of vanishing states from 22 to 8. Using this GSPN, the multiprocessor performance analysis thus becomes much simpler. Moreover, the structure of this new GSPN is such that multiprocessor systems with a larger number of memories and buses are simply represented by changing the initial marking. An increase in the number of processors requires, instead, changing the initial marking and lengthening the chain of places p_5 to p_9. This chain must, in fact, comprise as many places as there are processors in the system.

8.2.4 Compact Model

The GSPN models in figures 8.4 and 8.6 have the distinctive characteristic of being well suited to represent multiprocessor systems with a small number of memories and processors, respectively. In practice, however, it is much more common that multiprocessor systems comprise a large number of processors and memories, but very few buses. It is thus desirable to develop a GSPN model whose complexity only depends on the number of buses. This can again be done provided that a careful study of the multiprocessor behavior is made. The resulting GSPN model for the 5-processor, 3-memory, and 2-bus multiprocessor system is shown in figure 8.7. Only 5 places and 5 transitions (3 timed and 2 immediate) are necessary in this case. The meanings associated with each place and transition are summarized in table 8.4. Place p_1 as usual contains tokens representing processors executing in their private memory, and place p_2 contains tokens representing free buses. Transition t_1 represents the issuing of access requests, and place p_3 contains requests that have not yet been served. Tokens in place p_4 represent processors accessing common memories. Tokens in place p_5 represent processors requesting the same common memory as the one accessed by the token that has been in place p_4 longer. The firing of transition t_5 represents the end of the access to the memory for which processors in place p_5 are queued. The firing of transition t_4 represents the end of the access to a memory for which there is no outstanding request.

The two immediate transitions t_2 and t_3 model the memory choice: the firing of transition t_3 corresponds to choosing the memory that is being accessed by the processor in p_4. The choice of any other memory corresponds to the firing of transition t_2. The random switches that must be defined in the GSPN comprise transitions t_2 and t_3 and the switching distribution:

$$P\{t_2\} = 1 - \frac{1}{m}, \qquad P\{t_3\} = \frac{1}{m}, \tag{8.4}$$

where m is the number of common memories. Again the same switching distribution is valid for all the GSPN markings enabling both transitions t_2 and t_3.

Indeed, when a token enters p_3 three cases are possible:

1. All memories are idle ($m_4 = 0, m_2 = 2$). t_2 is the only enabled transition.
2. One memory is busy ($m_4 = 1, m_2 = 1$). Both t_2 and t_3 are enabled; t_3 fires with probability $1/m$, corresponding to the possibility of choosing the busy memory.
3. Two memories are busy ($m_4 = 2, m_2 = 0$). Neither t_2 nor t_3 is enabled, since the system comprises only two buses.

The policy for the bus arbitration is the same as in the previous models. The reachability set generated by this GSPN is exactly the same as obtained with the GSPN in figure 8.6. This model can accommodate any number of processors and memories for a fixed number of buses, b, which in our case is equal to 2. To extend the model to the case with $b > 2$, the chain t_3–p_5–t_5 must be split into $b - 1$ similar chains, and appropriate connections to the rest of the net must be introduced. The complexity of the net grows then linearly with the number of buses.

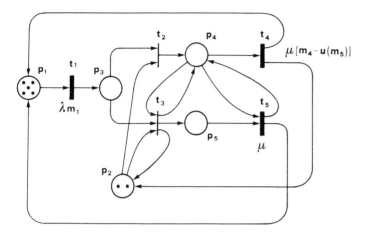

Figure 8.7
Compact GSPN model of the multiprocessor architecture shown in figure 8.1, in the case of 5 processors, 3 common memories, and 2 buses.

Table 8.4
Legend for the GSPN in figure 8.7

Places	
p_1	Active processors
p_2	Available buses
p_3	Processors waiting for accessing common memories
p_4	Processors accessing common memories
p_5	Processors queued for common memories
Transitions	
t_1	End of a processor activity
t_2	A processor selects an idle common memory
t_3	A processor selects a busy common memory
t_4	End of access to a memory with an empty queue
t_5	End of access to a memory with a nonempty queue

Table 8.5
Characteristics of the four GSPN models from the point of view of graphical complexity and cardinality of the reachability set (a multiprocessor system comprising 5 processors, 3 common memories, and 2 buses is assumed)

GSPN model	Number of places	Number of transitions		Number of markings	
		Timed	Immediate	Tangible	Vanishing
Figure 8.4	21	16	15	64	22
Figure 8.5	12	4	15	64	199
Figure 8.6	9	6	5	16	8
Figure 8.7	5	3	2	16	8

8.2.5 Remarks

It must be observed again that the three GSPN in figures 8.4, 8.6, and 8.7 model exactly the same system. Let us summarize how the different GSPN represent the system behavior:

1. The "explicit" request for a memory (memory choice) is made by processors only when a bus is available. This is obtained in the three models using a place (p_3) in which requests are collected upon generation, before the memory choice. These places are surrounded by a "barrier" of immediate transitions enabled only if a bus is available. This model feature was introduced to limit the number of markings of the GSPN reachability set, and hence the number of states of the Markovian model.
2. The bus arbitration is modeled by the immediate transitions t_3 to t_6, t_{13} to t_{16}, and t_{23} to t_{26} in figure 8.4, by the chain t_3 to t_6 in figure 8.6, and by the absence of an output arc from t_5 to p_2 in figure 8.7.

A further interesting comment concerns the way in which the same queuing policy is modeled by the GSPN in figures 8.6 and 8.7, with completely different topologies. The chain p_5 to p_9 in figure 8.6 maps into places p_4 and p_5 in figure 8.7. The number of tokens in p_5 (figure 8.7) corresponds to the position of the token in the chain p_6–p_9 (figure 8.6); note that $m_6 + m_7 + m_8 + m_9 \leq 1$ since only two buses are available. For example, if a processor is accessing a common memory, and three other processors are queued for the same memory, this situation is represented in the GSPN in figure 8.7 by $m_5 = 3$ and $m_4 > 0$, whereas in the GSPN in figure 8.6 we have $m_8 = 1$.

The characteristics of the four GSPN models, from the point of view of both the graphical complexity and the cardinality of the reachability set, are summarized in table 8.5.

8.3 Product Form Solution

The queuing network in figure 8.2 that is used to model the behavior of the class of multiple-bus multiprocessor systems that we are considering does admit a product form solution, even if it does not satisfy the requirements of the BCMP theorem. A proof of the local balance property (which implies the product form solution [TOWS75]) for this type of queuing networks was presented by the authors in [AJMO84], and was independently obtained by other researchers [IRAN84, LEBO86]. We briefly outline in this section the main results presented in [AJMO84].

Consider the GSPN model of a two-bus multiprocessor system shown in figure 8.7. Obviously, since two buses are available, only two memory modules can be simultaneously accessed. At any point in time, we shall refer to them as the "first" and "second" modules, depending on the order in which they have been referenced. Upon completion of a memory access, the module that is still being accessed (if there exists one) assumes always the name of "first" module.

From this GSPN model the reachability graph can be automatically derived together with the corresponding continuous-time Markov chain state transition rate diagram as described in chapter 4. The state transition rate diagram for the case of a $5 \times m \times 2$ system is shown in figure 8.8.

States are labeled by a triplet of natural numbers (v_1, v_2, n) with the following meaning:

v_1 represents the number of processors that requested the first memory module while another bus was still available (queue for the first memory module);
v_2 (either 0 or 1) represents the access to the second memory module;
n is the number of processors still waiting for a bus.

This triplet is related to the marking of the GSPN in the following way:

$$v_1 = m_5,$$
$$v_2 = u(m_4 - 1), \qquad (8.5)$$
$$n = m_3,$$

where $u(\cdot)$ is the unit-step function defined as $u(i) = 1$ for every integer $i > 0$, and $u(i) = 0$ otherwise.

The number L of states of the continuous-time Markov chain associated with the GSPN in figure 8.7 grows with the square of the number p of processors included in the system $[L = (p(p+1)/2) + 1]$. Even though this number is quite small when

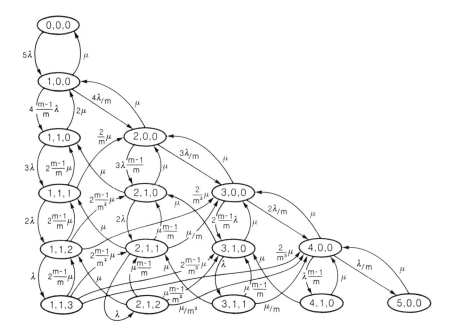

Figure 8.8
State transition rate diagram of the continuous-time Markov chain associated with the GSPN in figure 8.7 in the case of 5 processors and 2 buses.

compared with the size of the state space of the continuous-time Markov chain models presented in section 8.2, it still becomes quickly too large to allow a direct analysis of large-size multiprocessor systems of this type. Indeed, the exact solution of these continuous-time Markov chains (e.g., with Gauss elimination) has a computational complexity of order $O(p^6)$, so that systems with more than 30 processors are practically unsolvable.

An alternative approach to the solution of this model comes from the fact that it satisfies the local balance condition. This property can be proved by writing for all states in the Markov chain the global balance as well as the local balance equations, and then showing that the solution of the set of local balance equations also satisfies the set of global balance equations. For a detailed proof the reader is referred to [AJMO84].

Observe now the regular structure of the state transition diagram in figure 8.8. Each row of states corresponds to all markings that can be obtained keeping fixed the

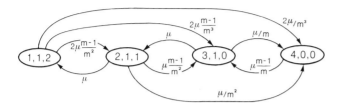

Figure 8.9
State transition rate diagram of the continuous-time Markov chain representing the bus-memory subsystem with 4 processors.

number of processors inside the bus-memory subsystem. A consequence of the local balance property is that the probability distribution over the states in a row, conditional on a given number N of processors in the subsystem, does not depend on the values of the arrival rate of requests and on the speed of the memory modules. This implies that this distribution can be obtained under the hypothesis of a constant number of processors using the bus-memory subsystem. The knowledge of conditional probabilities for all states in the same row (obtained independently of the solution of the initial problem) can be exploited in order to aggregate each row of states into a macrostate labeled with the number N of processors requesting memory access, using the techniques described in chapter 2.

The sets of conditional probabilities $P\{v_1, v_2, n|N\}$ for $N = 2, \ldots, p$ are obtained by sequentially solving $p - 1$ submodels with simple corresponding continuous-time Markov chains. These models can be derived from the GSPN in figure 8.7 in which transition t_1 is replaced by an immediate transition, and in which N tokens are initially placed in p_1. Each one of these submodels has exactly N distinct states. Figure 8.9 depicts the state transition rate diagram of the continuous-time Markov chain of the subsystem with a fixed number $N = 4$ of processors circulating in it. Obtaining the equilibrium state probability distribution for all these submodels has a computational complexity of order $O(p^4)$. However, owing to the regularity of the Markov chains of the "shorted" subsystem models for increasing number of processors N, we were able to solve the whole class of these chains in closed form, obtaining the expression for the state (conditional) probabilities [AJMO84]. Using this result, the aggregation technique mentioned previously allows the aggregation of each row of the original Markov chain into a macrostate characterized by the number of processors using the bus-memory subsystem. The transition rates from macrostate N are $(p - N)\lambda$ and $\mu_{eq}(N, m, 2)$ (remember that m is the number of external common memories, and that we are considering a two-bus system), where

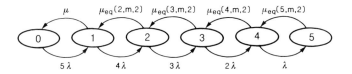

Figure 8.10
State transition rate diagram of the aggregated continuous-time Markov chain in the case of 5 processors and 2 buses.

$$\mu_{eq}(N, m, 2) = 2\mu m \frac{f(N, 2)}{f(N + 1, 2)} \tag{8.6}$$

and $f(N, 2)$ is recursively defined as follows:

$$\begin{aligned} f(1, 2) &= 1/2M, \\ f(i, 2) &= mf(i - 1, 2) + 2^{i-3}. \end{aligned} \tag{8.7}$$

The state transition rate diagram of the resulting aggregated continuous-time Markov chain is shown in figure 8.10. This corresponds to a very simple B-D process with $p + 1$ states. The steady state solution of this continuous-time Markov chain allows the computation of the processing power P of the system with a computational complexity of the order of the number of processors comprised in the system. The steady state probability distribution obtained in this way has a product form in which the processor and memory speed parameters appear in different factors:

$$P\{N\} = \frac{1}{G(p)} \frac{1}{(p - N)! \lambda^{p-N}} \frac{f(N + 1, 2)}{(2\mu m)^N}, \tag{8.8}$$

where $G(p)$ is a normalization constant making the probabilities sum to 1.

This result is extremely interesting, because it allows a very convenient (and inexpensive) exact performance analysis of systems with a very large number of processors, independently of the number of memory modules.

Combining the solution of the B-D continuous-time Markov chain with the conditional state probabilities, we can also obtain the general (closed form) expression for the initial continuous-time Markov chain steady state probabilities.

The results obtained for the two-bus case can be extended to the general case of b buses:

$$\mu_{eq}(N, m, b) = b\mu m \frac{f(N, b)}{f(N + 1, b)} \tag{8.9}$$

and

$$P\{N\} = \frac{1}{G(p)} \frac{1}{(p - N)!\lambda^{p-N}} \frac{f(N + 1, b)}{(b\mu m)^N}. \tag{8.10}$$

Moreover, the Markov chain steady state probabilities are

$$P\{v_1, \ldots, v_b, n\} = \frac{\prod_{i=0}^{b-1} (m - i)^{u(v_{i+1})}}{m^{(N-n)} b^{(v_b+n)} \prod_{j=1}^{P} c(j, v_1, \ldots, v_{b-1})} \rho(N), \tag{8.11}$$

where b represents, as usual, the number of buses in the system; the coefficient $c(\cdot)$ is defined as the factorial of the number of memory queues, among the first $b - 1$ memory modules, containing exactly j processors,

$$c(j, v_1, \ldots, v_{b-1}) = \left(\sum_{k=1}^{b-1} \delta(j, v_k)\right)!. \tag{8.12}$$

and

$$\rho(N) = (\lambda/\mu)^N \frac{p!}{(p - N)!} p(0, \ldots, 0, 0). \tag{8.13}$$

Equation (8.11) can be used to obtain the bus-memory subsystem equivalent service rate in those cases in which it is not known explicitly. Figure 8.11 depicts the aggregated queuing network that yields the processing power for these systems.

The load dependence function of the equivalent server is formally specified by the following expression:

$$\mu_{eq}(N) = E\left[\mu \sum_{i=1}^{b} u(v_i) \middle| N\right] \tag{8.14}$$

for $N = 1, 2, \ldots, p$.

Due to the product form property, a numerical evaluation of equation (8.14) is sufficient to make the queuing network in figure 8.11 solvable using the computationally efficient algorithms devised for the analysis of standard BCMP queuing networks outlined in chapter 3.

The complexity of the solution technique just described lies in the computation of the function $f(N, b)$ that is to be used in the expression of the equilibrium macrostate

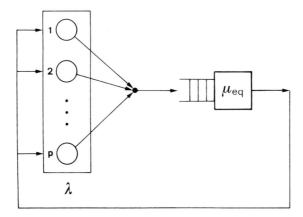

Figure 8.11
Aggregated queuing network model.

probabilities (8.10). A recursive relation is known in the cases $b = 2$ [see (8.7)] and $b = 3$ [AJMO84], but for larger numbers of buses it is necessary to obtain numerical results from the probabilities given in (8.11). In the cases in which either this computation is too heavy or the accuracy required of the analysis does not justify the computation, it can be appropriate to resort to the very simple queuing bounds that will be described in the next section.

The product form solution is a characteristic of these bus-memory subsystem models that extends beyond the simple queuing networks used for their analysis. This implies that a bus-memory service station can be embedded inside an otherwise BCMP queuing network, still retaining the product form property. Besides the theoretical relevance of this result, we note that this allows the extension of the above results to multiprocessor systems in which active times are generally distributed and possibly different for each processor. Indeed, the conditions of the BCMP theorem permit the existence in the network of infinite server stations with general distributions, possibly different for all customer classes (see chapter 3).

Further investigations have shown that the product form characteristic of the steady state solution of this class of multiprocessor system models is valid also when some of the restrictions originally imposed on the model are removed. One of the generalizations that were considered is that of allowing a nonuniform distribution of references among memory modules. However, it is possible to see that both the equal exponential distribution of the service time for each memory module and the FCFS bus-memory assignment policy are essential for preserving a product form solution.

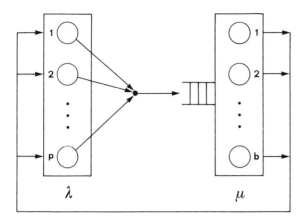

Figure 8.12
Queuing network to obtain an upper bound on the multiprocessor processing power.

Indeed, neither a Last Come First Served policy (with and without preemption), nor a priority discipline (with and without preemption) was found to yield a locally balanced model of the bus-memory subsystem.

8.4 Simple Queuing Bounds

Bounds on the multiprocessor processing power can be obtained from the analysis of very simple queuing systems whose solution is straightforward and can be obtained with very little computational effort.

8.4.1 Upper Bound

Very often in real systems the number of common memories greatly exceeds the number of buses. It is thus likely that whenever a processor issues a request, if a bus is available, the requested memory is also free. In other words, we may assume that blocking of processors is mainly due to buses. It is on these grounds that the upper bound on system performance is based.

The upper bound is obtained by assuming that interference is only due to buses. Memory interference is thus neglected. Processors are assumed to issue requests for buses after exponentially distributed active times, use the buses for exponentially distributed periods, then release the buses and return to the active state.

The upper bound is thus a machine repairman queuing network, as in figure 8.12.

The same queuing system is also called an $M/M/b$ queue with finite population (p customers).

This queuing system is analyzed using a B-D continuous-time Markov chain with birth and death rates [see (2.84)]

$$\lambda_k = \lambda(p-k), \quad 0 \le k \le p,$$
$$\mu_k = \begin{cases} k\mu, & 1 \le k < b \\ b\mu, & b \le k \le p, \end{cases} \quad (8.15)$$

where λ_k and μ_k are the birth and death rates when k customers are in the queue, including the one in service. That is, λ_k and μ_k are the access request rate and access completion rate, respectively, when $p - k$ processors are active.

π_k, the steady state probability of having k customers in the queue (probability of $p - k$ active processors), satisfies the relationships

$$\pi_k = \pi_{k-1} \frac{\lambda_{k-1}}{\mu_k} \quad (1 \le k \le p), \quad \sum_{k=0}^{p} \pi_k = 1 \quad (8.16)$$

and is obtained as

$$\pi_k = \begin{cases} \pi_0 \binom{p}{k} \left(\frac{\lambda}{\mu}\right)^k, & 0 \le k \le b \\ \pi_0 \binom{p}{k} \frac{k!}{b! b^{k-b}} \left(\frac{\lambda}{\mu}\right)^k, & b \le k \le p, \end{cases} \quad (8.17)$$

where

$$\pi_0 = \left[\left(1 + \frac{\lambda}{\mu}\right)^p + \sum_{j=b}^{p} \binom{p}{j} \left(\frac{j! b^{b-j}}{b!} - 1\right) \left(\frac{\lambda}{\mu}\right)^j\right]^{-1}. \quad (8.18)$$

The upper bound on the average number of active processors, P_u, is then evaluated as

$$P_u = \sum_{k=0}^{p} (p-k) \pi_k$$
$$= \frac{1}{1+(\lambda/\mu)} \left\{ p - (p-b)\pi_b \left[\frac{p-b-(b\mu/\lambda)}{(b\mu/\lambda) E_{1,p-b-1}(b\mu/\lambda)} + 1 \right] \right\}, \quad (8.19)$$

where $E_{1,p-b-1}(x)$ is the Erlang function of the first type of order $p-b-1$ with argument x, also called Erlang B function.

$$E_{1,j}(x) = \frac{(x^j/j!)}{\sum_{i=0}^{j}(x^i/i!)}. \tag{8.20}$$

P_u is an upper bound on the processing power of the system in figure 8.2. The tightness of the bound depends on the system load and on the number of common memories. The larger the number of memories, the tighter the bound.

8.4.2 Lower Bound

In order to obtain a lower bound on the average number of active processors in the system in figure 8.2 some pessimistic assumptions must be introduced. For the bound to be computationally simple, it is required that the simplified queuing system be solvable in closed form.

The lower bound is obtained assuming that the number of common memories is equal to the number of buses ($m = b$). The hypothesis is pessimistic since the number of resources in the system is reduced, and thus the simplified model shows a higher level of interference than would be obtained with the queuing system in figure 8.2.

Consider, for instance, the case in which $b - 1$ memories are being accessed, so that one bus is still available. When a processor issues a request in the real system (figure 8.2) it references a free memory with probability $(m - b + 1)/m$; then, since a bus is available, the memory can be accessed. In the simplified system the probability of referencing the only free memory is $1/m$, which is smaller than in the previous case, as we assumed that in the real system m is larger than b and b is larger than 1.

The lower bound queuing network is shown in figure 8.13. Processors issue requests for the common memories after exponentially distributed active periods. Each memory is selected at random with probability $1/b$. If the memory is available, it is accessed for an exponentially distributed time (a bus is certainly available); then the bus and the memory are released and the processor returns to the active state.

The approximate queuing network contains one infinite-server station with exponential service time and b FCFS single-server stations with exponential service time. The BCMP theorem can thus be quoted to state that the steady state probabilities can be written in product form. Since this is the case, the CHW theorem states that the exact solution can be found by replacing the b single-server stations with an equivalent server whose service function must be evaluated as described in chapter 3. Consider the bus-memory system in isolation as shown in figure 8.14, which is equivalent to the network in figure 8.13, where the infinite-server station has been shorted. Customers exiting from service immediately reenter a queue that they choose with uniform probability.

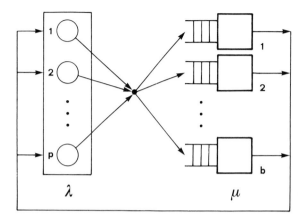

Figure 8.13
Queuing network to obtain a lower bound on the multiprocessor processing power.

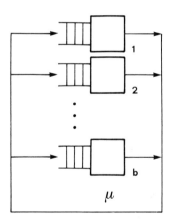

Figure 8.14
Bus-memory subsystem in isolation.

By conditioning on the number of customers in this system, k, the steady state pobability of n_1 customers being in the first queue, n_2 in the second, ..., and n_b in the bth queue is

$$P\{n_1, n_2, \ldots, n_b | k\} = 1 \bigg/ \binom{k+b-1}{b-1}. \tag{8.21}$$

Indeed, all distributions of customers are at steady state equally likely, and the number of possible distributions is equal to the number of ways that k balls can be put in b boxes, and is thus

$$\binom{k+b-1}{b-1}.$$

The ith server (common memory) is idle with probability

$$P\{n_1, n_2, \ldots, n_i = 0, \ldots, n_b | k\} = \binom{k+b-2}{b-2} \bigg/ \binom{k+b-1}{b-1}$$
$$= \frac{b-1}{k+b-1}, \tag{8.22}$$

since out of the

$$\binom{k+b-1}{b-1}$$

possible distributions

$$\binom{k+b-2}{b-2}$$

will be such that one queue is empty and the server is idle.

The utilization of each server is thus

$$P\{n_1, n_2, \ldots, n_i \neq 0, \ldots, n_b | k\} = 1 - \frac{b-1}{k+b-1} = \frac{k}{k+b-1}. \tag{8.23}$$

The service function of the system in figure 8.14 conditional on the number of customers in the system is then evaluated as

$$\mu_{eq}(k) = b\mu \frac{k}{k+b-1}. \tag{8.24}$$

It is now possible to replace the queuing network in figure 8.13 with the one in figure 8.11, where the single-server station is now load dependent, and its service function is the one given by (8.24).

We can again analyze this system using a continuous-time Markov chain B-D model. The birth and death rates are now

$$\lambda_k = \lambda(p - k), \qquad 0 \le k < p,$$
$$\mu_k = b\mu \frac{k}{k + b - 1}, \qquad 0 < k \le p. \tag{8.25}$$

Again the steady state probabilities satisfy the relationship (8.16), and can be expressed as

$$\pi_k = \pi_0 \left(\frac{\lambda}{b\mu}\right)^k \binom{p}{k} \frac{(b + k - 1)!}{(b - 1)!}, \qquad 0 \le k \le p, \tag{8.26}$$

where

$$\pi_0 = \left[\frac{1}{(b - 1)!} \sum_{k=0}^{p} \left(\frac{\lambda}{b\mu}\right)^k \binom{p}{k} (b + k - 1)!\right]^{-1}. \tag{8.27}$$

The lower bound on the average number of active processors can then be evaluated as

$$P_l = \sum_{k=0}^{p} (p - k)\pi_k. \tag{8.28}$$

P_l is a lower bound on the processing power of the system in figure 8.2. Again the tightness of the bound depends on the system load and on the number of common memories. In this case, however, the bound is tighter when the number of common memories is closer to the number of buses.

Note that the evaluation of the bounds does not depend on the number of common memories in the system. Actually the lower bound was evaluated by assuming a number of common memories equal to the number of buses, whereas the upper bound assumes an infinitely large number of common memories. It then follows that the range of values between the two bounds contains all possible values of processing power for any number of common memories in the range (b, ∞). When the number of memories is small (large), the processing power is closer to the lower (upper) bound.

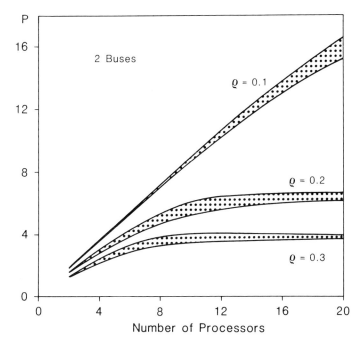

Figure 8.15
Processing power regions for a multiprocessor system with the architecture of figure 8.1 with 2 buses as a function of the number of processors, and for different values of the load factor ρ.

8.5 Numerical Results

The knowledge of the two bounds presented in the previous section allows processing power regions (which contain all values of processing power for a varying number of common memories) to be drawn versus the number of processors in the system, for a fixed number of buses, and for a fixed load, as shown in figure 8.15. Alternatively, it is possible to fix either the number of processors and the system load, and to show the processing power region as a function of the number of buses (figure 8.16), or the system configuration, and to show the processing power region versus the load factor ρ (figure 8.17).

A number of observations can be made from figures 8.15, 8.16, and 8.17. A diminishing return effect is clearly visible either when the number of processors is increased for a fixed number of buses (figure 8.15) or the number of buses is increased for a fixed

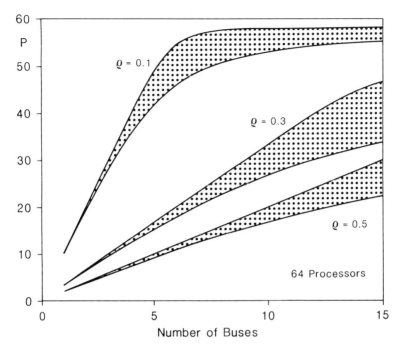

Figure 8.16
Processing power regions for a multiprocessor system with the architecture of figure 8.1 with 64 processors as a function of the number of buses, and for different values of the load factor ρ.

number of processors (figure 8.16). Moreover, as expected, the processing power curve is a monotonically decreasing function of the system load.

In the three figures we see that the two bounds start from the same value, diverge rather remarkably, and then tend to converge slowly again toward a common value.

The availability of the bounds is important for a first-order approximation analysis of the multiprocessor system performance and for determining, during the design stage, what configurations and loads are to be chosen in order to meet some specified performance criterion. By using the bounds, it is possible to choose rather accurately the most convenient number of processors and buses. Little can be said, however, about the number of common memories. We know that by setting $m = b$ we obtain the lower bound performance, and that by increasing the number of common memories the system performance increases toward the upper bound, but we do not know exactly how the processing power is affected by the presence of additional common memories. Moreover, once the configuration and load are determined, a precise quantification of

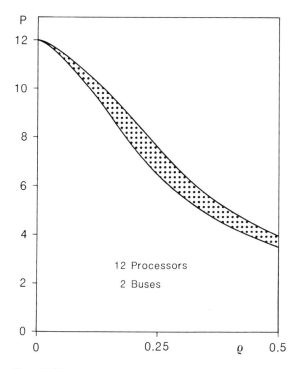

Figure 8.17
Processing power region for a multiprocessor system with the architecture of figure 8.1 with 12 processors and 2 buses as a function of the load factor ρ.

the system processing power is desired. Either GSPN models or the product form results given in the previous section can be used to obtain these exact results, and to analyze precisely the influence of the number of common memory areas on the system performance.

Consider, for example, a 12-processor, 2-bus system with load factor 0.3. Figures 8.15, and 8.17 tell us that the processing power of this multiprocessor lies between $P = 5.6$, and $P = 6.5$, independently of the number of common memories. The exact results of figure 8.18 show the processing power behavior when the number of common memories is varied from 2 to 10. For 2 memories the processing power is equal to the lower bound, as we already know. If the number of common memories is increased to 3, the processing power is increased to almost 6.2, thus obtaining 2/3 of the total possible improvement (the distance between the two bounds). Adding a 4th common memory module, we reach 85% of the total obtainable performance increase. With 5

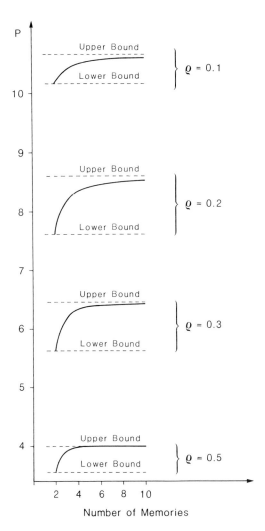

Figure 8.18
Processing power for a multiprocessor system with the architecture of figure 8.1 with 12 processors and 2 buses as a function of the number of common memory modules, and for different values of the load factor ρ.

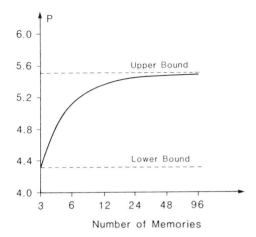

Figure 8.19
Processing power for a multiprocessor system with the architecture of figure 8.1 with 10 processors and 3 buses as a function of the number of common memories; load factor $\rho = 0.5$.

common memories we reach 90%, and with 10 we reach 96%. It is thus clear that it is not convenient to use more than 4–5 common memory modules in this multiprocessor, since the fractional performance improvement yielded by adding extra memories is negligible beyond these values.

Figure 8.18 shows a family of processing power results, always assuming a multiprocessor system comprising 12 processors and 2 buses. We can observe that the fractional performance improvement obtained increasing the number of common memories from 2 to 3 becomes larger and larger for increasing system load. With $\rho = 0.1$ the extra memory buys 48% of the distance between the two bounds; with $\rho = 0.5$ it buys 80% of the total achievable performance improvement. Moreover, we can see that the curves between the two bounds rise faster and faster for increasing loads: with $\rho = 0.5$, 4 common memories are practically sufficient to obtain the upper bound processing power. Note also that, in all cases, the upper bound becomes very soon more accurate than the lower bound, and that the upper bound performance can be approached with a relatively small number of common memories.

Similar results can be obtained also for other system configurations. For example, figure 8.19 shows the processing power of a system comprising 10 processors, 3 buses, and a variable number of common memories, with a load factor $\rho = 0.5$. Again, the two bounds are shown together with the exact results yielded by the exact models. In this case the convergence toward the upper bound is slower than in the two-bus system (note the logarithmic horizontal scale): over 10 common memories are necessary to obtain a processing power close to the upper bound.

References

[AJMO82] Ajmone Marsan, M., and Gerla, M., "Markov Models for Multiple Bus Multiprocessor Systems," *IEEE Transactions on Computers* C-31(3) (March 1982), 239–248.

[AJMO84] Ajmone Marsan, M., Balbo, G., Chiola, G., and Donatelli, S., "On the Product Form Solution of a Class of Multiple Bus Multiprocessor System Models," Proc. International Workshop on Modeling and Performance Evaluation of Parallel Systems, Grenoble, France, December 1984.

[CHAN78] Chandy, K. M., and Sauer, C. H., "Approximate Methods for Analyzing Queueing Network Models of Computer Systems," *ACM Computing Surveys* 10(3) (September 1978), 281–317.

[IRAN84] Irani, K. B., and Onyuksel, I. H., "A Closed Form Solution for the Performance Analysis of Multiple Bus Multiprocessor Systems," *IEEE Transactions on Computers* C-33(11) (November 1984), 1004–1012.

[KELL76] Keller, T. W., "Computer System Models with Passive Resources," Ph.D. Thesis, Computer Science Department, University of Texas at Austin, 1976.

[LEBO86] Le Boudec, J. Y., "A BCMP Extension to Multiserver Stations with Concurrent Classes of Customers," Proceedings PERFORMANCE '86, Raleigh, North Carolina, USA (May 1986).

[TOWS75] Towsley, D., "Local Balance Models of Computer Systems," Ph.D. Thesis, University of Texas at Austin, December 1975.

9 Single-Bus Multiprocessors with Distributed Common Memory

In chapters 7 and 8 we analyzed multiprocessor systems in which all common memories are at the same hierarchy with respect to processors. In this chapter we present simple Markovian models for the performance analysis of systems in which the common memory is split into separate modules that can be accessed with different rights and, possibly, at different speeds by the different processors.

From a physical point of view we can recognize, for each processor, local and external memory modules. A processor accesses its own local memory module with a single-level bus connection, and external memory modules with a multiple-level bus connection. There may also be memory modules that are not reachable from a given processor.

From a logical point of view we can identify private and common memories (again with respect to a given processor). Private memories are accessible only from the processor to which they are local. In all the architectures that we shall analyze, common memory modules are always accessible, although with different rights, from all processors. The common memory can be implemented either by using memory modules external to all processors or by distributing it in the nonprivate part of the local memories.

Three different common memory organizations, corresponding to three multiprocessor architectures, are analyzed and compared in this chapter. The three single-bus architectures that are considered comprise a set of p processors, made up of a CPU and a memory module connected by a bus. Other memory modules, which correspond to global resources, are present in the system. Details will be given separately for each architecture.

9.1 Modeling Assumptions

In order to be able to compare the effectiveness of the different architectures it is necessary to describe precisely the multiprocessor workload. Indeed, in this case the workload cannot be defined directly at the functional level (i.e., in terms of processor accesses to memory units) because the architecture is different from case to case, but it must be defined at some higher level of abstraction. From this workload, specified at the system level, the activity induced on the different architectures at a functional level can be derived; the performance indices obtained with this approach are then comparable in terms of the system level workload parameters. For this reason in this chapter (as well as in the next one) we assume that multiprocessors are operating in the message-passing environment described in chapter 5, and depicted in figure 5.8. Other types of workload could be assumed as well, resulting in similar models.

Processors are assumed to execute tasks that cooperate by passing messages. Tasks can communicate either with other tasks allocated to the same processor or with tasks allocated to other processors. Communication between tasks allocated to the same processor takes place through private memory only; no common resources (common memory and global bus) are involved in the message exchange operation. Communication between tasks allocated to different processors must use a "communication port" residing in common memory.

Given this system level workload model, it is possible to identify at the functional level active periods (CPU bursts) during which processors require access to local memories only, and access periods (transfer periods) that require the transfer of data to external memory areas to pass messages. Transfer period durations always depend on the length of the message being written in (read from) the external common memory, and are thus independent of the system architecture. CPU bursts, on the other hand, may have different average lengths in different architectures. Depending on the organization of the message-passing mechanism, CPU bursts may comprise accesses to local common memories needed to complete the delivery of the message to the destination task.

For the models to be "simple" and computationally not expensive it is necessary to introduce simplifying assumptions similar to those used in chapter 7:

1. The durations of CPU bursts and access periods are assumed to be exponentially distributed random variables with means $1/\lambda$ and $1/\mu$ respectively.
2. The interconnection structure is considered ideal. Zero time is required to establish or to release a path.
3. If a path cannot be established, the processor idles, waiting for the necessary resource(s).
4. An external access request from processor i is directed to a nonlocal memory j with probability $1/m$, where m is the number of nonlocal common memory modules.

The assumption of a continuous flow of instructions being executed by each processor implies that idle periods due to task synchronization are negligible or, equivalently, that the number of tasks allocated to processors is very large with respect to the number of processors itself.

In addition to the three processor states (ACTIVE, ACCESSING, QUEUED) already defined in chapter 7 we must consider the case when a processor is BLOCKED by some other processor accessing the common memory segment of its local memory.

With reference to the multitasking environment assumed as a common workload, we assume that, in order to produce a useful piece of information (a message), a task must execute for a random time with average $1/\lambda_t$.

The exchange of information between tasks is relevant to our models only in the case the communicating tasks reside on different processors, since only in this case are common memories used. The parameter we need, in order to study the contention for shared resources, is thus the rate of generation of messages exchanged among processors; in fact, we must not consider the activity induced by the exchange of messages among the tasks on the same processor. Thus we define $1/\lambda_p$ to be the average active time elapsing between subsequent messages sent out by the same processor toward communication ports.

A relationship between λ_t and λ_p is easy to obtain if the workload is composed of a set of identical tasks uniformly distributed among processors. Assume that p is the number of processors considered in the model, and that exactly k tasks are allocated to each processor. The number of tasks external to each processor is simply $k(p-1)$. If we assume a uniform reference model between tasks, the probability that task i sends a message to the input port of task j is $1/(kp-1)$ for all $j \neq i$. Thus we have

$$\lambda_p = \lambda_t \frac{k(p-1)}{kp-1}. \qquad (9.1)$$

Moreover, if we assume k to be very large, we can approximate λ_p as

$$\lambda_p = \lambda_t \frac{p-1}{p}. \qquad (9.2)$$

The relationship between λ_p and λ_t does not depend on the architecture, but only on the number of processors. The parameters λ_p and λ_t are both useful: λ_p allows the behaviors of the different models to be compared once the number of processors is fixed. λ_t is needed in order to compare the performance of each architecture when a different number of processors is used to execute the same (fixed) workload.

A relationship between λ, which is used to characterize the workload at functional level, and λ_p can be derived from the operating characteristics of each architecture, considering the two-step interprocessor communication scheme shown in figure 5.8. The details of this derivation will be provided with the discussion of the model used to represent each architecture.

Results are given in terms of ρ, ρ_p, and ρ_t, which are obtained as the ratios of λ, λ_p, and λ_t to μ. These quantities can be interpreted as the characterization of the workload seen by the model at the functional level (ρ), generated by a processor (ρ_p), and generated by a task (ρ_t) at the system level.

9.2 Architecture 1

Let us consider for a moment the multiprocessor architecture that was already analyzed in chapter 7, which in this chapter shall be identified as Architecture 1. The external common memory (see figure 7.1) is accessible only through the global bus. It contains all the communication ports. Contention may arise each time a message is written in (read from) common memory.

The behavior of this system at the message-passing level can be described as follows: processors execute segments of programs until they need to access common memory. After issuing a request for the global bus, processors may have to wait for the bus to become available. When the bus is allocated to a processor, the transfer of data takes place. In the message-passing environment described before, each message sent out by a process is eventually read by the destination process. The symmetry of the model implies that (on the average) the traffic of messages flowing out of a process (and hence of a processor) balances that flowing into the same process (or processor). Processor activity is thus interrupted with a rate (λ) that is twice the rate of generation of messages:

$$\lambda = 2\lambda_p. \tag{9.3}$$

The independence and exponential assumptions introduced in the previous section are discussed in chapter 7.

From the definition of processing power (7.14) the following closed form expression can be derived using (7.11):

$$P = \frac{\{\sum_{k=0}^{p} \rho^k [p!/(p-k)!]\} - 1}{\rho \sum_{k=0}^{p} \rho^k [p!/(p-k)!]}. \tag{9.4}$$

A recursive formulation of the above expression is

$$P(p) = \frac{p}{1 + \rho[p - P(p-1)]} \tag{9.5}$$

with $P(0) = 0$.

Equations (9.2) and (9.3) provide the following relationship between ρ, ρ_p, and ρ_t:

$$\rho = 2\rho_p = 2\rho_t \frac{(p-1)}{p}. \tag{9.6}$$

Using (9.6), equations (9.4) and (9.5) can be written in a form that will be used later for comparison purposes.

Chapter 9

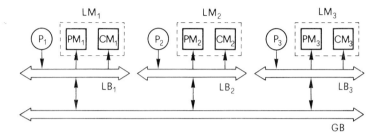

Figure 9.1
Structure of Architecture 2 in the case of three processors. Processing units are composed of a CPU (P_i), and of a local memory (LM_i) subdivided into a private segment (PM_i) and a common segment (CM_i). CPU and local memory are connected by a local bus (LB_i). Processing units are connected by a global bus (GB).

9.3 Architecture 2

As mentioned before, the common memory can be distributed on modules local to each processor. Architecture 2 assumes that local memories are (logically) divided into private and common areas. Common areas contain the communication ports of the associated processors. Each processor is connected to its own local memory segment by a local bus. A processor accesses a nonlocal common memory segment using its own local bus, the global bus, and the local bus connected to the destination common memory module, where the input port of the destination processor is located.

Figure 9.1 depicts a three-processor system organized according to this structure. Arbitration mechanisms are needed to manage global and local buses. Contention may arise for using each of the buses represented in the model.

We assume that processors waiting for the global bus and requesting a free common memory module are served according to an FCFS discipline. A processor that gains access to the global bus acquires priority to use any reachable resource and may preempt other processors. Processors preempted while active become blocked; processors preempted while queued maintain their state, but release their local bus. These policies avoid deadlocks and improve performance.

Figure 9.2 shows a GSPN model of the activity of a processor (say, processor 1) embedded in Architecture 2. The presence of a token in place p_1 represents a processor executing in its private memory if the local bus is available (a token in place p_2), or a blocked processor if p_2 is empty. At the end of the activity in the local memory, the processor selects a memory among the external ones (this selection is represented by the random switch $t_{12}, \ldots, t_{1j}, \ldots, t_{1p}$) and tries to access it. The access can be

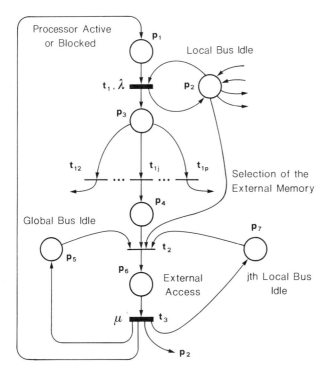

Figure 9.2
GSPN description of the activity of a processor in the system represented in figure 9.1.

performed if the processor local bus and the global bus are free (respectively, p_5, p_2 are not empty); moreover, while the access is in progress the local bus of the external memory is busy (p_7 is empty). Observe that the model does not consider the FCFS queuing policy for the access to the global bus.

In this architecture the system level workload described in figure 5.8 is executed in the following way. A message generated by a sender task on processor i is passed to the input port of a destination task allocated to processor j ($i \neq j$) using this mechanism: at the end of a CPU burst, processor i issues a request for the global bus. When available, the bus is seized by the processor together with the local bus j: a transfer period begins, and data are moved into the input port of processor j. The message is eventually received when the destination processor moves it from its input port to the task input port. This latter action is a transfer of data within the local memory of the destination processor and is thus considered, as anticipated in section 9.1, part of its activity, but must not be regarded as a contribution to the processing power.

As we observed in the previous section, the symmetry of the model implies that flows of incoming and outgoing messages balance. It follows that the mean length of a CPU burst can be considered as the sum of the mean time required to produce a message ($1/\lambda_p$) and the mean transfer period required to receive a message ($1/\mu$). Hence

$$\frac{1}{\lambda} = \frac{1}{\lambda_p} + \frac{1}{\mu}, \quad \text{or} \quad \lambda = \frac{\lambda_p \mu}{\lambda_p + \mu}. \tag{9.7}$$

Because of the blocking phenomenon due to one processor accessing the local memory of another one, Architecture 2 cannot be modeled directly as a simple queuing system. A GSPN model could be effectively used, but in this case a Markov chain model can be directly constructed. The state of the system can be described with the $2p$-tuple

$$(m_1, s_1; m_2, s_2; \ldots; m_p, s_p), \tag{9.8}$$

where m_i is the index of the memory module referenced by processor i and s_i is the state of processor i.

s_i can take the values

2 active,
1 accessing an external common memory module,
0 blocked,
$-k$ queued for the global bus: kth in queue.

The symmetry of the system can be used to lump this Markovian model as described in chapter 2, in order to reduce the number of states. Aggregated states require a less detailed description. The state definition in the lumped chain is given by the triplet

$$(n_a, n_e, n_b), \tag{9.9}$$

where

n_a = number of active processors.
n_e = number of processors either accessing an external common memory area or queued for the global bus,
n_b = number of blocked processors (which were active and have been preempted by an external access).

An important property of the lumped model is its size, which grows only linearly with the number of processors in the system: the analysis of systems in which a very large number of processors cooperate thus becomes feasible. The state transition rate diagram of the lumped Markov chain for the general case of p processors is shown in figure 9.3, and the expressions for the transition rates are given in table 9.1.

Notice that λ transitions correspond to the generation of an access request by one of the active processors; μ transitions correspond to the completion of common memory accesses.

Processors requesting the use of the global bus when it is busy wait in queue for their turn. Upon completion of an access to the external common memory, the global bus is immediately seized by one of the queued processors. A new message transfer begins and the corresponding destination processor becomes blocked unless it was already waiting in the global bus queue. Depending on the state of this target processor, the system moves into a state with either one or zero blocked processors. We call the transitions associated with the first alternative μ-type transitions, while μ'-type transitions correspond to the second one. Given a state $\mathbf{s} = (n_a, n_e, n_b)$, the access request generation rate is proportional to the number of active processors n_a; the total access completion rate is μ whenever n_e is larger than zero. If n_e is less or equal than 2, only μ-type transitions may take place because when the accessing processor completes its access at most one processor is queued for the global bus, and it will surely block an active processor. If n_e is larger than 2, then two cases are possible: upon the end of an access a processor seizes the bus and may access either the local memory of one of the $n_e - 2$ processors queued for the global bus or the local memory of an active processor. The first alternative corresponds to a μ'-type transition and, due to the uniform probability distribution, may occur with probability $(n_e - 2)/(p - 1)$. The second alternative corresponds to a μ-type transition, and may occur with probability $1 - (n_e - 2)/(p - 1)$.

Due to the regularity of the structure of the lumped Markov chain, it is not difficult to set up a program that automatically generates the states of the chain. The equilibrium probabilities of the states of the lumped chain are then easily evaluated by solving a system of linear equations.

Let S be the state space of the Markov chain, $\mathbf{s}$ be a state, and $\pi_\mathbf{s}$ be its equilibrium state probability. The processing power of the multiprocessor system is given by the following expression:

$$P = (1 - \rho) \sum_{\mathbf{s} \in S} n_a(\mathbf{s}) \pi_\mathbf{s}. \tag{9.10}$$

The factor $1 - \rho$ is introduced to account for the message read time included in the CPU bursts as expressed by (9.7); the fraction of CPU burst actually used to generate a message is indeed

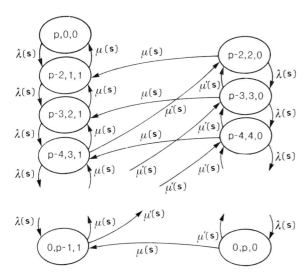

Figure 9.3
State transition rate diagram of the lumped continuous-time Markov chain model of Architecture 2 in the general case of p processors.

Table 9.1
Transition rates of the lumped Markov chain model of Architecture 2 (figure 9.3)

$\lambda(\mathbf{s}) = n_a \lambda$

$\mu(\mathbf{s}) = \begin{cases} \left(1 - \dfrac{n_e - 2}{p - 1}\right)\mu, & n_e > 2 \\ \mu, & n_e \leq 2 \end{cases}$

$\mu'(\mathbf{s}) = \dfrac{n_e - 2}{p - 1}\mu, \qquad n_e > 2$

where $\mathbf{s} = (n_a, n_e, n_b)$;
note that $\mu(\mathbf{s}) + \mu'(\mathbf{s}) = \mu$
$\qquad n_a + n_e + n_b = p$

Table 9.2
Architecture 2; closed form expressions of processing power of multiprocessor systems comprising two, three, and four processors

Number of processors	Processing power
2	$\dfrac{2(1-\rho)}{1+2\rho}$
3	$\dfrac{3(1-\rho^2)}{1+3\rho+3\rho^2}$
4	$\dfrac{4(1-\rho)(9+36\rho+59\rho^2+52\rho^3+24\rho^4)}{9+54\rho+149\rho^2+236\rho^3+208\rho^4+96\rho^5}$

$$\frac{(1/\lambda)-(1/\mu)}{(1/\lambda)} = 1 - \rho. \tag{9.11}$$

Closed form expressions for the processing power of this architecture with two, three, and four processors are given in table 9.2, as functions of ρ.

The following definitions of ρ in terms of ρ_p and ρ_t [see equations (9.2) and (9.7)]

$$\rho = \frac{\rho_p}{1+\rho_p} = \frac{\rho_t}{\rho_t + [p/(p-1)]}; \tag{9.12}$$

allow the equations of table 9.2 to be used for comparison purposes.

9.4 Architecture 3

An improvement on Architecture 2 can be obtained using a double-port memory module [CHAN80] to implement the common part of the local memory of each processor. Common memory modules are thus directly accessible from external processors through the global bus.

No contention arises either on local buses or on double-port memories that support two simultaneous accesses. Contention is in this case only due to the sharing of the global bus that is arbitrated according to an FCFS policy. Figure 9.4 depicts the structure of Architecture 3 in the case of a two-processor system. Note that processors are not allowed to access the common section of their own local memory through the global bus.

The activity of one processor is modeled by the GSPN in figure 9.5. A token in p_1 represents the processor in its active state; when t_1 fires, the processor tries to

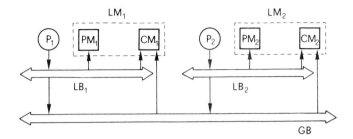

Figure 9.4
Structure of Architecture 3 in the case of two processors. Processing units are composed of a CPU (P_i), and of a local memory (LM_i) subdivided into a private segment (PM_i) and a common segment (CM_i). CPU and local memory are connected by a local bus (LB_i). Common memory areas are also connected to the global bus (GB) that links processing units.

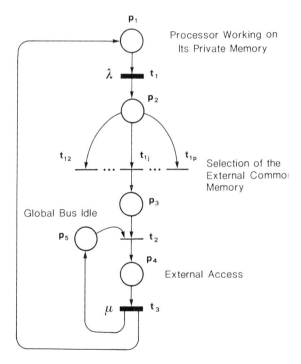

Figure 9.5
GSPN description of the activity of a processor in the system represented in figure 9.4.

access an external common memory. The selection is made by the random switch $t_{12},\ldots,t_{1j},\ldots,t_{1p}$; then the jth external common memory can be accessed if the global bus is available. It must be observed that, in a single-global bus system, the external memory is always available because only one external access is possible; moreover, one external access and one internal access are simultaneously possible on the same common memory. As in the previous case, the FCFS policy for the accesses to the global bus is not modeled.

The execution of the system level workload involves a sequence of operations very much similar to that described in the previous section for Architecture 2. Because of the double-port memory, writing a message in the input port of the destination processor does not block its activity. Again CPU bursts include the action of moving a message from the processor input port to the task input port, both located in the processor local memory, so that the relationship between λ and λ_p remains the one described by equation (9.7)

Since the global bus is the only element that may cause contention, the Markovian model of Architecture 3 is again a "machine repairman" model, and we can use the results of section 9.2 for the evaluation of this architecture.

The closed form expression of processing power given for Architecture 1 can be used, but, as in the case of Architecture 2, it must be reduced by a factor $(1-\rho)$ that accounts for the time needed to transfer a message within the local memory between processor and task input ports. We thus obtain

$$P = (1-\rho)\frac{\{\sum_{k=0}^{p}\rho^{k}[p!/(p-k)!]-1\}}{\rho\sum_{k=0}^{p}\rho^{k}[p!/(p-k)!]}, \tag{9.13}$$

and the recursion becomes

$$P(p) = \frac{p(1-\rho)}{1+\rho\{p-[P(p-1)/(1-\rho)]\}}. \tag{9.14}$$

Substituting for ρ its definition in terms of ρ_p and ρ_t, given by (9.12), equations (9.13) and (9.14) become again useful for comparison purposes.

9.5 Architecture 4

When a double-port memory is not available, a variation of Architecture 3 can be obtained by implementing the common memory modules as shown in figure 9.6, which depicts the structure of Architecture 4 in the case of a two-processor system.

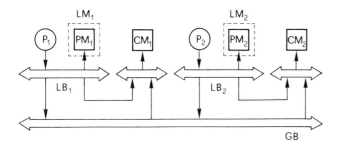

Figure 9.6
Structure of Architecture 4 in the case of two processors. Processing units are composed of a CPU (P_i), and of a private memory (PM_i) [which coincides with the local memory (LM_i)]. CPU and private memory are connected by a local bus (LB_i). Common memories (CM_i) are connected to the local bus of the processor with which they are associated and to the global bus (GB) that links processing units.

Each common memory module contains the input port of its associated processor. Nevertheless, common memory modules are external to all processors.

As in Architecture 3, processors are not allowed to access their associated common memory segments through the global bus. Only one processor is allowed to access a common memory module at each point in time. Contention arises for the use of the global bus and of the common memory modules. Arbitration mechanisms are needed for managing the global bus and the common memory buses. As in Architecture 2, the global bus is arbitrated according to an FCFS policy, and, to improve performance, priority is given to access requests coming from the external processor through the global bus: a processor accessing its associated common memory module may thus be preempted.

The activity of a processor in Architecture 4 is modeled by the GSPN in figure 9.7. A token in p_1 represents the processor in its active state. In this case t_1 and t_2 are simultaneously enabled. The firing of t_1 models the end of the active state and the request of an access to the local common memory. The access can be performed provided that the local common memory is free. The firing of t_2 models the beginning of an access to the external common memory, which is selected according to the random switch $t_{12}, \ldots, t_{1j}, \ldots, t_{1p}$. The access can be performed if the global bus and the external common memory are both available. Also in this case the policy for the bus access is not modeled.

In this architecture the system level workload is executed as in Architecture 3. A message generated by a sender task on processor i is passed to the input port of a destination task allocated to processor j ($i \neq j$) using the following mechanism: at the

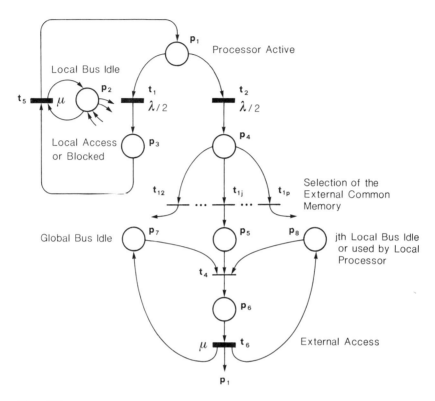

Figure 9.7
GSPN description of the activity of a processor in the system represented in figure 9.6.

end of a CPU burst, processor i issues a request for the global bus. When available, the bus is seized by the processor together with the bus of the destination common memory module. A transfer period begins and data are moved into the input port of processor j. During this transfer period processor j is blocked if reading messages from its input port. The message is eventually received when the destination processor moves it from its input port to the task input port. In this architecture (as in Architecture 1) the latter action is considered a transfer period, since it involves an external memory access. Processor activity is thus interleaved with external common memory accesses to read and write messages. Because of the symmetrical workload assumption, incoming and outgoing message flows balance. Processor activity is thus interrupted at a rate (λ) that is twice the rate of message generation, so that the relation between λ and λ_p is the same as in (9.3).

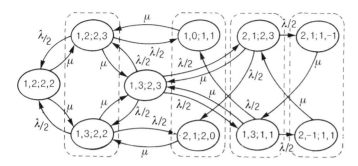

Figure 9.8
State transition rate diagram of the continuous-time Markov chain model of Architecture 4 in the case of 2 processors.

9.5.1 Continuous-Time Markov Chain Models

Architecture 4 can be modeled by a continuous-time Markov chain with the same state definition as in (9.8). The only difference is that now we must distinguish whether the processor accesses its associated common memory module or an external one. We shall thus use $s_i = 3$, meaning processor i is active, and $s_i = 2$ to represent processor i accessing its associated common memory module.

The complete Markov chain for the two-processor case has the state transition rate diagram shown in figure 9.8.

Lumping the Markov chain corresponding to the general case is not as straightforward as for Architecture 2. While we are only interested in first-order performance indices related to the average number of active processors, a reduction in the state description, which takes into account the state of each processor and neglects the destination of the external reference, does not meet the theoretical conditions for the lumpability of the original Markov chain. The destination of the memory reference of processors waiting in queue, as well as that of the processor working on external common memory, is thus important. A direct application of the lumpability criterion to the transition probability matrix of the Markov chain underlying the original model is computationally not feasible due to the complexity of the problem, even when a small number of processors are considered. The inherent symmetry of the model can be exploited, however, to obtain a first reduction of the state space size allowing a direct solution of slightly more complex systems.

This reduction, although exact, does not completely exploit the power of the lumpability criterion.

Table 9.3
Number of states of the Markov chain models of Architecture 4 as a function of the number of processors

Number of processors	Number of states	
	Original chain	Lumped chain
2	10	6
3	128	25
4	3784	173
5	—	1784

The state description we have chosen to perform this reduction step has a structure similar to that of the original model. The only difference is that processors are ordered according to their activity state (i.e., active processors, queued processors, ... are grouped together) without distinguishing among processor indices, but distinguishing among memory reference indices.

The state definition used to describe the lumped model is thus the following ordered list:

$$(m_{1st}, s_{1st}; \ldots; m_{ith}, s_{ith}; \ldots; m_{pth}, s_{pth}), \qquad (9.15)$$

where the position of each pair does not necessarily correspond to the index of the associated processor. The memory reference of the ith pair indicates the position held by the destination processor in the ordered list.

By using this state description, a substantial reduction in the size of the state space is achieved (see table 9.3), and an algorithm can be devised to generate automatically the transition matrix of the lumped Markov chain. Unfortunately, the size of the state space of the lumped chain keeps growing combinatorially with the number of processors considered in the model. The exact computation of the performance indices is thus feasible only for small models.

Applying this reduction technique to the two-processor chain in figure 9.8, aggregating the states comprised within dashed boxes, we obtain the Markov chain in figure 9.9, which can be easily solved, giving as result for the processing power

$$P = \frac{4(\rho + 1)(\rho + 2)}{3\rho^3 + 11\rho^2 + 10\rho + 4}. \qquad (9.16)$$

As the number of system components increases, the analysis of the model becomes more and more complex.

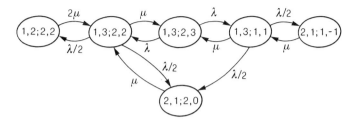

Figure 9.9
State transition rate diagram of the lumped Markov chain model of Architecture 4 in the case of 2 processors.

9.5.2 Generalized Stochastic Petri Net Models

Since in this case the main difficulty of the analysis lies in the correct state definition for a compact Markov chain model, we can take advantage of a GSPN representation of the system operations. Indeed, if we succeed in constructing a compact GSPN model of the system, we can automatically obtain from it an equivalent Markov chain model whose state space is a subset of the GSPN reachability set.

Consider first (figure 9.10) a detailed GSPN model of a two-processor system. The left side of the net models the behavior of one processor: the presence of a token in p_1 indicates that it is in its active state. The two timed transitions t_1 and t_3 are concurrently enabled and have the same meaning as t_1 and t_2 of the GSPN in figure 9.7. The firing of t_3 models a request of access to the external common memory; the firing of t_1 is a request of access to the local common memory.

After the firing of t_3, two different events can arise. In the first case, when a token is in p_{14} to signify that the second processor is already accessing the same common memory (i.e., its local common memory), t_7 fires and a token moves to p_9. The presence of a token in p_9 models the access of the first processor to the external common memory, while the second processor is preempted. When t_{17} fires, the first processor ends its access, the global bus is released, and a token returns to p_{14}; that is, the second processor can continue its access to the local common memory. In the second case, when the other processor is not accessing its local common memory (one token in p_3), t_5 fires and a token moves to p_7. The firing of t_{15} models the end of the external access.

If, otherwise, the first processor exits from its active state with the firing of t_1, a local access is about to begin and a token moves to p_{11}. t_{11} and t_9 model again the case that the other processor is or is not accessing the same memory. The firing of t_{11} moves a token to p_{10} (the second processor is accessing the nonlocal common memory and the first one is preempted), whereas the firing of t_9 allows the first processor to begin its

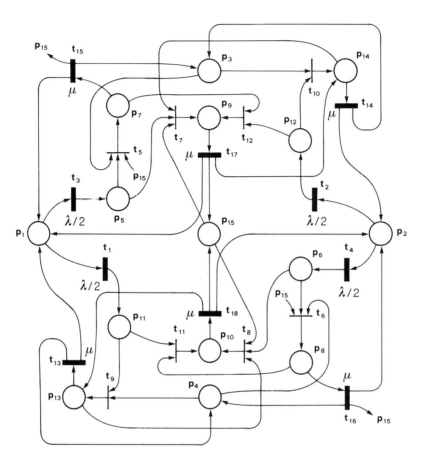

Figure 9.10
GSPN model of Architecture 4 in the case of 2 processors.

Table 9.4
Legend for the GSPN in figure 9.10

Places	
$p_1, (p_2)$	Processor 2 (1) is active.
$p_3, (p_4)$	Common memory 1 (2) available.
$p_5, (p_6)$	Processor 1 (2) requests the nonlocal common memory.
$p_7, (p_8)$	Processor 1 (2) accesses the nonlocal common memory; processor 2 (1) is not preempted.
$p_9, (p_{10})$	Processor 1 (2) accesses the nonlocal common memory; processor 2 (1) is preempted.
$p_{11}, (p_{12})$	Processor 1 (2) requests the local common memory.
$p_{13}, (p_{14})$	Processor 1 (2) accesses the local common memory.
p_{15}	The global bus is available.
Transitions	
$t_1, (t_2)$	Processor 1 (2) requests the local common memory.
$t_3, (t_4)$	Processor 1 (2) requests the nonlocal common memory.
$t_5, (t_6)$	Processor 1 (2) begins the access to the nonlocal common memory; processor 2 (1) is not preempted.
$t_7, (t_8)$	Processor 1 (2) begins the access to the nonlocal common memory; processor 2 (1) is preempted.
$t_9, (t_{10})$	Processor 1 (2) begins the access to the local common memory.
$t_{11}, (t_{12})$	Processor 1 (2) cannot access the local common memory; it is preempted.
t_{13}, t_{14}	End of access to the local common memory.
$t_{15}, t_{16}, t_{17}, t_{18}$	End of access the the nonlocal common memory.

access to the local common memory. Table 9.4 describes in detail the meaning of places and transitions of the GSPN in figure 9.10.

To develop a detailed and complete GSPN model of Architecture 4 with more than two processors, we associate with each processor a subnet containing places and transitions that represent the different processor states (active, accessing, queued, blocked). Preemption and other synchronization mechanisms are modeled using inhibitor arcs in order to keep the model as small as possible. Figure 9.11 depicts such a detailed GSPN model in the case of a three-processor system. This model will be used as a reference for the development of more compact models.

The reachability set of this GSPN comprises 68 tangible markings, and thus the associated continuous time Markov chain comprises 68 states. This number compares very favorably with the 128 states of the original Markov chain model described previously for this same case (see table 9.3). This reduction is due to the "memory choice" mechanism: in the GSPN model processors select the memory module to be accessed through the global bus only after seizing the bus, while in the Markov

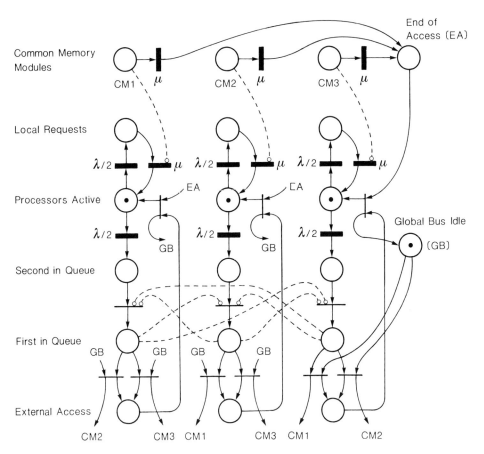

Figure 9.11
Detailed GSPN model of Architecture 4 in the case of 3 processors.

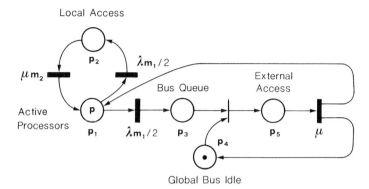

Figure 9.12
First draft of the compact GSPN model.

chain model the choice is performed when processors leave the active state; both alternatives obviously lead to the same throughput estimation. A further reduction in the dimension of the GSPN reachability set can be obtained if we assume a "random selection" policy for the bus allocation instead of FCFS. This modification of the multiprocessor system behavior does not alter the system processing power. With this further simplification the reachability sets of the GSPN models of the systems with three and four processors comprise 62 and 340 tangible markings, respectively, as compared with the 128 and 3784 states in table 9.3.

Observing the modular structure of the GSPN in figure 9.11, and recalling the assumptions of uniform processor behavior introduced previously, we can be optimistic about the possibility of constructing a more compact GSPN model of the multiprocessor system. Since we are only interested in the overall system processing power, rather than in individual processor performance, it is not necessary to represent the processor identity in the model. The compact GSPN model we are developing can thus be built by refining the one shown in figure 9.12, which represents a gross approximation of the system behavior, and hence of the GSPN system model shown in figure 9.11, since it does not take into account the preemption operated by memory access requests arriving from the global bus on processors accessing their shared memory module.

In order to take into consideration this feature of the system, we refine the model by splitting place p_5 of the GSPN in figure 9.12 in the two places p_6 and p_7 in figure 9.13 that represent these conditions: "global access with preemption" and "global access without preemption". The probability of entering either one of these

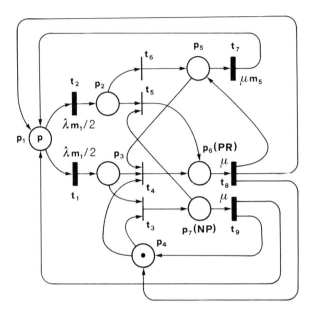

Figure 9.13
First refinement of the compact GSPN model. Random switch firing probabilities:

$$\begin{cases} P\{t_3\} = 1 - \dfrac{m_5}{p-1} \\ P\{t_4\} = \dfrac{m_5}{p-1}, \end{cases} \qquad \begin{cases} P\{t_5\} = \dfrac{1}{p-1} \\ P\{t_6\} = \dfrac{p-2}{p-1} \end{cases} \text{ if } m_7 = 1.$$

$$\begin{cases} P\{t_5\} = 0 \\ P\{t_6\} = 1 \end{cases} \text{ if } m_7 = 0,$$

places is determined by simply counting the number of (equally likely) possibilities. Furthermore, a subnet is substituted for place p_2: before accessing its shared memory module, the processor must decide whether to be preempted by a global access or not (the selection is made by the random switch of immediate transitions t_5 and t_6). In the case of a two-processor system we can thus formulate the refined GSPN model shown in figure 9.13, whose tangible reachability graph exactly coincides with the 6-state "lumped" Markov chain model in figure 9.9. The caption for the GSPN in figure 9.13 is given in table 9.5. However, if we try to use this GSPN model to analyze systems comprising more than two processors (by adding tokens into place p_1 and rearranging transition probabilities), we obtain results that are (slightly) different from those obtained with the GSPN in figure 9.11.

Table 9.5
Legend for the GSPN in figure 9.13

Places

p_1	Processors are active.
p_2	Processors try to access the local common memory.
p_3	Processors try to access the nonlocal common memory.
p_4	The global bus is available.
p_5	A processor accesses the local common memory.
p_6	A processor accesses the nonlocal common memory, preempting another processor.
p_7	A processor accesses the nonlocal common memory without preempting other processors.

Transitions

t_1	End of active state, access to the local common memory.
t_2	End of active state, access to the nonlocal common memory.
t_3	A processor begins to access the nonlocal common memory without preemption.
t_4	A processor begins to access the nonlocal common memory, preempting another processor.
t_5	A processor cannot access its local memory and is preempted.
t_6	A processor begins the access to its local common memory.
t_7	End of the access to the local common memory.
t_8, t_9	End of the access to the nonlocal common memory.

If we carefully examine the tangible reachability graphs of the GSPNs in figures 9.11 and 9.13 in the case of three processors, we realize that the former is "almost" lumpable into the second one. The only states that do not meet the lumpability condition are those in which a global access to the memory module of a processor already waiting for the global bus takes place; indeed, in this case no preemption may occur until the present global memory access is completed, and we must then inhibit transition t_5 of the GSPN in figure 9.13. We can thus further refine the GSPN in figure 9.13 by splitting place number 7 into two different conditions: "no preemption yet" and "no preemption possible." We obtain then the GSPN in figure 9.14. The topology of this GSPN model is independent of the number of system components. The caption for the GSPN in figure 9.14 is given in table 9.6. The GSPN in figure 9.14 was validated by comparing its results with those of the detailed model for systems comprising up to four processors. The number of tangible GSPN markings, and hence the number of states of the associated Markov chain model, is $L = \lceil (3p^2 - p)/2 \rceil + 1$, where p is the number of processors in the system.

The GSPN model in figure 9.14 will be used to obtain processing power results for multiprocessor systems comprising more than five processors.

The comparison of the processing power results with those of other architectures is made possible by substituting for ρ its definition in terms of ρ_p and ρ_t, given by (9.6).

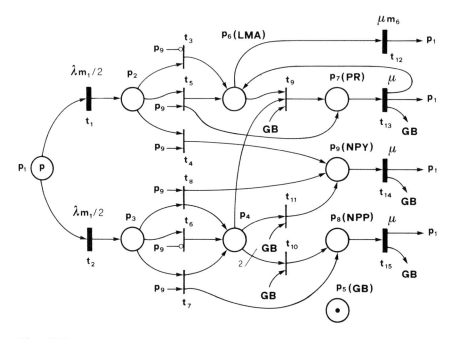

Figure 9.14
Second refinement of the compact GSPN model. Random switch firing probabilities:

$$\begin{cases} P\{t_4\} = \dfrac{m_1}{1+m_1} \\ P\{t_5\} = \dfrac{1}{1+m_1}, \end{cases}$$

$$\begin{cases} P\{t_7\} = \dfrac{1}{1+m_1} \\ P\{t_8\} = \dfrac{m_1}{1+m_1}, \end{cases}$$

$$\begin{cases} P\{t_9\} = \dfrac{m_6}{1+m_1+m_4+m_6} \\ P\{t_{10}\} = \dfrac{m_1}{1+m_1+m_4+m_6} \\ P\{t_{11}\} = \dfrac{1+m_4}{1+m_1+m_4+m_6}. \end{cases}$$

Table 9.6
Legend for the GSPN in figure 9.14

Places

p_1	Processors are active.
p_2	Processors try to access the local common memory.
p_3	Processors try to access the nonlocal common memory.
p_4	Processors try to access the nonlocal common memory.
p_5	The global bus is available.
p_6	A processor accesses the local common memory.
p_7	A processor accesses the nonlocal common memory, preempting another processor.
p_8	A processor accesses the nonlocal common memory without preempting other processors; preemption is possible.
p_9	A processor accesses the nonlocal common memory without preempting other processors; preemption is not possible.

Transitions

t_1	End of active state, access to the local common memory.
t_2	End of active state, access to the nonlocal common memory.
t_3, t_4	A processor requests to access the local common memory without preemption.
t_5, t_9	A processor cannot access the local common memory.
t_6, t_7, t_8 t_{10}, t_{11}	A processor begins to access the nonlocal common memory.
t_{12}, t_{13}	End of the access to the local common memory.
t_{14}, t_{15}	End of the access to the nonlocal common memory.

9.6 Architecture Comparison

We start the architecture comparison by considering the two-processor case, as it is the first step toward multiprocessing, and points out some results that become less obvious (but not less important) in larger systems.

Figure 9.15 shows the processing efficiency (the processing power normalized with respect to the number of processors p) versus ρ_p, the process or communication load, for the four two-processor architectures. The same results are given in closed analytical form in table 9.7. These results support the considerations used to develop the four architectures, as Architecture 3 is superior to 4, which, in turn, is better than 2. These considerations imply that Architectures 2 and 3 provide, respectively, lower and upper bounds on the performance of Architecture 4.

The relative behavior of Architectures 1 and 2 is very interesting: for light loads, Architecture 1 outperforms 2; this is rather surprising because Architecture 1 generates twice as many accesses to the global bus. This result is due to the fact that, with light

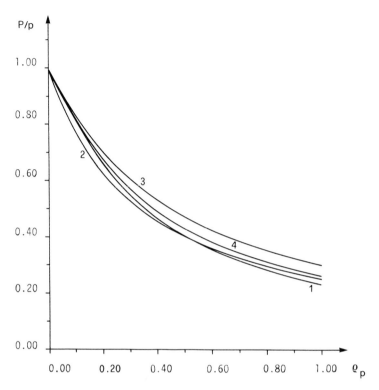

Figure 9.15
Normalized processing power for two-processor systems versus ρ_p, Architectures 1–4.

Table 9.7
Closed form expressions of processing power of two-processor systems

Architecture	Processing power
1	$\dfrac{2(1 + 2\rho_p)}{1 + 4\rho_p + 8\rho_p^2}$
2	$\dfrac{2}{1 + 3\rho_p}$
3	$\dfrac{2(1 + 2\rho_p)}{1 + 4\rho_p + 5\rho_p^2}$
4	$\dfrac{2(1 + 2\rho_p)(1 + \rho_p)}{1 + 5\rho_p + 11\rho_p^2 + 6\rho_p^3}$

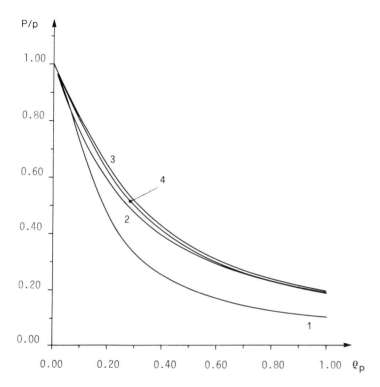

Figure 9.16
Normalized processing power for five-processor systems versus ρ_p, Architectures 1–4.

loads, the average queuing delay is very low, thus making negligible the additional contention introduced by Architecture 1. With Architecture 2, on the other hand, every access to an external common memory area preempts a processor, whose probability of working on its local memory is very high under light load conditions. This same argument explains why Architecture 2 is the only one for which the derivative of P with respect to ρ_p is negative for $\rho_p = 0$. In all other cases we have a null derivative at $\rho_p = 0$. The break-even point between Architectures 1 and 2 is at $\rho_p = 0.5$; for higher loads Architecture 2 becomes advantageous. Low loads should, however, be considered as most significant for comparison purposes because well-designed multiprocessor systems should operate in this region, if the problem decomposition into tasks and task allocation to processors is aimed at reducing communication overhead.

For very low leads we see that the behaviors of Architectures 1, 3, and 4 are very similar. For two-processor systems we can thus conclude that, whenever the bus is not

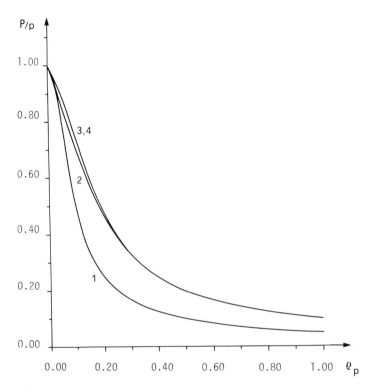

Figure 9.17
Normalized processing power for ten-processor systems versus ρ_p, Architectures 1–4.

the system bottleneck, Architecture 1 is not a bad choice, considering the simplicity of its implementation.

Considering now more complex systems, we present in figure 9.16 the processing efficiency of a five-processor system organized according to the four different architectures; figure 9.17, instead, shows the processing efficiency of a ten-processor system.

The results provided by the two-, five-, and ten-processor systems show some trends that allow us to make general statements about the behavior of the different architectures. The ranking of architectures made for the two-processor case remains valid also in more complex situations. Increasing the number of processors, the performances of Architectures 2, 3, and 4 become very similar to each other, up to the point that differences become negligible in the case of the ten-processor system even for very light loads. Architecture 3 no longer gives a noticeable advantage as it did in

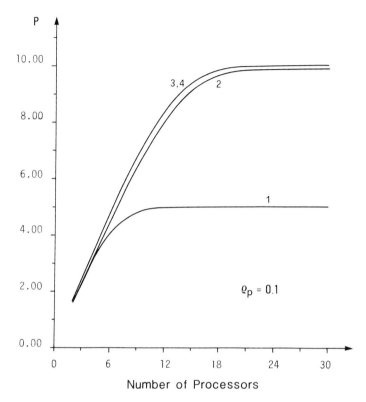

Figure 9.18
Processing power of the four architectures versus number of processors for $\rho_p = 0.1$.

the two-processor case. The similar behavior of Architectures 2, 3, and 4 for heavily loaded large systems can be intuitively explained by the bottleneck effect of the global bus; in these conditions processors are mainly queued for the global bus, so that other contention and blocking phenomena tend to disappear.

A further consideration is that the crossover between Architectures 1 and 2 now takes place for very low loads, and, when the communication load increases, Architecture 1 behaves significantly worse than the others.

In figure 9.18 we have shown the processing power of the four architectures versus the number of processors in the system, for a fixed processor communication load $\rho_p = 0.1$. The same considerations made for figures 9.16 and 9.17 can be drawn from this figure too. It provides strong evidence that Architecture 1 is a bad choice for large systems, and that the performance of Architecture 4 is very close to that of

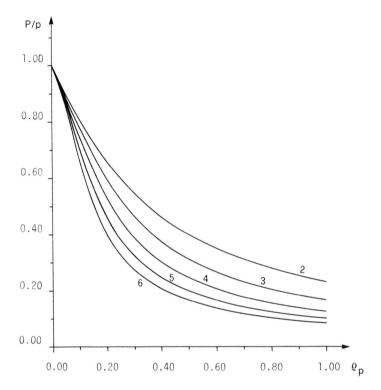

Figure 9.19
Architecture 1; normalized processing power versus ρ_p; number of processors from two to six.

Architecture 3. Note also that this figure shows a crossover between Architectures 1 and 2, for increasing system size.

The behavior of each architecture when the number of components is increased is presented in figures 9.19–9.22 which show, respectively, the normalized processing power of Architectures 1–4 versus ρ_p for varying system size. It can be noted that Architecture 1 shows the largest performance reduction for increasing number of processors and communication load. Moreover, for very low loads Architectures 3 and 4 yield very similar performances, superior to those of the other two architectures. This can be seen by comparing the slopes of the curves for low communication loads. Denormalizing the results for Architecture 1, we observe that high communication loads induce such a contention for the global bus as almost to nullify the advantage expected when adding new processors. The same phenomenon, for higher loads, is observed for the other architectures too. For all architectures these figures show how

Chapter 9   221

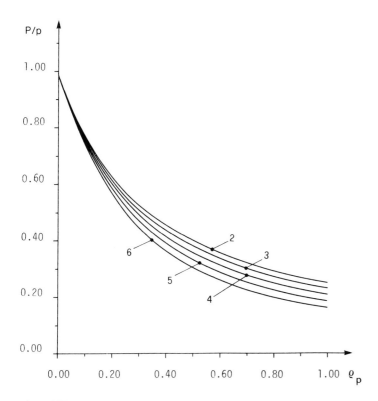

Figure 9.20
Architecture 2; normalized processing power versus ρ_p; number of processors from two to six.

the potential processing power provided by new processors translates into actual processing power only when the communication load is kept low.

These results are obviously biased by the fact that the models discussed here explicitly neglect performance losses due to synchronization among tasks and/or processors. In large multiprocessor systems, our assumption of the processors executing a continuous flow of instructions (that is, the number of tasks being much larger than the number of processors) may not be justified, making these conclusions rather optimistic.

All of the previous results were derived using the assumptions introduced in section 9.1, which allowed us to obtain simple Markovian models of the multiprocessor system behavior. Real systems do not quite possess those characteristics, but it is generally recognized that Markovian queuing models provide robust performance estimates with respect to changes in the hypotheses (see, for example, [BUZE77]).

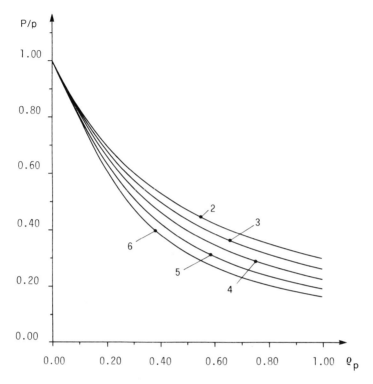

Figure 9.21
Architecture 3; normalized processing power versus ρ_p; number of processors from two to six.

More precise statements can be made about some of the assumptions introduced in section 9.2. The hypothesis of exponentially distributed access times is conservative with respect to all distributions with coefficients of variation smaller than one; in particular, if the message duration is fixed, or can vary only within given limits, the actual performance will be better than predicted by our models. The approximation introduced by the exponential distribution assumptions would be less satisfactory if the real system were characterized by service time distributions with coefficients of variation greater than one; it should be noted that most of the resource allocation schemes implemented in real systems tend to keep this factor low, and hence tend to limit the approximation errors produced by these assumptions. The uniform distribution of load among processors is a conservative assumption too: since a processor cannot interfere with itself, the worst case is obtained when all processors generate messages with the same rate.

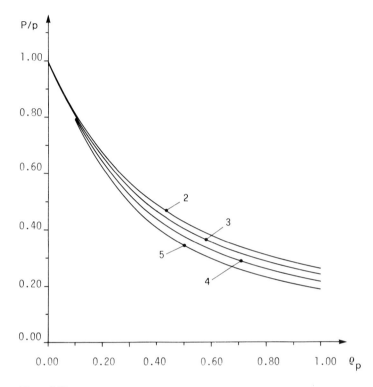

Figure 9.22
Architecture 4; normalized processing power versus ρ_p; number of processors from two to five.

References

[BUZE77] Buzen, J. P., and Potier, D., "Accuracy of the Exponential Assumption in Closed Queuing Models," Proc. 1977 SIGMETRICS/CMG Int. Conf. Computer Performance, Modeling, Measurement, Management, Washington, DC, November 1977.

[CHAN80] Chang, S. S. L., "Multiple-Read Multiple-Write Memory and Its Applications," *IEEE Trans. on Computers* C-29(8) (August 1980), 689–694.

10 Multiple-Bus Multiprocessors with Distributed Common Memory

In the previous chapter we derived models for analyzing the contention for shared resources in several single-bus multiprocessor architectures. In this chapter the analysis is extended to multiple-bus multiprocessor systems. The assumptions used in the derivation of Markovian models of the system behavior are the same as those described in chapter 9.

In some cases the extension to the general multiple-bus case is feasible. In the cases in which this is not possible either we confine the study to the case of two buses or we somewhat simplify the assumptions on multiprocessor operations.

10.1 Architecture 1

The multiprocessor architecture in which common memory modules are connected only to global buses was already analyzed in detail in chapter 8. It will be considered again in this chapter for comparison purposes, and it will be referred to as Architecture 1.

The relation between λ and λ_p in this case is the same as in (9.3).

10.2 Architecture 2a

The second architecture that we consider in this chapter is obtained by distributing the common memory into modules local to each processor in the same way as was done for Architecture 2 in chapter 9. Each processor's local memory is divided into two parts: a private area and a common area. Figure 10.1 shows a two-bus multiprocessor system comprising four identical modules, and represents the smallest system for which the availability of a second global bus is relevant to the performance analysis. Nonlocal segments of common memory can be reached using one of the global buses and the local buses of the destination and the origin processor.

Architecture 2a is a possible extension to the multiple-bus case of Architecture 2 of chapter 9. For this architecture we confine the analysis to the two-bus case. Another possible extension will be called Architecture 2b, and will be considered in the next section.

Processors that gain access to one of the global buses may preempt processors working on their local memory. Preempted processors become blocked. We assume that processors waiting for a global bus and requesting a free common memory module are served according to an FCFS discipline.

In order to compare the performance of this architecture with others, we assume

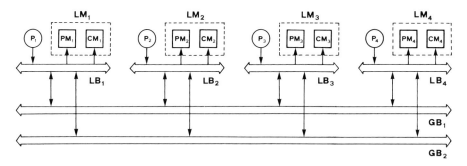

Figure 10.1
Structure of Architecture 2a with four processors composed of CPU (P_i), and of a local memory (LM_i) subdivided into private memory (PM_i) and common memory (CM_i). CPU and local memory are connected by a local bus (LB_i). The interconnection network is composed of two global buses (GB_i).

the workload model already described in section 9.1. The exchange of messages is performed as described in section 9.3; (9.7) thus applies also in this case.

The state definition is identical to the one used for the single-bus case, and is given by the $2p$-tuple [see (9.8)]

$$(m_1, s_1, \ldots, m_p, s_p) \tag{10.1}$$

where m_i is the index of the memory module addressed by processor i and s_i is the state of processor i.

As in previous cases, lumping can be used to reduce the size of the state space of the Markov chain, but the number of states still keeps growing combinatorially with the number of modules. For example, in the case of four processors and two buses, the exact reduced chain comprises 27 states, and its structure is shown in figure 10.2. The complexity of the Markov chain obtained for this simple case suggests that approximate models should be sought for the analysis of larger systems.

In the following, we introduce two approximate models obtained by reducing the information included in the Markov chain state definition, but still assuming a Markovian behavior in the evolution through the state space.

The first approximate model is named Approximation G (where G pretentiously stands for good). In this case the system state is described by the quadruplet

$$(n_a, n_e, n_b, n_o), \tag{10.2}$$

where

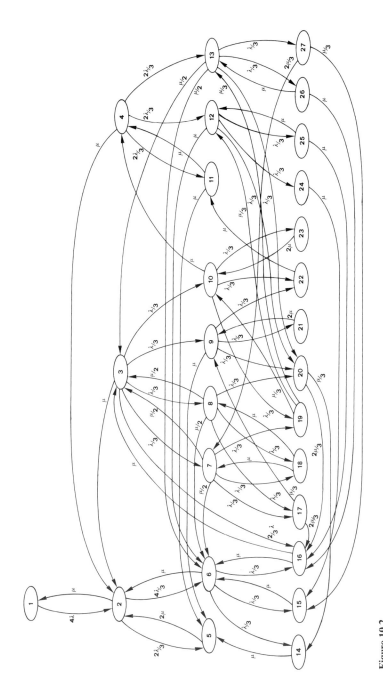

Figure 10.2
State transition rate diagram of the Markov chain model of Architecture 2a with four processors.

n_a is the number of processors accessing a local memory;
n_e is the number of processors accessing an external common memory module;
n_b is the number of blocked processors;
n_o is the number of processors queued for an external resource (that can be either busy or free), whose local bus is being used by some other processor.

Note that $p - (n_a + n_e + n_b + n_o)$ processors, whose local bus is not used by any external processor, are queued for shared resources currently not available.

The evaluation of the transition rates is performed assuming that all the states of the original chain, which are grouped in one state of the approximate chain, have equal steady state probabilities (see section 2.5). This assumption is not met by the exact chain, and an error is thus introduced in the reduction process.

The resulting chain contains $5(p - 2)$ states. Figures 10.3a and 10.3b show the structure of the approximate chain in the general case of p processors, separating the transitions corresponding to a new access request (λ transitions) from those corresponding to the completion of an access (μ transitions). Tables 10.1 and 10.2 give the expressions of the transition rates as functions of the parameter $z = 2/(p - 1)$, and of the state level

$$l = \begin{cases} p - n_a - 1, & p > n_a \\ 0, & p = n_a. \end{cases}$$

In figure 10.4 the approximate Markov chain obtained with Approximation G in the case of four processors is shown. Table 10.3 lists the states in figure 10.2 that correspond to each state in figure 10.4. Note the remarkable simplification with respect to the exact lumped chain in figure 10.2. The number of states is reduced from 27 to 10.

In many cases the level of detail in the representation of the system used in Approximation G and the corresponding accuracy in the estimate of the processing power are not worth the complexity of the model solution. A simpler model comprising a smaller number of states might then be desirable, even if this reduction is paid by a loss in accuracy. This simpler model is named Approximation F (where F pretentiously stands for fast), and it describes the system behavior using a Markov chain whose state is defined by the triplet

$$(n_a, n_e, n_{bo}), \tag{10.3}$$

where

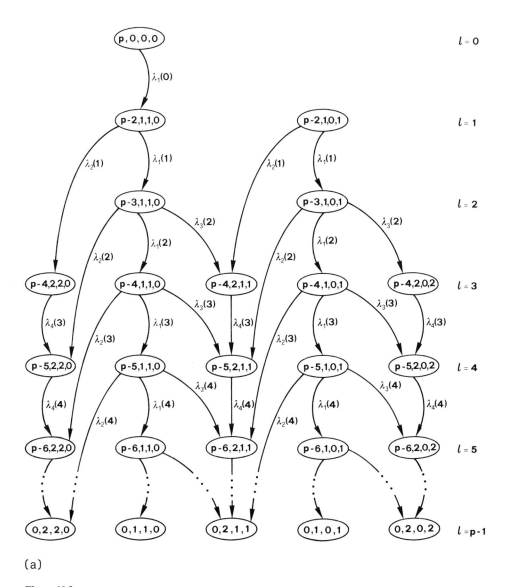

(a)

Figure 10.3
State transition rate diagram of the approximate Markov chain model of Architecture 2a (Approximation G): (a) λ transitions; (b) μ-transitions.

Chapter 10

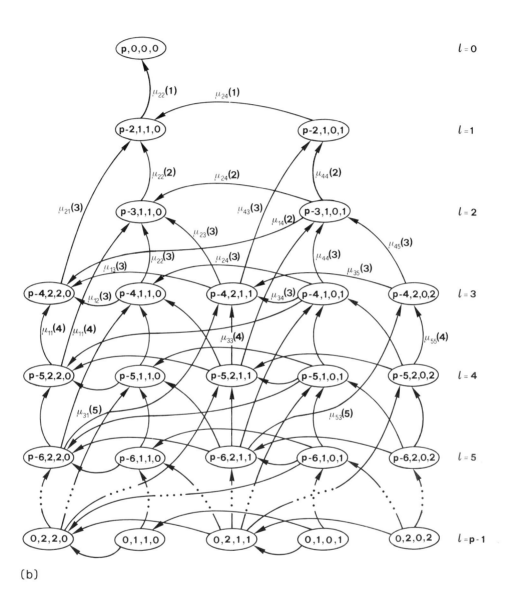

(b)

Figure 10.3 (continued)

Table 10.1
Expressions of the transition rates associated with λ transitions for Architecture 2a, Approximation G

$$\lambda_1(z,l) = \begin{cases} \dfrac{2+z}{z}\lambda & l = 0 \\ (2-lz)\lambda & l \geq 1 \end{cases}$$

$$\lambda_2(z,l) = \begin{cases} \dfrac{(2-lz)[2-(l+1)z]}{2z}\lambda & l \geq 1 \\ 0 & \text{otherwise} \end{cases}$$

$$\lambda_3(z,l) = \begin{cases} \dfrac{(l-1)}{2}(2-lz)\lambda & l \geq 2 \\ 0 & \text{otherwise} \end{cases}$$

$$\lambda_4(z,l) = \begin{cases} \dfrac{2-lz}{z}\lambda & l \geq 3 \\ 0 & \text{otherwise} \end{cases}$$

with $z = \dfrac{2}{p-1}$

Table 10.2
Expressions of the transition rates associated with μ transitions for Architecture 2a, Approximation G

$$\mu_{22}(l) = \begin{cases} \mu & l = 1 \\ 2^{-(l-2)}\mu & l \geq 2 \\ 0 & \text{otherwise} \end{cases}$$

$$\mu_{12}(l) = \begin{cases} \mu - \mu_{22}(l) & l \geq 2 \\ 0 & \text{otherwise} \end{cases}$$

$$\mu_{21}(z,l) = \begin{cases} 2 \cdot z^{l-3}\mu & l \geq 3 \\ 0 & \text{otherwise} \end{cases}$$

$$\mu_{31}(z,l) = \begin{cases} (l-4)z\dfrac{1-z^{l-3}}{1-z} & l \geq 5 \\ 0 & \text{otherwise} \end{cases}$$

$$\mu_{11}(z,l) = \begin{cases} 2\mu - [\mu_{11}(z,l) + \mu_{31}(z,l)] & l \geq 4 \\ 0 & \text{otherwise} \end{cases}$$

$$\mu_{23}(z,l) = \begin{cases} z^{l-2}\mu & l \geq 3 \\ 0 & \text{otherwise} \end{cases}$$

$$\mu_{13}(z,l) = \begin{cases} \dfrac{2-(l-1)z}{2}\dfrac{1-z^{l-2}}{1-z}\mu & l \geq 3 \\ 0 & \text{otherwise} \end{cases}$$

Table 10.2 (continued)

$$\mu_{43}(z,l) = \begin{cases} z^{l-3}\mu & l \geq 3 \\ 0 & \text{otherwise} \end{cases}$$

$$\mu_{53}(z,l) = \begin{cases} (l-4)\dfrac{z}{2}\dfrac{1-z^{l-3}}{1-z}\mu & l \geq 5 \\ 0 & \text{otherwise} \end{cases}$$

$$\mu_{33}(z,l) = \begin{cases} 2\mu - [\mu_{23}(z,l) + \mu_{13}(z,l) + \mu_{43}(z,l) + \mu_{53}(z,l)] & l \geq 4 \\ 0 & \text{otherwise} \end{cases}$$

$$\mu_{44}(z,l) = \begin{cases} \dfrac{(l-1)2^{-(l-1)}}{l}(1+z)\mu & l \geq 2 \\ 0 & \text{otherwise} \end{cases}$$

$$\mu_{34}(z,l) = \begin{cases} \dfrac{1-2^{-(l-1)}}{2l}[(2l-3)z + 2(l-2)]\mu & l \geq 3 \\ 0 & \text{otherwise} \end{cases}$$

$$\mu_{14}(z,l) = \begin{cases} \dfrac{1-2^{-(l-1)}}{l}(2-lz)\mu & l \geq 2 \\ 0 & \text{otherwise} \end{cases}$$

$$\mu_{24}(z,l) = \begin{cases} \mu - [\mu_{44}(z,l) + \mu_{34}(z,l) + \mu_{14}(z,l)] & l \geq 1 \\ 0 & \text{otherwise} \end{cases}$$

$$\mu_{45}(z,l) = \begin{cases} 2z^{l-2}\mu & l \geq 3,\, p \geq 6 \\ 0 & \text{otherwise} \end{cases}$$

$$\mu_{35}(z,l) = \begin{cases} 2(1-z)\mu & l=3,\, p \geq 6 \\ \dfrac{1}{2(l-1)(l-2)(1-z)^3}\{(4l^2 - 12l + 8) \\ \quad - (4l^3 - 16l^2 + 28l - 24)z \\ \quad + (l^4 + 4l^3 - 55l^2 + 164l - 174)z^2 \\ \quad - (4l^4 - 18l^3 - 18l^2 - 202l - 318)z^3 \\ \quad + (6l^4 - 40l^3 + 68l^2 + 64l - 262)z^4 \\ \quad - (4l^4 - 30l^3 + 74l^2 - 34l - 98)z^5 \\ \quad + (l^4 - 8l^3 + 23l^2 - 20l - 12)z^6 \\ \quad - (4l^2 - 18l + 26)z^{l-2} + (2l^3 - 4l^2 - 24l + 86)z^{l-1} \\ \quad - (4l^3 - 20l^2 + 2l + 122)z^l \\ \quad + (2l^3 - 20l^2 + 36l + 66)z^{l+1} \\ \quad + (4l^2 - 4l - 24)z^{l+2}\}\mu & l \geq 4,\, p \geq 6 \\ 0 & \text{otherwise} \end{cases}$$

$$\mu_{55}(z,l) = \begin{cases} 2\mu - [\mu_{45}(z,l) + \mu_{35}(z,l)] & l \geq 4,\, p \geq 6 \\ 0 & \text{otherwise} \end{cases}$$

with $z = \dfrac{2}{p-1}$

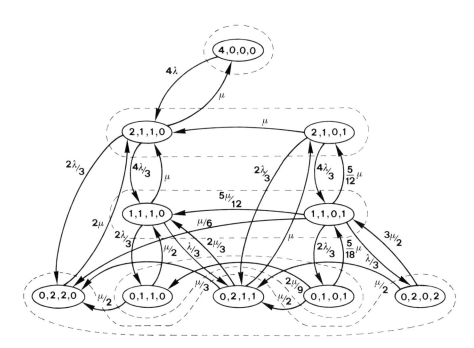

Figure 10.4
State transition rate diagram of the approximate Markov chain model of Architecture 2a with four processors (Approximation G).

Table 10.3
Correspondence between the states of the Markov chain in figure 10.4 and those of the Markov chain in figure 10.2

States of the MC in figure 10.4	States of the MC in figure 10.2
4, 0, 0, 0	1
2, 1, 1, 0	2
2, 1, 0, 1	3, 4
1, 1, 1, 0	6
1, 1, 0, 1	7, 8, 9, 10, 12, 13
0, 2, 2, 0	5
0, 1, 1, 0	14, 15
0, 2, 1, 1	16
0, 1, 0, 1	17, 19, 20, 22, 24, 27
0, 2, 0, 2	11, 18, 21, 23, 25, 26

n_a is the number of processors accessing a local memory;
n_e is the number of processors accessing an external common memory module;
n_{bo} is the number of processors whose local bus is being used by some external processor (n_{bo} is the sum of n_b and n_o in Approximation G).

In this case all states defined by Approximation G, whose elements n_a and n_e are equal and in which the sum $n_b + n_o$ is constant, are merged. The transition rates are evaluated from those of Approximation G, assuming that the merged states have equal steady state probabilities. The resulting approximate chain contains $2(p - 1) - 1$ states.

Figures 10.5a and 10.5b show the structure of the reduced chain yielded by Approximation F in the general case of p processors. Table 10.4 gives the expression of the transition rates as a function of the parameters z and l.

In figure 10.6 the approximate Markov chain obtained with Approximation F in the case of four processors and two buses is shown. Each state in figure 10.6 corresponds to one of the encased sets of states in figure 10.4. The state space now comprises only five states; a remarkable improvement in the solution complexity is thus obtained. This improvement may be vital for the analysis of large systems whose study is not feasible using the exact Markovian model.

10.3   Architecture 2b

An improvement in performance with respect to Architecture 2a can be obtained if we avoid the states in which a processor (say processor i) is prevented from reaching an external common memory module only by an external processor using the local bus of processor i. Architecture 2b is an extension of Architecture 2 in chapter 9 that allows this performance improvement. Figure 10.7 shows a multiprocessor system comprising three modules and two buses and again represents the smallest significative configuration with two buses. Note that Architecture 2b does not yield any improvement over Architecture 2a in the single-global bus case. In fact, if only one global bus is available, this architecture behaves exactly like Architecture 2 in chapter 9. In this case a processor does not need its own local bus to reach an external common memory module: it is connected to its local bus and to the global buses through separate interfaces. A processor reaches an external common memory module using a global bus and the local bus of the destination processor. The local common memory module is, instead, reached using the local bus.

An arbitration mechanism is needed for local and global buses. We assume that

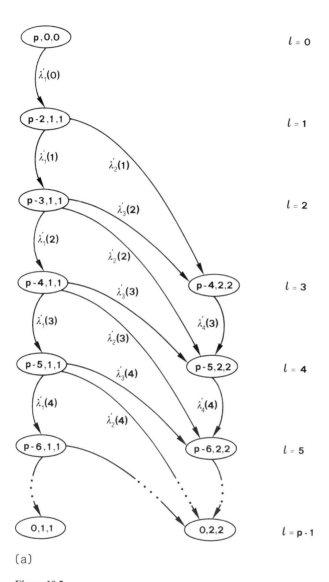

(a)

Figure 10.5
State transition rate diagram of the approximate Markov chain model of Architecture 2a (Approximation F): (a) λ transitions; (b) μ transitions.

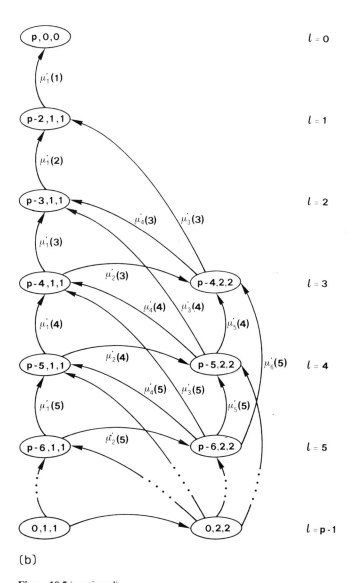

(b)

Figure 10.5 (continued)

Table 10.4
Expressions of the transition rates associated with λ transitions and μ transitions for Architecture 2a, Approximation F

$$\lambda'_1(z,l) = \begin{cases} \dfrac{2+z}{z}\lambda & l=0 \\ (2-lz)\lambda & l \geq 1 \end{cases}$$

$$\lambda'_2(z,l) = \begin{cases} \dfrac{(2-lz)[2-(l+1)z]}{2z}\lambda & l \geq 1 \\ 0 & \text{otherwise} \end{cases}$$

$$\lambda'_3(z,l) = \begin{cases} \dfrac{(l-1)}{2}(2-lz)\lambda + \dfrac{1-2^{-(l-1)}}{2l}(2-lz)\cdot\mu & l \geq 2 \\ 0 & \text{otherwise} \end{cases}$$

$$\lambda'_4(z,l) = \begin{cases} \dfrac{2-lz}{z}\lambda & l \geq 3 \\ 0 & \text{otherwise} \end{cases}$$

$$\mu'_1(z,l) = \begin{cases} \dfrac{2^{-l}}{l}[(3l-1)+(l-1)z]\mu & l \geq 2 \\ \dfrac{\mu}{2} & l = 1 \\ 0 & \text{otherwise} \end{cases}$$

$$\mu'_2(z,l) = \begin{cases} \left\{[1-2^{-(l-1)}]\dfrac{(3l-2)}{2l} - \dfrac{1}{2} + [1-2^{-(l-1)}] \right. \\ \left. \cdot\dfrac{(2l-3)}{4l}z\right\}\mu & l \geq 3 \\ 0 & \text{otherwise} \end{cases}$$

$$\mu'_3(z,l) = \begin{cases} z^{l-3}\mu & l \geq 3 \\ 0 & \text{otherwise} \end{cases}$$

$$\mu'_4(z,l) = \begin{cases} z^{l-2}\mu & l \geq 3, p \geq 6 \\ 0 & \text{otherwise} \end{cases}$$

Table 10.4 (continued)

$$\mu'_5(z,l) = \begin{cases} 2\mu - \dfrac{1}{6(l-1)(l-2)(1-z)^3}\{(6l^2 - 18l + 12) \\ \qquad - (2l^3 + 5l^2 - 21l + 6)z \\ \qquad + (l^4 - 19l^2 + 84l - 126)z^2 \\ \qquad - (4l^4 - 20l^3 - l^2 + 165l - 296)z^3 \\ \qquad + (6l^4 - 40l^3 + 68l^2 + 64l - 262)z^4 \\ \qquad - (4l^4 - 30l^3 + 74l^2 - 34l - 98)z^5 \\ \qquad + (l^4 - 8l^3 - 23l^2 - 20l - 12)z^6 \\ \qquad + (6l^2 - 18l + 12)z^{l-3} - (3l^3 - 3l^2 - 18l + 70)z^{l-2} \\ \qquad + (9l^3 - 46l^2 + 53l + 124)z^{l-1} \\ \qquad - (9l^3 - 59l^2 + 84l + 114)z^l \\ \qquad + (3l^3 - 30l^2 + 59l + 52)z^{l+1} \\ \qquad + (4l^2 - 4l - 24)z^{l+2}\}\mu & l \geq 4,\ p \geq 6 \\ 0 & \text{otherwise} \end{cases}$$

$$\mu'_6(z,l) = \begin{cases} (l-4)\dfrac{z}{2}\dfrac{1-z^{l-3}}{1-z}\mu & l \geq 5 \\ 0 & \text{otherwise} \end{cases}$$

with $z = \dfrac{2}{p-1}$

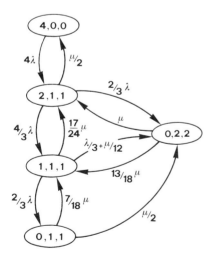

Figure 10.6
State transition rate diagram of the approximate Markov chain model of Architecture 2a with four processors (Approximation F).

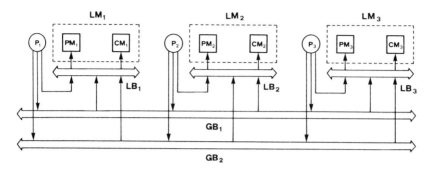

Figure 10.7
Structure of Architecture 2b with three processors composed of CPU (P_i), and of a local memory (LM_i) subdivided into private memory (PM_i) and common memory (CM_i). CPU and local memory are connected by a local bus (LB_i). The interconnection network is composed of two global buses (GB_i).

requests coming from the global bus can preempt local accesses. Processors may thus be blocked. An FCFS policy is assumed for processors queued for a global bus.

The system level workload is the same as described in the case of Architecture 2 in chapter 9, so that (9.7) applies. Also in this case we confine the analysis to two-bus systems.

The exact Markovian description is again based upon the state definition (10.1). The state transition rate diagram of the exact chain in the case of four processors is shown in figure 10.8.

Approximate models can be derived using the same technique described in the case of Architecture 2a.

Approximation G is now somewhat simpler than in the previous case, since we have eliminated the case of processors queued for an external common memory, whose local bus is currently busy. The state is thus described by the triplet

$$(n_a, n_e, n_b), \tag{10.4}$$

where

n_a is the number of processors accessing a local memory;
n_e is the number of processors accessing an external common memory module;
n_b is the number of blocked processors.

Note that $p - (n_a + n_e + n_b)$ processors are queued for either a global bus or a common memory currently not available.

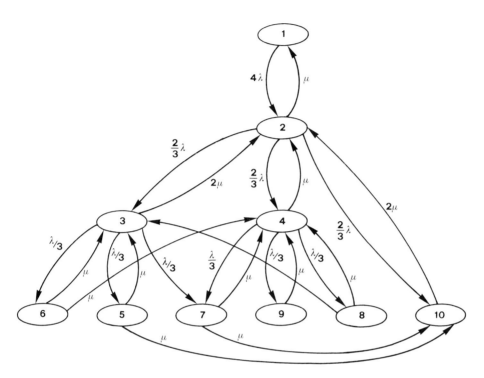

Figure 10.8
State transition rate diagram of the Markov chain model of Architecture 2b with four processors.

The transition rates of the approximate Markov chain are evaluated using the technique described in the previous section. The approximate chain contains $4(p-1)-2$ states. Figures 10.9a and 10.9b show the structure of the approximate chain in the general case of p processors separating the transitions corresponding to a new access request (λ transitions) from those corresponding to the completion of an access (μ transitions). Tables 10.5 and 10.6 give the expressions of the transition rates of the approximate model as functions of $z = 1/(p-1)$ and l.

In the case of four processors and two buses the approximate chain contains only seven states, and is shown in figure 10.10. In the case of three processors the reduction step yields the exact result, which can easily be written in closed form:

$$P = \frac{12(1-\rho^2)}{(2+3\rho)^2}. \tag{10.5}$$

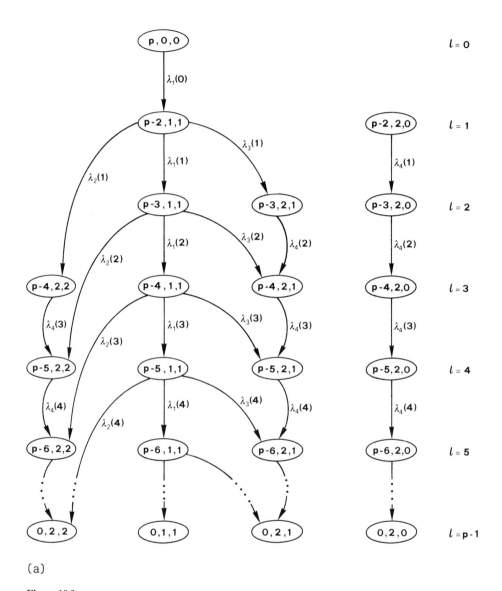

Figure 10.9
State transition rate diagram of the approximate Markov chain model of Architecture 2b (Approximation G): (a) λ transitions; (b) μ transitions.

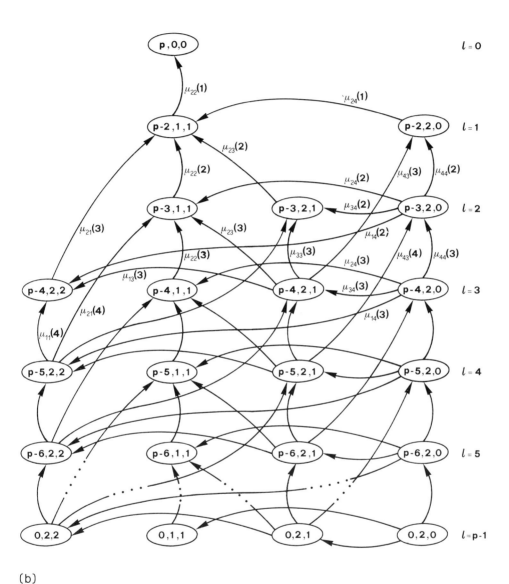

(b)

Figure 10.9 (continued)

Table 10.5
Expressions of the transition rates associated with λ transitions for Architecture 2b, Approximation G

$$\lambda_1(z,l) = \begin{cases} \dfrac{1+z}{z}\lambda & l = 0 \\ (1-lz)\lambda & l \geq 1 \end{cases}$$

$$\lambda_2(z,l) = \begin{cases} \dfrac{(1-lz)(1-(l+1)z)}{z}\lambda & l \geq 1 \\ 0 & \text{otherwise} \end{cases}$$

$$\lambda_3(z,l) = \begin{cases} l(1-lz)\lambda & l \geq 1 \\ 0 & \text{otherwise} \end{cases}$$

$$\lambda_4(z,l) = \begin{cases} \dfrac{1-lz}{z}\lambda & l \geq 1 \\ 0 & \text{otherwise} \end{cases}$$

with $z = \dfrac{1}{p-1}$

Table 10.6
Expressions of the transition rates associated with μ transitions for Architecture 2b, Approximation G

$$\mu_{21}(z,l) = \begin{cases} 2z^{l-3}\mu & l \geq 3 \\ 0 & \text{otherwise} \end{cases}$$

$$\mu_{31}(z,l) = \begin{cases} 2(l-3)z\dfrac{1-z^{l-3}}{1-z}\mu & l \geq 4 \\ 0 & \text{otherwise} \end{cases}$$

$$\mu_{11}(z,l) = \begin{cases} 2\mu - [\mu_{21}(z,l) + \mu_{31}(z,l)] & l \geq 4 \\ 0 & \text{otherwise} \end{cases}$$

$$\mu_{22}(z,l) = \begin{cases} \mu & l \geq 1 \\ 0 & \text{otherwise} \end{cases}$$

$$\lambda_{23}(z,l) = \begin{cases} \dfrac{l}{(l-1)}z^{l-2}\mu & l \geq 2 \\ 0 & \text{otherwise} \end{cases}$$

Table 10.6 (continued)

$$\mu_{13}(z,l) = \begin{cases} \dfrac{1}{(l-1)(1-z)^2}\{l-(l^2+l-3)z+(2l^2-4l+1)z^2 \\ \quad +(l-1)(l-2)z^3-lz^{l-2}+(l+1)(l-1)z^{l-1} \\ \quad +(l-1)z^l\}\mu & l \geq 3 \\ 0 & \text{otherwise} \end{cases}$$

$$\mu_{43}(z,l) = \begin{cases} \dfrac{z}{(l-1)(1-z)^2}\{(l^2-5l+8)-(l-1)(l-2)z \\ \quad +(l-2)z^2-2z^{l-2}+(l-2)z^{l-1}\}\mu & l \geq 3 \\ 0 & \text{otherwise} \end{cases}$$

$$\mu_{33}(z,l) = \begin{cases} 2\mu - [\mu_{23}(z,l)+\mu_{13}(z,l)+\mu_{43}(z,l)] & l \geq 3 \\ 0 & \text{otherwise} \end{cases}$$

$$\mu_{24}(z,l) = \begin{cases} \dfrac{2l}{(l^2-l+1)}z^{l-1}\mu & l \geq 1 \\ 0 & \text{otherwise} \end{cases}$$

$$\mu_{14}(z,l) = \begin{cases} \dfrac{2l}{(l^2-l+1)}(1-lz)\dfrac{1-z^{l-1}}{1-z}\mu & l \geq 2 \\ 0 & \text{otherwise} \end{cases}$$

$$\mu_{34}(z,l) = \begin{cases} \dfrac{1}{(l^2-l+1)(1-z)^2}\{2(l-1)^2-2(l^3-3l^2+5l-3)z \\ \quad +2(l^3-2l^2+4l-4)z^2-2(l^2-2)z^3 \\ \quad +2(l-1)z^{l-1}-2(2l^2-2l-1)z^l \\ \quad +2(l^2-2)z^{l+1}\}\mu & l \geq 2,\ p \geq 6 \\ 0 & \text{otherwise} \end{cases}$$

$$\mu_{44}(z,l) = \begin{cases} 2\mu - [\mu_{24}(z,l)+\mu_{34}(z,l)+\mu_{14}(z,l)] & l \geq 2 \\ 0 & \text{otherwise} \end{cases}$$

with $z = \dfrac{1}{p-1}$

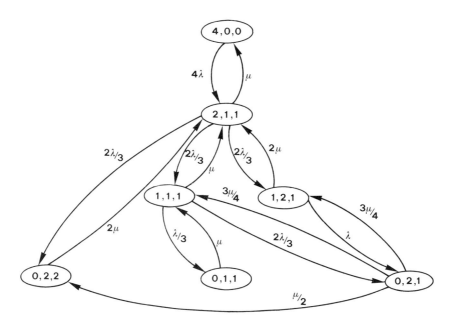

Figure 10.10
State transition rate diagram of the approximate Markov chain model of Architecture 2b with four processors (Approximation G).

10.4 Architecture 3

Architecture 3 requires the availability of multiple-port memories supporting several simultaneous accesses, which are used to implement the common parts of the processors' local memories. Common memory areas are thus directly accessible from the global buses. The structure of a multiprocessor system comprising three modules and two buses is shown in figure 10.11. In this case the only sources of contention are the global buses.

The system level workload considered in this case is the same as that described in the case of Architecture 3 in the previous chapter; thus once more (9.7) applies.

This architecture can be analyzed for any number of buses using a finite population queuing model. Using standard notation the multiprocessor system can be modeled by an $M/M/b/p/p$ queue. This model is the same as the one that was used to obtain an upper bound to the processing power in the case of Architecture 1 with multiple buses in section 8.4.1.

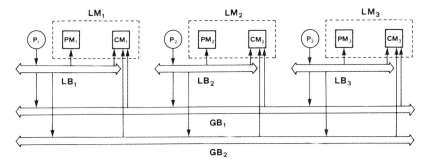

Figure 10.11
Structure of Architecture 3 with three processors composed of CPU (P_i), and of a local memory (LM_i) subdivided into private memory (PM_i) and common memory (CM_i). CPU and local memory are connected by a local bus (LB_i). The interconnection network is composed of two global buses (GB_i).

The processing power P for this architecture can be put in closed form, obtaining

$$P = \frac{1-\rho}{1+\rho}\left\{p - (p-b)\pi_b\left[\frac{p-b-(b/\rho)}{(b/\rho)E_{1,p-b-1}(b/\rho)} + 1\right]\right\}, \tag{10.6}$$

where $E_{1,p-b-1}(b/\rho)$ is the Erlang function of the first type of order $p - b - 1$, with argument b/ρ, given by (8.20), and

$$\pi_b = \frac{[p!/(b!b^{k-b})]\rho^p}{\left\{(1+\rho)^p + \sum_{j=b}^{p}\binom{p}{j}\left[\frac{b^{b-j}j!}{b!} - 1\right]\rho^j\right\}}. \tag{10.7}$$

Note that (10.6) is very similar to (8.19), the only difference being the factor $(1 - \rho)$, which stems from the fact that, as in (9.13), the processing power is reduced to account for the time needed to transfer a message within the local memory between processor and task input port (see figure 5.8).

10.5 Architecture 4

As in the single-bus case, Architecture 4 is similar to Architecture 3, the only difference being that the common parts of the processors' local memories cannot support several simultaneous accesses. Common memory areas are thus accessible through a local bus. The structure of a multiprocessor system comprising three processors and two buses is shown in figure 10.12.

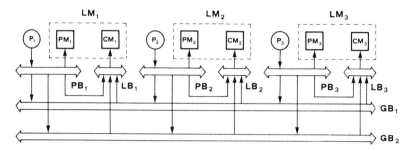

Figure 10.12
Structure of Architecture 4 with three processors composed of CPU (P_i), and of a local memory (LM_i) subdivided into private memory (PM_i) and common memory (CM_i). CPU and local memory are connected by a local bus (LB_i). The interconnection network is composed of two global buses (GB_i).

The system level workload considered in this case is the same as that described in the case of Architecture 4 in the previous chapter; thus (9.3) applies.

The direct analysis of the behavior of Architecture 4 in the case of multiple buses with either Markov chains or GSPN models appears to be rather complex. However, if we simplify the assumptions on the multiprocessor operations, an explicit representation of the contention for shared resources using a queuing network model is possible. The changes that must be introduced in the modeling assumptions for this purpose are the following:

1. When processors issue access requests, if a bus is free, it is seized, regardless of whether the referenced memory module is accessible; if necessary, processors wait in queue for the destination memory module to become available without releasing the global bus.
2. No preemption of external accesses over local accesses is allowed.

These new modeling assumptions represent a multiprocessor system whose behavior is substantially different from that described in the previous sections. The impact that these modifications have on the overall system performance will be discussed when presenting numerical results. Figure 10.13 depicts a queuing network model of Architecture 4 under the new assumptions, and in which queuing may occur at the global bus and at the common memory modules. Processors are represented as delay elements. Common memory access requests can be viewed as customers requiring service from the common memory modules. Upon completion of their service, access requests return to their corresponding processor stations, where they are delayed before repeating

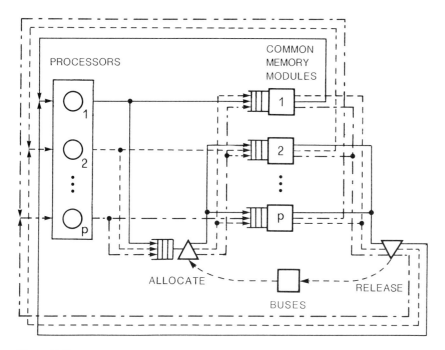

Figure 10.13
Queuing network representation of Architecture 4.

the memory access cycle. This delay represents processor activity between subsequent access requests (CPU burst).

The queuing network in figure 10.13 is a model with passive resources (the global buses), as described in chapter 3. Approximate solution of these models can be obtained by using the decomposition and equivalence techniques that were outlined in section 3.8.

Let us identify the common memory modules as a single-common memory subsystem loaded by processors with memory access requests. At any point in time up to p access requests can be queued or receive service from the memory subsystem, but only b of them can be external requests (if b buses are available). An aggregated model such as that in figure 10.14 can be obtained by replacing the memory subsystem with an equivalent station whose service characteristics are computed using a set of controlled experiments.

A further simplification can be obtained when the identity of the access requests (issuing processor identifier) is removed and a set of requests belonging to two different

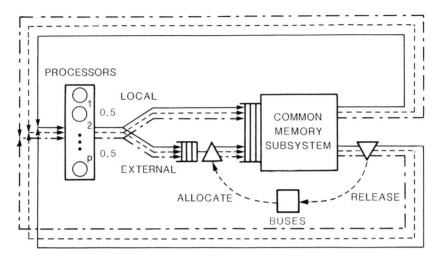

Figure 10.14
Flow equivalent representation of the memory subsystem.

classes (the class of local requests and the class of external requests) is assumed to load the common memory subsystem. This abstract view of the multiprocessor system can be used to represent multiprocessors comprising an arbitrary, but finite, number b of buses. The resulting model is that in figure 10.15.

The success of this aggregation technique relies on the possibility of replacing the common memory subsystem with a memory flow equivalent station so that the behavior of the processors is left unchanged by such a substitution. The functional characteristics of the equivalent service station are obtained by computing the response time of the memory subsystem to access requests of the two classes, assuming the memory subsystem itself to be kept under a fixed load. As mentioned in chapter 3, this technique is known to be exact when the original model is of the product form type, while providing approximate results in the other cases [CHAN75]. The controlled experiments for the computation of the parameters of the equivalent memory station are performed on a model that can be obtained from the original queuing network (figure 10.13) by short-circuiting the processor and bus servers, and by assuming that fixed mixes of memory access requests are continuously asking for service from the memory modules. Figure 10.16 depicts the multiclass network used to perform the controlled experiments in the general case of a p processor system. Each class in this model is a closed path throughout the network that can be used by one customer. A class is said to be *alive* if the customer of that class is present in the model, and it is

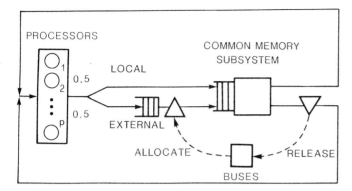

Figure 10.15
Aggregate representation of the queuing network in figure 10.13.

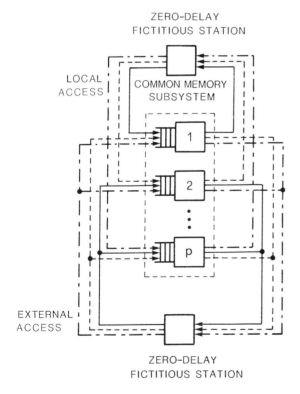

Figure 10.16
Model for the computation of the parameters of the equivalent station.

said to be *dead* otherwise. The first p classes represent local common memory requests. A fictitious station (with zero mean service time) is added to the model to accumulate the global throughput of local requests provided by the memory subsystem. Local requests do not interfere with each other, since they visit different memory modules. The other p classes represent the external common memory requests. Each one of these last classes visits $p - 1$ memory modules. The global behavior of the external access requests is collected, adding another fictitious station with zero mean service time (see figure 10.16).

A request mix is characterized by having n classes ($n = 1, 2, \ldots, p$) simultaneously alive. The symmetry of the system allows the identification of a request mix with any distribution of n requests over the $2p$ different classes with the constraints that classes i and $p + i$ ($i = 1, 2, \ldots, p$) cannot be simultaneously alive (a processor issues either a local request or an external request), and that the number of external classes simultaneously alive cannot exceed the number of available buses b. Let n_l and n_e represent the number of local and external classes that are alive in a given request mix. A request mix is identified by the pair (n_l, n_e). Two request mixes are considered different when the corresponding pairs are different.

Let $X_l(n_l, n_e)$ represent the throughput of the first fictitious station when the memory subsystem is loaded with the (n_l, n_e) request mix; similarly, let $X_e(n_l, n_e)$ represent the throughput of the second fictitious station under the same subsystem load. These two quantities represent the rates of local and external requests satisfied by the memory subsystem under given loads. Their reciprocals can be interpreted as mean response times. The behavior of the memory subsystem (the service function of the equivalent memory station) is represented by the set of mean response times obtained by loading the memory subsystem with all the possible request mixes.

The computation of the service function of the memory equivalent station is completed assuming that the memory subsystem responds with a rate of service $X(n_l, b)$ every time it is actually loaded with a request mix (n_l, n_e) such that $n_e > b$. When the bus interconnection network is made up of p buses, and thus behaves as a crossbar switch, the original model is a product form network and the aggregation process is exact. When the number of buses (b) is smaller than the number of processors (p), the aggregation process leads to an approximate queuing network model of the multiprocessor system that in general does not satisfy the conditions for a product form solution [BALB83], but that can nevertheless be solved with an efficient technique proposed by Herzog [HERZ75]. The accuracy of the approximation degenerates with the decreasing number of buses and has a worst case represented by the single-global bus interconnection structure.

The results of this approximate analysis of the multiple bus model shown in figure 10.15 have been successfully validated with a detailed simulation of the original system model. Tables 10.7 and 10.8 present the validation results in which simulation interval estimates are obtained using the regenerative method ([IGLE78, LAVE78]) with 95% confidence interval and 5% width. The approximation of the analytical results is, in the cases we have considered, very good, so that they are covered by the confidence intervals provided by the simulation. In the analysis of a three-processor system and single global bus, exact results can be used to check the behavior of the approximation method in worst-case conditions. The very good agreement found between the results obtained with the two techniques suggests the possibility of using this fast aggregation method in the analysis of larger-size multiple-bus systems.

10.6 Numerical Results

In this section we present numerical values of two-bus multiprocessor system processing power obtained using the models presented in this chapter and, in some cases, compare them with simulation results. Simulation results are given with their associated 99% confidence interval.

Before comparing the performances of the four architectures, we discuss the accuracy of the approximate models developed for Architectures 2a and 2b.

Figure 10.17 presents processing power results in the case of Architecture 2a, for different values of the load factor ρ, as a function of the number of processors. Simulation results are compared with the approximate results yielded by Approximations F and G. A numerical comparison with the exact results is given in table 10.9, in the case of four processors. Approximation G shows a very good accuracy, and provides very slightly pessimistic estimates in the case of high loads and large systems, when the processing power curve has reached saturation. In the four-processor case, results from table 10.9 indicate that Approximation G provides an almost exact estimate. Approximation F is, instead, less accurate, particularly in the case of medium loads. In fact, it can be viewed as a sort of first-order approximation to the multiprocessor system's processing power.

Figure 10.18 shows processing power results in the case of Architecture 2b, for different values of the load factor ρ, as a function of the number of processors in the system. Results obtained with Approximation G are compared with simulation results. A numerical comparison with the exact results is given in table 10.10, where the four-processor case is considered. Again Approximation G shows a very good accuracy

Table 10.7
Processing power of a three processor system in the case of Architecture 4, for 1, 2, and 3 buses (comparison of the approximate analytical results against the interval estimates obtained with simulation; in the case of 1 bus the exact solution obtained with the GSPN models of chapter 9 is also presented)

	Processing power									
	1 bus				2 buses			3 buses		
			Simulation			Simulation			Simulation	
$\rho = \lambda/\mu$	GSPN	QN	Low	Up	QN	Low	Up	QN	Low	Up
0.05	2.850	2.850	2.70	2.99	2.853	2.71	2.99	2.853	2.70	2.99
0.1	2.704	2.701	2.56	2.83	2.713	2.58	2.85	2.713	2.57	2.84
0.2	2.427	2.419	2.29	2.53	2.455	2.34	2.58	2.456	2.38	2.58
0.3	2.189	2.167	2.05	2.26	2.228	2.13	2.35	2.230	2.12	2.34
0.4	1.963	1.948	1.85	2.04	2.030	1.94	2.14	2.033	1.93	2.13
0.5	1.776	1.759	1.73	1.91	1.859	1.78	1.96	1.862	1.78	1.96
0.6	1.616	1.598	1.57	1.73	1.709	1.61	1.77	1.714	1.63	1.80
0.8	1.358	1.340	1.28	1.41	1.466	1.38	1.52	1.473	1.39	1.53
1.0	1.163	1.147	1.11	1.22	1.278	1.21	1.33	1.286	1.21	1.33

Table 10.8
Processing power of a four-processor system in the case of Architecture 4, for 1, 2, and 3 buses (comparison of the approximate analytical results against the interval estimates obtained with simulation)

	Processing power											
	1 bus			2 buses			3 buses			4 buses		
		Simulation			Simulation			Simulation			Simulation	
$\rho = \lambda/\mu$	QN	Low	Up	QN	Low	Up	QN	Low	Up	QN	Low	Up
0.05	3.797	3.61	3.99	3.803	3.62	3.99	3.803	3.62	3.99	3.803	3.62	3.99
0.1	3.592	3.42	3.78	3.615	3.44	3.80	3.615	3.43	3.79	3.615	3.44	3.80
0.2	3.199	3.03	3.34	3.266	3.10	3.41	3.269	3.13	3.46	3.269	3.13	3.46
0.3	2.846	2.71	2.99	2.957	2.80	3.09	2.963	2.82	3.11	2.963	2.79	3.08
0.4	2.542	2.39	2.64	2.686	2.45	2.70	2.698	2.58	2.84	2.698	2.58	2.84
0.5	2.283	2.14	2.36	2.451	2.34	2.59	2.467	2.40	2.66	2.467	2.38	2.61
0.6	2.065	1.97	2.17	2.247	2.10	2.31	2.267	2.16	2.38	2.267	2.15	2.37
0.8	1.723	1.62	1.79	1.915	1.82	2.01	1.941	1.82	2.01	1.943	1.90	2.10
1.0	1.472	1.36	1.50	1.660	1.60	1.77	1.691	1.64	1.81	1.692	1.64	1.81

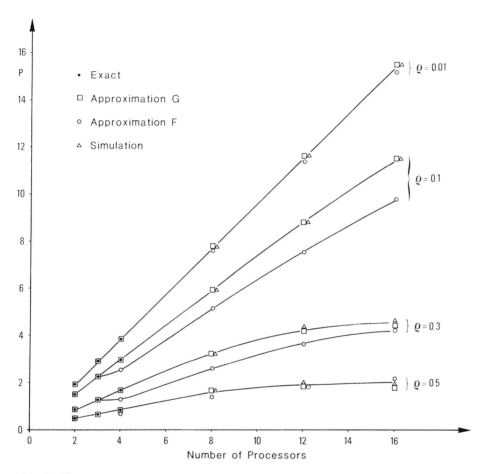

Figure 10.17
Processing power of Architecture 2a multiprocessor systems versus the number of processors, for different loads.

Table 10.9
Comparison of exact, approximate, and simulation results in the case of Architecture 2a with four processors, for varying load factors

$\varrho = \lambda/\mu$	Processing power			Simulation (99% confidence interval)
	Exact	App. G	App. F	
0.01	3.882	3.882	3.807	3.881 ± 0.049
0.1	2.971	2.971	2.568	2.982 ± 0.033
0.3	1.660	1.661	1.283	1.672 ± 0.028
0.5	0.908	0.910	0.683	0.918 ± 0.017
0.7	0.438	0.440	0.329	0.442 ± 0.007

and the estimate is slightly pessimistic for large systems and high loads. In the case of four processors the results of Approximation G are almost exact.

A comparison of the processing power provided by the architectures considered in this chapter in the case of two buses is shown in figure 10.19 for a fixed load $\rho_p = 1.0$, as a function of the number of processors in the system. As expected, Architecture 3 provides better processing power results than Architecture 2b, which in turn is superior to Architecture 2a. In the case of large systems, however, once the saturation has been reached, the differences tend to disappear, since the two global buses become the system bottleneck. Already in the case of twelve processors, with the load considered, differences are negligible. The bounds on the processing power of Architecture 1 show that in the case of large- or even medium-size systems, the performance yielded by this architecture is much worse than with the three other alternatives considered in this book. This same conclusion was also reached in the previous chapter in the single-bus case.

A separate comment is necessary for Architecture 4. Intuitive arguments based on the system structure suggest that (similarly to what happens in the single bus case) the processing power curve for this architecture lies between those of Architectures 3 and 2b. While this is true if the assumptions on the bus management policy are the same for the three architectures, the intersection between the processing power curves of Architectures 2b and 4 observed in figure 10.19 is due to the degradation of the overall system performance induced by the modifications in the assumptions on the bus management policy introduced to obtain a tractable queuing network model of Architecture 4.

A comparison of the processing power results in the cases of one and two buses

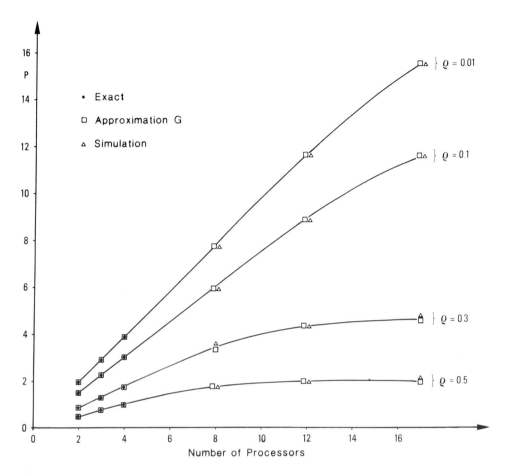

Figure 10.18
Processing power of Architecture 2b multiprocessor systems versus the number of processors, for different loads.

Table 10.10
Comparison of exact, approximate, and simulation results in the case of Architecture 2b with four processors, for varying load factors

	Processing power		
$\varrho = \lambda/\mu$	Exact	App. G	Simulation (99% confidence interval)
0.01	3.882	3.882	3.878 ± 0.049
0.1	2.992	2.992	3.009 ± 0.028
0.3	1.724	1.726	1.733 ± 0.025
0.5	0.972	0.974	0.973 ± 0.009
0.7	0.480	0.481	0.480 ± 0.010

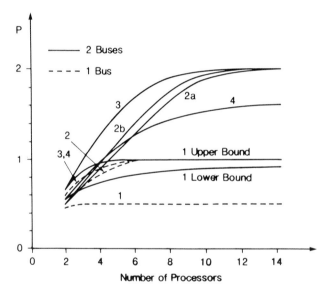

Figure 10.19
Processing power versus number of processors for a fixed load $\rho_p = 1.0$ in the cases of double-bus multiprocessor architectures (solid lines) and of the corresponding single-bus architectures (dashed lines).

(dashed lines and solid lines, respectively, in figure 10.19) shows that at saturation the two-bus system processing power is twice as large as for the single-bus system. This result is very intuitive: at saturation the system bottleneck is the interconnection network, whose bandwidth is proportional to the number of buses. Moreover, we can see that the performance curve of double-bus multiprocessor systems reaches saturation when the number of processors is approximately twice as large as necessary to saturate the processing power of single-bus systems.

Finally, it is interesting to note that the difference in performance between Architecture 2 and Architecture 3 is much larger in the case of two buses than in the single-bus case. Thus the use of multiple-port memories seems to be of interest mainly for high-performance, multiple-bus multiprocessor systems.

References

[BALB83] Balbo, G., and Bruell, S. C., "Computational Aspects of Aggregation in Multiple class Queueing Network," *Performance Evaluation*, 3(3) (August 1983), 177–185.

[CHAN75] Chandy, K. M., Herzog, U., and Woo, L., "Approximate Analysis of General Queueing Networks," *IBM J. of Res. and Dev.* 19(1) (January 1975), 43–49.

[HERZ75] Herzog, U., Woo, L., and Chandy, K. M., "Solution of Queueing Problems by a Recursive Technique," *IBM J. of Res. and Dev.* 19(3) (May 1975), 295–300.

[IGLE78] Iglehart, L. D., "The regenerative Method for Simulation Analysis," in *Current Trends in Programming Methodology*, Vol. 3, K. M. Chandy and R. T. Yeh, Eds., Prentice-Hall, Englewood Cliffs, NJ, 1978.

[LAVE78] Lavenberg, S. S., "Regenerative Simulation of Queueing Networks," IBM Research Report RC-7087, 1978.

11 Other Aspects of Multiprocessor Performance Evaluation

In the previous chapters we have discussed analytical models of contention for the physical shared resources (buses and memories) in multiprocessor systems. Although in some cases the reader may have been discouraged by the model complexity, the environment we have assumed has been relatively simple. Indeed, many more performance reduction factors than we considered exist in multiprocessors. The two most obvious phenomena that can be mentioned are the existence of synchronization at the software level and the possibility of faults that may reduce the numbers of operating modules in the system. The study of the influence of such phenomena on the behavior of multiprocessor systems has just started, and few results exist in the literature. This is probably due to the fact that a direct extension of the models that we have previously described to incorporate the new system behavior patterns induces a very significant increase in the model complexity, as will be shown in this chapter. On the other hand, no ad hoc modeling technique has yet been developed for these problems.

Two examples will be presented: the first one describes the modeling of the synchronization of tasks in single-processor and two-processor systems. Results show that, as is intuitively expected, the effects of this behavior may induce a much more significant performance reduction than the contention for shared resources, particularly when the communication load is low.

The second example presents the analysis of a multiprocessor system in which components are subject to failures and repairs. It is very easy to understand that faults may substantially reduce the multiprocessor processing power, but often quantifying this performance reduction is not simple. For some applications, however, this quantification may be vital, since the multiprocessor fault tolerance could be the primary goal of the analysis.

Another very important issue that should be raised in a book on peformance analysis is the validation of models with measurement results. Also in this case few results exist in the literature, since the validation of a model requires the existence of a real multiprocessor system on which the measurement must be performed. The validation of some of the analytical results presented in chapter 9 is done with measurements performed on a real prototype multiprocessor system developed at the Department of Electronics of the Politecnico di Torino, named TOMP [CONT81]. Validating the analytical results with measurements on an actually existing system is extremely important, since it demonstrates the power of the analytical modeling approach, and thus generates confidence in the accuracy of the performance predictions that it yields.

Chapter 11

11.1 Synchronization of Tasks

In order to provide a simple example of the analysis of the effects of task synchronization, we consider a single-processor system to which is allocated a given number of tasks. Tasks communicate with each other by writing messages to mailboxes associated with receiver tasks. Each task may originate a communication request specifying whether it desires to send or to receive data, as well as the identity of the requested task. After issuing a communication request, the requesting task idles, waiting for the requested task to respond. At the end of the communication both tasks resume operations. The partner task is selected according to a uniform distribution. Each task is assumed to issue a communication request after a random, exponentially distributed running time, characterized by the parameter λ. The message length is assumed to be an exponentially distributed random variable, so that the times needed to read and write messages are also exponentially distributed, with parameter μ.

The processor schedules its active tasks according to a round robin discipline. Let τ be the average of the random variable representing the time slice allocated to each running task, and let σ be the average of the random variable representing the time needed to switch from one task to another one. For the sake of simplicity we assume that the time slice and switch time are exponentially distributed random variables, but generalizations can be easily studied [AJMO84]. Finally, we assume that when a communication request has been issued for a given task, this task is switched into execution, and is processed until it becomes ready to communicate.

The processing power in this case is defined as the sum of the fractions of time the processor devotes to the execution of tasks. We thus exclude from the computation of P the time spent switching tasks, as well as the time spent reading and writing messages.

By using these assumptions, the behavior of a single-processor system can be represented by the GSPN model in figure 11.1.

Tasks ready for execution and awaiting their time slice are represented by tokens in place p_1. The task presently running is represented by a token in p_2. The switching of the running task is represented by a token in p_3.

The initial marking of the GSPN contains a number of tokens equal to T_1, the number of tasks allocated to the processor. One token is initially put in place p_2, whereas the remaining $(T_1 - 1)$ tokens are put in place p_1. Note that, for any marking, only one token can be in p_2. When a running task issues a communication request, a token is put in either p_4 or p_5, depending on whether the request entails a receive or a send operation. The token in p_4 (p_5) represents the pair of communicating tasks. The receive sequence is as follows: the task from which data are requested in switched to

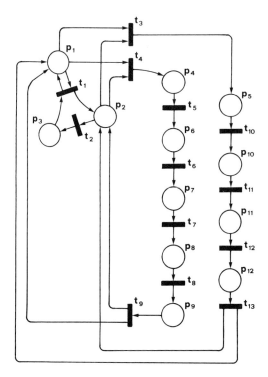

Figure 11.1
Detailed GSPN model of the communication between tasks in a single-processor system.

execution (transition t_5) and runs until data are ready (place p_6 and transition t_6); data are then sent to the other task (p_7 and t_7), which is switched to execution (p_8 and t_8), so that it can read its message (p_9). The receiver task then returns to running state and the sender task returns to ready state (t_9). The send sequence is as follows: the sender task writes a message (p_5 and t_{10}); the receiver task is switched to execution (p_{10} and t_{11}); it runs until it issues a receive request (p_{11} and t_{12}); then it reads the message (p_{12}) and returns to running state while the sender task returns to ready state (t_{13}). This sequence is only one of the many possible alternatives: note that in this case at the end of the communication procedure the receiver task always returns to running state while the sender task returns to ready state. Other possible sequences of operations can be easily modeled with simple modifications of the GSPN. The meanings associated with each place and transition are summarized in table 11.1, where transition firing rates are also given, together with the initial marking.

Chapter 11

Table 11.1
Description of the GSPN in figure 11.1

Places		Number of tokens in initial marking	Transitions		Firing rates
p_1	Ready tasks	$T_1 - 1$	$t_1, t_5,$	End of switch	$1/\sigma$
p_2	Running task	1	t_8, t_{11}		
p_3	Switch	0	t_2	Start switch	$1/\tau$
p_4	Switch to sender	0	t_3	Issue send request	$\lambda/2$
p_5, p_7	Writing message	0	t_4	Issue receive request	$\lambda/2$
p_6	Sender running	0	t_6	Ready to write	λ
p_8, p_{10}	Switch to receiver	0	t_7, t_{10}	End of write	μ
p_9, p_{12}	Reading message	0	t_9, t_{13}	End of read	μ
p_{11}	Receiver running	0	t_{12}	Ready to read	λ

The GSPN in Figure 11.1 can be simplified as shown in figure 11.2 by observing that the sequences of operations performed in the case of a send request and of a receive request differ only in that the receive sequence comprises one more switching of tasks and in the order in which operations are executed. The order of execution of operations is irrelevant in the estimation of the system processing power. The meanings of places and transitions in this GSPN are explained in table 11.2. A further simplification is obtained by noting that the number of tasks allocated to the single-processor system does not influence the Markov chain underlying the GSPN (provided that $T_1 \geq 2$), thus place p_1 can be removed from the model, and the GSPN in figure 11.3 is obtained. The meanings associated with places and transitions in this GSPN are explained in table 11.3. This last GSPN is extremely simple: it only comprises 6 places and 8 transitions. Moreover, only one token that moves from place to place exists in the GSPN. This implies that the state transition rate diagram of the associated Markov chain is topologically identical to the GSPN, and that it can be obtained by substituting arcs and transitions, with directed arcs weighted with transition firing rates. Since the Markov chain model comprises only 6 states, we can evaluate a closed form expression for the system processing power by summing the steady state probabilities of states in which the token is either in p_1 or in p_4:

$$P = \frac{2}{2[1 + (\lambda/\mu)] + (3/2)\lambda\sigma + (\sigma/\tau)}. \tag{11.1}$$

This expression allows the investigation of the combined effect on system performance of the four parameters used in the description of the system operations. It is interesting

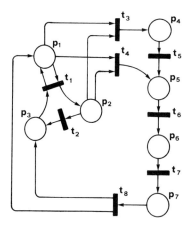

Figure 11.2
First reduction of the GSPN in figure 11.1.

Table 11.2
Description of the GSPN in figure 11.2

Places		Number of tokens in initial marking	Transitions		Firing rates
p_1	Ready tasks	$T_1 - 1$	t_1	End of switch	$1/\sigma$
p_2	Running task	1	t_2	Start switch	$1/\tau$
p_3	Switch	0	t_3	Issue receive request	$\lambda/2$
p_4	Switch to sender	0	t_4	Issue send request	$\lambda/2$
p_5	Run	0	t_5	End of switch	$1/\sigma$
p_6	Write	0	t_6	Ready to write	λ
p_7	Read	0	t_7	End of write	μ
			t_8	End of read	μ

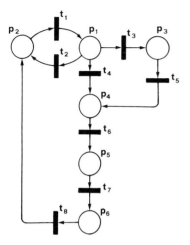

Figure 11.3
Second reduction of the GSPN in figure 11.1.

Table 11.3
Description of the GSPN in figure 11.3

Places		Number of tokens in initial marking	Transitions		Firing rates
p_1	Running task	1	t_1	End of switch	$1/\sigma$
p_2	Switch	0	t_2	Start switch	$1/\tau$
p_3	Switch to sender	0	t_3	Issue receive request	$\lambda/2$
p_4	run	0	t_4	Issue send request	$\lambda/2$
p_5	Write	0	t_5	End of switch	$1/\sigma$
p_6	Read	0	t_6	Ready to write	λ
			t_7	End of write	μ
			t_8	End of read	μ

to observe that, due to the structure of the Markov chain state transition rate diagram, this result holds independently of the distribution of read and write times, and of task switching time, as long as the average values corresponding to these three operations are $1/\mu$, $1/\mu$, and σ, respectively.

The extension of the performance analysis to a two-processor system raises no conceptual difficulty, but does require accounting for the specific architecture of the multiprocessor system. Considering for example, the case of Architecture 4 in chapter 9, we must distinguish the cases in which the two communicating tasks are allocated either to the same processor or to different processors. Moreover, in the latter case it is necessary to specify in the model whether the requested task is ready, running, or already communicating with a third task. A detailed GSPN model describing the behavior of the system can be constructed [AJMO84]. The model is quite complex, and is not shown here. From this GSPN model it is possible to derive the numerical results presented in figure 11.4.

Curve a provides processing power results for the single-processor case, assuming a time slice average duration $\tau = 0.1$ and an average switching time $\sigma = 0.001$. Note that the single-processor performance depends separately on λ, and on μ, not only on their ratio. Results were derived by setting $\lambda = 1$ and varying μ, as well as by setting $\mu = 1$ and varying λ. The two alternatives yield almost identical results, so that they are not distinguishable on the graph.

Curve b in figure 11.4 gives processing power results for the two-processor case, assuming that two tasks are allocated to each processor. Also in this case the curve provides results obtained by setting $\lambda = 1$ and varying μ, as well as by setting $\mu = 1$ and varying λ. Note that for $\rho = \lambda/\mu = 0$ curve b reaches the value $P = 2$, but then descends steeply, getting very close to the vertical axis for small values of ρ. A diminishing return effect is clearly visible, since the two-processor system does not yield twice as much processing power as the single-processor system.

For comparison purposes we have also drawn in figure 11.4 curve c, which shows the results found in chapter 9 by modeling only the effect of contention for shared resources. Curve c is obtained from the expression given in the bottom row of table 9.7. The comparison of the two curves indicates that the synchronization of tasks entails a significantly more important performance reduction than the contention for system shared resources, particularly in the case of lightly loaded systems. Actually, a precise comparison of the two curves is not possible, since the modeling assumptions used in the development of the two models are somewhat different. In chapter 9 we assumed that the exchange of information among tasks allocated to the same processor causes no performance loss, since no shared resource is involved in this operation. Here

Chapter 11

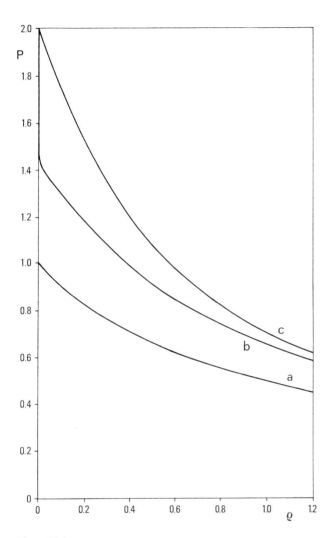

Figure 11.4
Processing power results for the single-processor system (curve a), and for the two-processor system (curves b and c).

we have instead modeled the degradation due to synchronization of tasks allocated to the same processor. Nevertheless, it is interesting to see that the two curves behave similarly, and that both indicate that the ideal processing power ($P = 2$) is reduced to half for communication loads of the order of 0.5 (0.4 in one case, and 0.6 in the other one). It is thus clear that high efficiencies can be achieved only if the communication load is kept very low. The significant difference between the two curves, referring to the two-processor case, is that if we only consider contention for shared resources, we can approach a processing power $P = 2$ by keeping the communication load low (e.g., with $\rho = 0.03$ we get $P \approx 1.9$). If, instead, we take into account the effect of task synchronization, it is virtually impossible to obtain processing power values higher than $P = 1.5$, since the communication load cannot be reduced arbitrarily if cooperation among tasks is necessary.

11.2 Failure of System Components

As we pointed out in chapter 5, one of the potential advantages of multiple-processor systems over single-processor units is the increase in reliability and availability. The availability $A(t)$ of a system is the probability that the system is operational at a given instant of time, independently of previous faults, whereas the reliability $R(t)$ of a system is the conditional probability that a system has survived the interval $0-t$, provided that the system was correctly operating at time $t = 0$. These two parameters are expected to increase in a multiprocessor with respect to a single-processor system. The redundancy of physical resources can indeed be exploited to replace faulty modules, and thus obtain a reconfiguration of the system at a lower performance level.

When system modules are subject to failures it is necessary to introduce the concept of coverage, that is, the probability of the system successfully recovering from a failure. Obviously the recovering from a faulty condition cannot be complete, and this fact suggests the possibility of integrating reliability and performance models. Meyer [MEYE78] defined a performance measure, called performability, that gives the probability of a system performing at a given level of accomplishment.

We shall not discuss in detail reliability and performability analysis of multiprocessors systems, which are beyond the scope of this book; instead, we simply analyze here the performance of the single-bus multiprocessor system shown in figure 11.5 in the presence of faults. The system architecture is the same as the one shown in figure 7.1; but in this case we explicitly assume that the shared resource is composed of two independent modules CM_1 and CM_2. The system considered here is very simple, and the analysis is confined to the functional level. It must be observed that a correct and

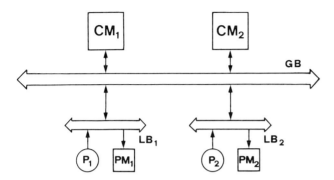

Figure 11.5
Bus-oriented multiprocessor system.

complete analysis of these problems must not ignore the interaction between hardware and software and can therefore be better performed at the system level.

A GSPN model of the multiprocessor system operations is shown in figure 11.6. The assumptions on the multiprocessor workload are the same as described in chapter 9. Tokens in place p_1 represent active processors. The firing of t_1 represents the request for an access, so its firing rate is $m_1 \lambda$, where λ is the common memory request rate of each processor. The selection of the memory to be accessed is made by means of the random switch t_2–t_3. We assume that the two memories are requested with equal probabilities. A token in either p_3 or p_4 indicates that the memory has been selected, but it is not yet available. When the memory becomes free, the token moves from p_3 (p_4) to p_7 (p_8). The firing of t_6 (t_7), at rate μ, indicates the end of the access; therefore, when the transition fires, a processor becomes again active (a token moves to p_1), and the common memory and the bus are released.

Starting from the fault-free model in figure 11.6, it is possible to derive the GSPN model of the system with failures and repairs by just adding new places and transitions. The GSPN model considering faults and repairs is shown in figure 11.7, where heavy lines represent the fault-free system operations, light lines represent failures, and dashed lines represent repairs.

The firing of t_8 means that one active processor goes out of service (a token moves to p_{10}), and the firing of t_9 indicates the end of the repair activity. The firing rates of t_8 and t_9 are, respectively, $m_1 f_p$ and $m_{10} r_p$, where f_p is the processor failure rate and r_p the processor repair rate. Transition t_{15} (t_{19}) represents the failure of CM_1 (CM_2), while it is not accessed. A token in p_{11} (p_{12}) indicates that CM_1 (CM_2) has failed. The

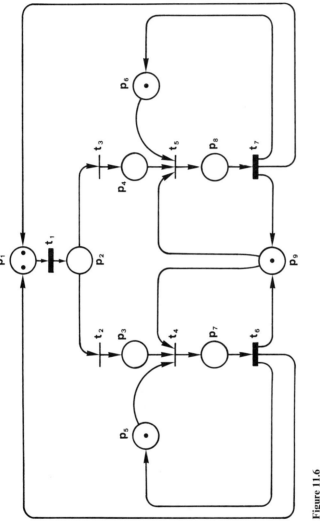

Figure 11.6
Fault-free GSPN model of the system in figure 11.5.

firing of t_{16} (t_{20}) means that the memory has been repaired. The memory failure rate is f_m, and the memory repair rate is r_m. A token in p_9 indicates that the bus is not used. The firing of t_{23} corresponds to a bus failure (rate f_b), and that of t_{24} (rate r_b) to a bus repair.

When a processor is accessing CM_1 (CM_2), a token is present in p_7 (p_8); the access can abort because of a failure of the processor, the memory, or the bus. Transition t_{13} (t_{17}) fires if the failure is due to the processor, t_{14} (t_{18}) fires if the failure is due to the memory, and t_{21} (t_{22}) fires if the failure is due to the bus. In the case of memory failure [firing of t_{14} (t_{18})], the accessing processor waits for the memory to be repaired.

The meaning of places and transitions in figure 11.7 is summarized in table 11.4, where firing rates of timed transitions and firing probabilities of immediate transitions are also given.

As usual, to measure the effectiveness of the system we use the system processing power, defined as the mean number of active processors, i.e., the average number of tokens in p_1.

The processing power was evaluated considering different hypotheses concerning the way the system can fail and how it reacts to a failure. If we assume, for example, that the bus is not subject to failure, transitions t_{21} to t_{24}, and place p_{13}, are eliminated with the associated input and output arcs. If processors can recognize the faulty condition of a memory and then do not try to access it, the inhibitor arcs from p_{11} (p_{12}) to t_2 (t_3) are introduced in the model. The firing probabilities of t_2 and t_3 are consequently altered.

Results are obtained assuming the following numerical values:

$$\mu = 1,$$
$$\lambda = \rho\mu,$$
$$f_p = f_m = f_b = f = 10^{-4}, \quad (11.2)$$
$$r_p = r_m = r_b = 10f.$$

Curve 1 in figure 11.8 shows the steady state processing power of the fault-free system obtained from the GSPN in figure 11.6 versus the load factor $\rho = \lambda/\mu$. Curves 2 (3) and 4 (5) give the system peformance assuming the bus cannot (can) fail and the presence or absence, respectively, of the inhibitor arcs in the GSPN in figure 11.7.

It must be observed that the limits for $\rho \to 0$, of curves 2–5, are equal, because, in the limiting case, it is not relevant whether faulty memories are recognized and whether the bus fails or not, since the common memory accesses are extremely rare.

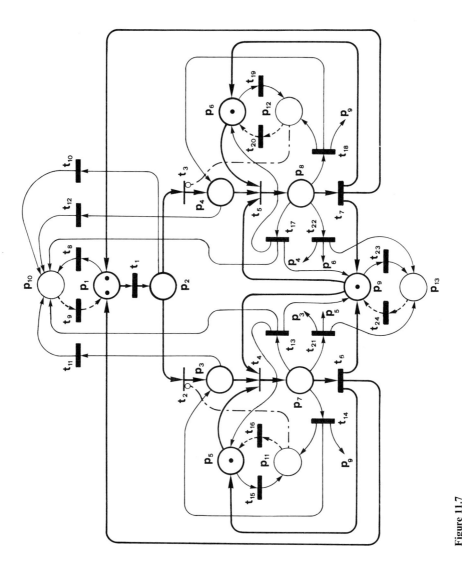

Figure 11.7
GSPN model of the system in figure 11.5 with failures and repairs.

Table 11.4
Description of the GSPN in figure 11.7

Places		Number of tokens in initial marking
p_1	Active processors	1
p_2	Processors requesting access	0
p_3	Processors waiting for CM_1	0
p_4	Processors waiting for CM_2	0
p_5	CM_1 not accessed	1
p_6	CM_2 not accessed	1
p_7	Processor accessing CM_1	0
p_8	Processor accessing CM_2	0
p_9	Free bus	1
p_{10}	Failed processors	0
p_{11}	Failed CM_1	0
p_{12}	Failed CM_2	0
p_{13}	Failed bus	0

Transition		Firing rates or probabilities
t_1	Processor issues access request	$m_1 \lambda$
t_2	Access request to CM_1	$1/2$
t_3	Access request to CM_2	$1/2$
t_4	Beginning of the access to CM_1	1
t_5	Beginning of the access to CM_2	1
t_6	End of the access to CM_1	μ
t_7	End of the access to CM_2	μ
t_8	Active processor fails	$m_1 f_p$
t_9	Processor is repaired	$m_{10} r_p$
t_{10}	Processor fails	$m_2 f_p$
t_{11}	Processor fails	$m_3 f_p$
t_{12}	Processor fails	$m_4 f_p$
t_{13}	Processor fails during an access	f_p
t_{14}	CM_1 fails during an access	f_m
t_{15}	CM_1 fails when it is not accessed	f_m
t_{16}	CM_1 is repaired	r_m
t_{17}	Processor fails during an access	f_p
t_{18}	CM_2 fails during an access	f_m
t_{19}	CM_2 fails when it is not accessed	f_m
t_{20}	CM_2 is repaired	f_m
t_{21}	Bus fails	f_b
t_{22}	Bus fails	f_b
t_{23}	Bus fails when it is not used	f_b
t_{24}	Bus is repaired	r_b

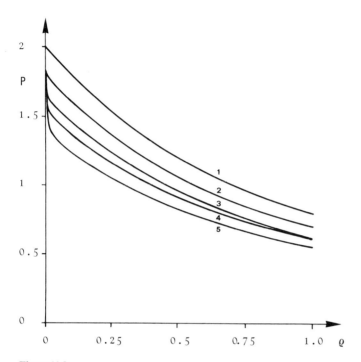

Figure 11.8
Steady state processing power of the multiprocessor system in figure 11.3 versus the load factor ρ.

11.3 Prototype Measurements and Model Validation

Measurements were performed on the three-processor TOMP prototype shown in figure 11.9. TOMP is an implementation of Architecture 4, chapter 9. The aim of the measurements was to validate the stochastic models used in the performance analysis of the system, with respect to the study of contention for physical resources, rather than to model applications or system control software. For this reason the workload applied to the real system closely approximates the model assumed in chapter 9. Thus each processor runs a cyclic process corresponding to the sequential execution of a CPU burst and a common memory access. The CPU burst consists of a sequence of operations on the private memory; let T_p represent the time required for the execution of each elementary operation, and N_p the number of operations in a sequence. A common memory access is a sequence of elementary read or write operations on a common memory area that can be either local or external; each elementary operation

Chapter 11

Figure 11.9
The prototype TOMP multiprocessor system.

requires a time T_a' when directed to the local common memory module and a time T_a'' when directed to an external common memory module. The number of elementary operations needed to perform an external access sequence is N_a. The quantities N_p and N_a approximate exponentially distributed random variables. By the assumptions introduced in chapter 9, the probabilities of accessing either local or external common memory modules are

$P\{\text{accessing local common memory}\} = 0.5$

and

$P\{\text{accessing each external common memory}\} = 0.25$.

The experimental values of processing power were obtained with direct measurements of three signals on each processor module. These signals (named GREQ, GSERV, and LREQ) are active whenever the following conditions hold:

GREQ: the processor has requested the global bus, but access has not been granted yet;
GSERV: the processor is using the global bus to access an external common memory module;
LREQ: the processor is either waiting to access its common memory module or accessing it.

The measurement instrumentation (figure 11.10) is composed a 5-MHz pulse generator, a simple gating logic circuit, and a set of pulse counters.

Defining f_m to be the pulse frequency, and N_x to be the number of pulses measured by the counter associated with signal x over a fixed measure time T_m, we obtain the fraction of time during which signal x is active, $F(x)$:

$$F(x) = \frac{N_x}{f_m T_m}. \tag{11.3}$$

The fraction of time during which processor i is not active, $F_i(\text{NACT})$, can be evaluated as

$$F_i(\text{NACT}) = F_i(\text{GSERV}) + F_i(\text{GREQ}) + F_i(\text{LREQ}), \tag{11.4}$$

and the processing power is

$$P = 3 - \sum_{i=1}^{3} F_i(\text{NACT}). \tag{11.5}$$

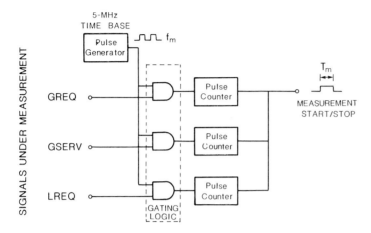

Figure 11.10
Block diagram of the measurement setup.

For each measurement the value of the load factor ρ may be estimated as

$$\rho = \frac{N_a T_a}{N_p T_p}, \tag{11.6}$$

where T_a is the common memory access time.

Since in the TOMP prototype the access to a common memory module has different durations for the local and the external processors, we assume (as a first-order approximation) for T_a the mean of the two values T_a' and T_a''; thus

$$T_a = \frac{T_a' + T_a''}{2}. \tag{11.7}$$

The measured values of processing power, obtained as in (11.5), versus the load factor, as given by equation (11.6), are plotted in figure 11.11 (curve *a*).

Several approximations introduced in the description of the system workload, and some architectural features that were not taken into account in the models, cause the parameter ρ to represent inexactly the real load of the multiprocessor system. The impact of these approximations on the estimate of the parameter ρ can be substantial, and a more careful derivation of its value is needed. In the following paragraphs we discuss some of these phenomena in order to derive a new formula for the evaluation of the load factor.

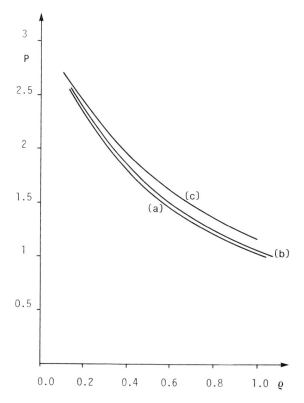

Figure 11.11
Processing power of a three-processor TOMP system. Comparison of the analytical results (curve c) versus the measurement results (curves a and b).

(A) Nonexponential Distributions

At the beginning of each CPU burst each processor computes three uniformly distributed random numbers by means of a shift register and of an irreducible polynomial of order 32 [PETE61]. The first random number is 2 bits wide and it is used to determine which common memory area is to be accessed during the next access period. The other two random numbers are used as pointers in logarithmic conversion tables to obtain the two random numbers N_a and N_p. Therefore the exponential distributions of the CPU burst and of the access period are, in fact, approximated by truncated geometric distributions. N_a can vary between 1 and 2^{16}, and N_p can vary between a minimum number N_c and a maximum $N_c + 2^{16}$. N_c is the number of internal cycles needed to evaluate the three random numbers.

(B) Internal Operations

Individual common memory accesses, although being part of a single sequence, are separated by a short interval T_i corresponding to processor operations; this fact allows a partial interleaving of the operations of different processors on the global bus and increases the mean CPU burst duration by a factor proportional to the mean access time. We can then correct the load factor ρ as follows:

$$\rho' = \frac{N_a T_a}{N_p T_p + N_a T_i}. \tag{11.8}$$

(C) Memory Refresh

The private memory of each of the prototype processors was implemented using dynamic memories refreshed by the processor itself. The refresh operations are performed in parallel with the execution of the workload process, and their effect is to increase the CPU burst duration by a factor T_r/T_{ir}, where T_r is the time required to execute a refresh operation and T_{ir} is the time interval between two successive refresh operations. Therefore the load factor ρ can be further corrected as

$$\rho'' = \frac{N_a T_a}{N_p T_p (1 + T_r/T_{ir}) + N_a T_i}. \tag{11.9}$$

(D) Global Bus Arbitration

The arbitration is executed by a distributed synchronous logic that assigns the bus to one processor at a time following a fixed priority policy. The arbitration process consumes some time while all the requesting processors are held waiting. This time can vary between two limits, T_{armn} and T_{armx}. In order to consider the impact of the global bus arbitration on the load factor ρ we can add to each external common memory access time T_a'', the average bus arbitration time T_{ar}, estimated as

$$T_{ar} = \frac{T_{armn} + T_{armx}}{2}; \tag{11.10}$$

hence we obtain the corrected common memory access time T_a''', given by

$$T_a''' = \frac{T_a' + T_a'' + T_{ar}}{2}, \tag{11.11}$$

and the load factor ρ can be finally corrected, obtaining

$$\rho''' = \frac{N_a T_a'''}{N_p T_p (1 + T_r/T_{ir}) + N_a T_i}. \tag{11.12}$$

The measured values of processing power versus the corrected load factor ρ''' are shown in figure 11.11 (curve *b*). Curve *c* in the same figure shows for comparison purposes the results yielded by the analytical models presented in chapter 9.

The comparison between the measured values and the analytical model estimates confirms the validity of the modeling approach we have used. The performance predictions are very accurate in spite of the differences between the actual prototype behavior and the assumptions concerning system operations used in the development of the model, where an abstract view of the system behavior neglects the actual details of the elementary operations executed by the prototype.

References

[AJMO84] Ajmone Marsan, M., Chiola, G., and Conte, G., "Performance Models of Task Synchronization in Computer Systems," Proc. First International Conference on Computers and Application, Peking, June 1985.

[CONT81] Conte, G., DelCorso, D., Gregoretti, F., and Pasero, E., "TOMP80—a Multiprocessor Prototype," Proc. EUROMICRO 81, Paris, France, September 1981.

[MEYE78] Meyer, J. F., "On Evaluating the Performability of Degradable Computing Systems," Digest Eighth Intern. Fault-Tolerant Computing Symposium, IEEE Comp. Society, Toulouse, France, 1978.

[PETE61] Peterson, W., and Weldon, E., *Error Correcting Codes*, MIT Press, Cambridge, MA, 1961.

Index

Approximation
  binomial, 128–129
  Rau's, 127
  Strecker's, 129–131, 135–136
Arbiter, 108, 114
Availability of a multiprocessor, 111, 266

Bandwidth, 257
Birth-and-death
  process, 27–29, 40, 45–46, 143, 176, 180, 184
  rates, 27, 29, 40, 45–46, 143, 180, 184
Blocking
  in multiprocessors, 179, 197, 219
  in queuing networks, 66
Bottleneck, 108, 117, 218, 219, 254, 257

Cache memory, 116
Classification
  of crossbar models, 121–122
  of distributed systems, 101–104
Computational complexity, 30, 60–65, 67–69, 95, 97, 98, 160, 174–177, 179, 192, 205
Concurrency, 73, 83
Confidence interval, 251
Conflict, 39, 75, 88, 110, 119, 147
Conservative assumption, 222
Convergence, 147, 186, 189
Crossbar, 106–108, 111, 119–136, 139, 158, 250
Cycle
  in Markov chains, 26, 37, 94
  memory, 121, 130–131, 247
  in multiprocessors, 115–116, 119, 128
  in queuing networks, 52, 64, 142

Data base, 102, 104, 142
Deadlock, 195
Diminishing return, 185, 264
Distribution
  Coxian, 47–50, 57, 71
  Erlang, 127, 147–148, 151–153, 156
  exponential, 11, 24–25, 30, 37, 40, 46–47, 51–57, 63, 71, 83–84, 87–88, 126, 139–147, 150, 153, 158, 178–179, 181, 192, 194, 222, 259, 274, 276
  geometric, 12, 17, 119, 121, 128, 130, 276
  hyperexponential, 147–153, 156
  Poisson, 30, 49, 125
DMA (direct memory access), 105

Eigenvalue, 68
Erlang B function, 180–181, 245

Failure, 112, 259, 266–272
Fault, 258, 266–269

Fault tolerance, 258
FCFS (first come first served) policy, 56–58, 63, 66, 70, 140–141, 143–158, 163, 178, 181, 195–196, 200, 202–203, 211, 224, 238
Finite state machine, 78

Granularity, 101, 103

Hierarchy, 106, 191

Interconnection network, 102, 105–111, 113–117, 119, 137, 158, 192, 225, 238, 245–246, 250, 257
  blocking, 110
  multistage, 109–111
  packet switched, 101, 109–111
  topology, 102–103, 114

LCFS (last come first served) policy, 57, 126, 146, 179
Level of detail of a model, 73, 112–113, 119, 227
Local area network, 102, 104, 106
Locality, 121, 132

Markov chain
  absorbing state, 14, 15, 22
  aggregation of states, 30–35, 68, 175–176, 197, 206
  aperiodic, 15–16, 18
  aperiodic state, 15, 36
  backward recurrence time, 25
  Chapman-Kolmogorov equation, 13, 20, 23
  decomposition, 56, 68
  embedded, 25–27, 35–36, 48–50, 93–97, 144, 147
  ergodic, 15–18, 22–26, 29–31, 33, 46, 55–56, 84
  ergodic state, 15–16, 22
  finite, 16, 18, 30, 33, 83
  forward recurrence time, 24–25
  homogeneous, 11–13, 15, 18, 20, 22, 28, 53, 73
  infinitesimal generator, 23, 33, 84
  irreducible, 15–16, 18, 22, 26, 28, 36
  isomorphic to SPN, 73, 83–84
  Kolmogorov forward and backward equations, 21, 23
  lumping, 31–34, 160–161, 197–199, 205–207, 212–213, 225, 227
  macrostate, 30–35, 68–69, 175, 177
  periodic, 26, 36
  periodic state, 14, 36
  recurrence time, 14–15, 19, 23–25, 36, 94
  recurrent, 26
  recurrent state, 14–15, 22, 36
  sojourn time, 11, 12, 17, 24–26, 35–37, 94, 97
  transient state, 14–15, 22, 29, 36

visit, 16, 26, 36–37, 94–96
visit ratio, 16, 26
Measurement, 1–2, 5, 260, 272–278
Microcomputer, 102
Microprocessor, 111
MIMD (multiple instruction multiple data) system, 104
Minicomputer, 102, 107, 111
Modularity, 111, 137
Multiport memory, 114, 200, 202, 244, 257

Packet switch, 142
Parallelism, 73, 103, 111
Parallel system, 73, 101–103, 111
Performability, 266
Performance
  criterion, 186
  degradation, 114, 139
  difference, 257
  estimate, 82, 221
  improvement, 188–189, 233
  increase, 111, 187
  index, 60, 62–63, 116, 121, 141–142, 151, 157, 191, 205–206, 220
  loss, 221, 264
  measure, 1, 30, 266
  model, 82, 137, 266
  objective, 117
  prediction, 258, 278
  reduction, 258, 264
Period
  access, 137, 192, 276
  active, 147, 158, 181, 192
  idle, 115, 192
  observation, 41–43
  queuing, 115
  transfer, 115, 192, 196–197, 204
Petri net model
  available token, 81–82
  ergodic, 84
  finite reachability set, 78, 93
  folding, 167–169
  inhibitor arc, 76–78, 150, 209, 269
  reachability graph, 172–173, 212
  reachability set, 78, 83, 89, 91, 93, 165, 167, 169–170, 172, 207, 209, 211
  reachability tree, 78–79, 85–86
  refinement, 211–214
  tangible marking (or state), 92–97, 165, 167, 169, 209, 211–213
  vanishing marking (or state), 92–98, 165, 167, 169
Pipeline, 103–104

Poisson process, 29–30, 49, 51–54, 56
Preemption, 56, 126, 146, 174, 195, 197, 203, 207, 209, 211–213, 215, 217, 224, 238, 246

Queue and queuing network
  aggregation, 66, 68–69, 71, 178, 247–251
  approximation, 50, 66–71, 247
  BCMP, 55–58, 60, 63, 66–67, 69, 71, 145–147, 173, 177–178, 181
  convolution, 61–63, 65
  decomposition, 67–68, 125, 247
  finite population, 143–144, 180, 244
  finite waiting room, 40, 67
  infinite server, 143, 145–146, 181
  Little's formula, 42–44, 62, 64–65, 141, 143, 145
  machine repairman model, 139, 179, 202
  multiclass, 63, 248
  Pollaczek-Khintchin mean value formula, 50, 125
  supplementary variable technique, 144
  visit, 53, 55, 64
  visit ratio, 55

Reconfiguration, 112, 266
Recursion, 28–29, 61–65, 127, 176, 178, 194, 202
Regenerative method, 251
Reliability, 111, 112, 266
Repair, 258, 267, 269–271
Round robin, 140, 259

SIMD (single instruction multiple data) system, 104
Simulation, 2–3, 112, 117, 251–257
SISD (single instruction single data) system, 104
Synchronization, 73, 83, 101, 104, 111–112, 114, 116, 120–121, 123, 192, 209, 221, 258–259, 265–266
Systolic array, 102–103

Taxonomy, 101, 118
Throughput, 53, 62, 64, 66, 80, 98, 142, 211, 250
Traffic 41, 194

Validation, 213, 251, 258, 272
VLSI (very large scale integrated), 103, 107, 111, 118

Workload, 1–2, 101, 112, 114, 116–117, 137–138, 147, 158, 191–193. 202–203, 225, 238, 244, 246, 267, 272, 275, 277

The MIT Press, with Peter Denning as consulting editor, publishes computer science books in the following series:

Artificial Intelligence, Patrick Winston and Michael Brady, editors

Computer Systems, Herb Schwetman, editor

Foundations of Computing, Michael Garey, editor

Information Systems, Michael Lesk, editor

Logic Programming, Ehud Shapiro, editor

Scientific Computation, Dennis Gannon, editor